THE OXFORD

CHEKHOV

VOLUME VII

STORIES
1893–1895

Translated and edited by
RONALD HINGLEY

OXFORD UNIVERSITY PRESS
OXFORD LONDON NEW YORK
1978

Oxford University Press, Walton Street, Oxford OX2 6DP

OXFORD LONDON GLASGOW
NEW YORK TORONTO MELBOURNE WELLINGTON
IBADAN NAIROBI DAR ES SALAAM LUSAKA CAPE TOWN
KUALA LUMPUR SINGAPORE JAKARTA HONG KONG TOKYO
DELHI BOMBAY CALCUTTA MADRAS KARACHI

British Library Cataloguing in Publication Data

Chekhov, Anton Pavlovich
  The Oxford Chekhov.
  Vol. 7: Stories, 1893–1895
  I. Title   II. Hingley, Ronald
  891.7'2'3   PG3455.A1   78-40064

  ISBN 0-19-211388-7

Printed in Great Britain by
Richard Clay (The Chaucer Press) Ltd.,
Bungay, Suffolk.

To

HARRY WILLETTS

CONTENTS

PREFACE

IT has been a pleasure to return to *The Oxford Chekhov* after a long, strenuous and enjoyable interval devoted to writing two books: *A New Life of Anton Chekhov*, which appeared in 1976, and a more general study, *The Russian Mind*, which was published in 1977 (New York) and 1978 (London). The former work supersedes my earlier *Chekhov: a Biographical and Critical Study* (1950), and complements the continuing systematic translation of Chekhov's writings on which I have been engaged since 1962.

All the versions in the present volume are published for the first time, excepting only *The Russian Master*, which has already appeared in the paperback selection *Chekhov: Eleven Stories* issued by the Oxford University Press in 1975. For the present reissue of the story some minor zoological corrections have been made. The 'Egyptian pigeons' have become 'turtle-doves', and my gophers have been caused to 'squeak' rather than whistle as the result of representations kindly made to the publisher by an anonymous correspondent more conversant than I with these intriguing rodents; incidentally, though, the only sound which the gopher is recorded as emitting over the centuries (by the *Oxford English Dictionary*, in 1841) is the rejected 'whistle'.

(a) Sources and Conventions

This volume contains Chekhov's entire output of fiction first published between December 1893 and February 1895 inclusive. The translations are based on the Russian text and variants as printed in vol. viii of the twenty-volume *Complete Collection of the Works and Letters of A. P. Chekhov* (Moscow, 1944–51), here referred to as '*Works, 1944–51*'.

The treatment of proper names, of colloquial and uneducated Russian speech, of terms of abuse, of institutional and administrative terms, and of dates, follows the lines laid down in detail in the Prefaces to volumes previously published: in the order vols. iii, viii, ii, i, v, vi and ix.

(b) Titles

Though great care has been taken throughout this edition to find the

most appropriate rendering for the titles of Chekhov's works, only one
of those in the present volume might seem sufficiently controversial to
require explanation. This is *The Russian Master*, for which the only
traced previous translator, Constance Garnett, has *The Teacher of
Literature*. But that is, with respect, the merest translationese. Though
the dictionaries do not recognize the fact, the term which constitutes
the Russian title (*Учитель словесности*) was regularly applied in
Russian nineteenth-century schools to masters who specialized in
teaching *Russian* language and literature rather than the languages and
literatures of other cultures. Now, if I ask one of my sons in Oxford,
England, who set him an essay on Shakespeare for his school homework, he will tell me that it was his 'English master'; and he will not,
repeat not, assert that it was his 'teacher of literature'. One would
think the point somewhat obvious, were it not that I find an American
reviewer (described in the byline as an 'Instructor of Humanities') of
my *New Life of Anton Chekhov* vectoring in from humanity at large to
instruct me in particular on the care which Chekhov took over his
titles: something which I had, as it happens, contrived to notice for
myself. The same reviewer has also sought to advertise an assumed
expertise in this technically difficult field by summarily dismissing
certain of my titles, including *The Russian Master*, as containing what
she calls 'egregious errors'.[1] These criticisms would be more impressive
had not the Instructor of Humanities herself committed the egregious
error of endorsing the inaccurate *Teacher of Literature*. Nor do her other
objections to my versions of Chekhov's titles (*The Artist's Story* and *A
Hard Case*) carry the slightest conviction, coming as they do from
someone who has chosen to ignore, or is blissfully unaware of, the
reasons which I have rightly or wrongly advanced—often at considerable length and risk of pedantry—for settling upon this or that rendering. All this, including specific discussions of the pilloried *Artist's Story*
and *A Hard Case*, was to be found in Preface after Preface to published
volumes of *The Oxford Chekhov*.[2] One sometimes wonders why one
bothers.

(c) *Notes and Notebooks*

An attempt has been made in the Notes (pp. 265–8) to cope briefly
but adequately with the task of identifying nearly three dozen

[1] Anne Frydman, *The New Leader* (New York), 27 Sept. 1976.
[2] *The Oxford Chekhov*, vol. vi, pp. ix–x; vol. viii, p. xi; vol. ix, pp. x–xi.

Muscovite localities to which reference is made in *Three Years*. The text has not, however, been burdened with the new names or successions of names which these streets, boulevards etc. may have acquired in the post-1917 period.

References to Chekhov's 'Notebooks' in the Appendixes are to his *Zapisnyye knizhki*, as published in *Works*, 1944–51, vol. xii.

(d) Acknowledgements

The text has been thoroughly revised several times by my wife, and also by Jeremy Newton, a pupil-turned-mentor who has acquitted himself splendidly in both capacities. Enthusiastic gardeners, all three of us, we have tried to cope adequately with the horticultural intricacies of *The Black Monk*—itself the work of a distinguished fellow-gardener. For advice on many a technical point of translation, some of it purveyed in the appropriately named Gardener's Arms (Plantation Road, Oxford), I am indebted to Harry Willetts, and am also delighted to salute his signal services to the art of translation from the Russian by dedicating this volume to him. For advice on points of detail I am also grateful to Clare Powell and John Fennell, as for help with the typing to Susan Henny, who produced the original draft version, and who has shared the clerical labours with my wife.

RONALD HINGLEY

Frilford, Abingdon
1978

INTRODUCTION

THE longest story in this volume, *Three Years*, differs from the rest of Chekhov's mature writings in being topographically anchored, during the greater part of the action, to the city of Moscow. The other mature works, by contrast, tend to avoid being so specific about background. Even in the same story we find Chekhov characteristically coy about the identity of the unspecified provincial home town of Julia Belavin, while elsewhere most of his provincial towns are similarly anonymous, and nearly all his village names are invented. He may go so far as to indicate that some happening occurs in 'T—— County' or 'the town of N', but for the most part he will not even say that much. And even when presenting Moscow in earlier major works he had sometimes been deliberately vague; we may, for instance, safely infer from certain buried indications that the outstanding *Dreary Story* (1889) has a Muscovite setting, but never are we informed of this in so many words.

In *Three Years*, however, Chekhov fairly wallows in the topography of Moscow, mentioning well over thirty localities which can be identified in gazetteers of the period. And though it has not been thought necessary to equip the present volume with a Moscow street plan of the 1890s, anyone in possession of the recently reissued *Baedeker's Russia 1914* can easily trace, for example, young Kostya Kochevoy's daily walk from Pyatnitsky Road to the Second High School on Razgulyay Square. He may accompany Julia and the Panaurov girls on their drive down the Little Dmitrovka to the Tver Road and Filippov's Café, or indulge in many another pleasant excursion of the imagination.

Equally untypical of Chekhov is the precise date which he casually implies near the end of *Three Years*. Writing in 1894, he has one of his characters described as being in America for 'the Exhibition'. In the context this must be identified with the World's Columbian Exposition at Chicago, Illinois, a major international event of the year 1893. Evidently Chekhov specifically conceived the action of *Three Years* as ending about a year before the writing of the story, and for once did not mind making this evident.

Abandoning spatial and temporal vagueness—broadly characteristic, not only of his own work, but also of other Russian fiction-writers and indeed of Russians in general—Chekhov paid the Moscow of *Three*

Years the compliment of describing it in some detail. He alludes to its concerts and art exhibitions, its cafés and churches, its past and its future. The effect is to remind us of what we might easily forget when reading his other mature works: that he was himself very much a Muscovite by adoption. Between the ages of nineteen and thirty-two he was a permanent resident of the city, Russia's former and future capital—even though he might leave it for long periods during the summer, and had absented himself for nearly eight months during his visit to the penal settlement of Sakhalin in 1890. Of the 'two capitals', as Russians would describe Moscow and St. Petersburg (the actual capital at this period), Moscow was the better known to Chekhov.

Before he was ready to describe Moscow in such detail, Chekhov first had to leave it. When he began writing *Three Years* in late 1894 he had already been living in the country for some time: on the estate at Melikhovo, nearly fifty miles south of Moscow, which he had bought in early 1892. His move to this rural retreat had been provoked by the utter detestation in which he had come to hold the big city. But Chekhov the newly established countryman was soon—typically enough—hankering for Moscow again, and was able to return at will, since the city was only a few hours' journey by train and carriage from his new home. Not only had absence made his heart grow fonder of Moscow, it had also given him the detachment and sense of distance which he often seemed to require before he was ready to incorporate a theme in fiction. He once remarked that he could only compose 'in retrospect. That's the only way I can write: from memory. I've never done live portraits from nature. I need my memory to sieve the subject, leaving behind—as on a filter-paper—only what is essential and typical.'[1]

Yet another anomalous feature of *Three Years* is its strong sociological or genre-description bias. One of the finest features of the story is the portrayal of Laptev's, those memorable old-fashioned haberdashery suppliers. More concerned on the whole to depict the general human situation than to insist on specifics, Chekhov here descends on the Moscow merchant class for all the world as if he were a *bytopisatel* (detailed chronicler of some aspect of Russian life) such as the country's most renowned dramatist of the previous generation, Alexander Ostrovsky. Old Laptev and his clerks might, indeed, have stepped straight out of one of Ostrovsky's many plays set in mercantile Mos-

[1] Letter to F. D. Batyushkov, 15 Dec. 1897.

cow. So too might 'the Beetle' and many another figure in *A Woman's Kingdom*.

To mention the Russian merchant is to be reminded that imperial Russian society was formally divided into specific social estates with one or other of which every citizen must, by law, be registered. They included the peasants (overwhelmingly preponderant numerically), the small but influential gentry and the priestly caste, as well as the merchant class (*kupechestvo*) to which the Laptevs belong. But 'merchant' is too narrow a rendering since the concept embraces those of 'industrialist', 'businessman', 'tradesman' and 'shopkeeper' as well. We also note that, in *Three Years*, Alexis Laptev's brother Theodore conceives the idea of transferring from the merchant's estate to the more prestigious gentry (*dvoryanstvo*). But the notion is put forward as a symptom of his developing mental instability, since the estates, though formally maintained in their strict compartments until 1917, were already losing much of their significance by the late nineteenth century. No one much cared, by now, whether he was a gentleman or not—certainly not Chekhov himself. Belonging to none of the regular categories, he was eventually forced by bureaucratic pressures to have himself inscribed as that absurdity, a retired civil servant.[1]

Unusual though *Three Years* is in fastening so firmly on a merchant setting, it is not unique—as another notable story in the present volume reminds us. This is *A Woman's Kingdom*, where the heroine is a prominent—albeit unenthusiastic—industrialist, and where the Christmas celebrations of her household once more capture the spirit of an Ostrovsky, Leskov or other Russian *bytopisatel*. There is also the mill-owning setting to *A Case History* (1898), a story which is to be found in volume ix of the present edition. Each of these three works presents some facet of a milieu which we are amazed to find the mature Chekhov portraying so rarely, since he had sprung from it himself. It was as the son of a provincial grocer that he had been born in 1860 in the south Russian port of Taganrog, and his father had been formally inscribed on the rolls of the local merchant class before his debts had driven him to run away to Moscow.

Once settled in Moscow, Chekhov's father had been employed for many years as a clerk by the firm of Gavrilov. This was (like 'Laptev's' in *Three Years*) a wholesale haberdashery store, and it also employed Chekhov's cousin Michael. Chekhov knew the establishment as a young man, and he undoubtedly used it as a model for 'Laptev's'. But

[1] Hingley, *A New Life of Anton Chekhov*, p. 173.

though Gavrilov's remained his main adult link with the world of commerce and industry, he had also met local industrialists when organizing precautions at Melikhovo against an advancing cholera epidemic in the summers of 1892 and 1893.

All these experiences helped to inspire his three major merchant or business stories, *A Woman's Kingdom*, *Three Years* and *A Case History*, which not only depict the Russian merchant class but do so from a remarkably uniform standpoint. The workers and humbler employees are all background figures, never developing into major characters. And they are always shown as victims of the 'system', so that the three stories can be read, by those with the necessary inclinations, as indictments of nascent Russian capitalism. Yet here is no black-and-white confrontation of grasping employer and victim-worker, since the employers too are regularly portrayed, for all their wealth and potential freedom of action, as helpless victims of a situation from which they derive little or no fulfilment. Alexis Laptev in *Three Years*, Anne Glagolev in *A Woman's Kingdom*, the Lyalikov heiress in *A Case History*—all are presented as trapped by predicaments from which they are as ill equipped to escape as are the humblest of their sweated labourers or office boys.

Work, it seems, is equally frustrating, whether one has to perform it oneself or is placed in the no less difficult position of having to live off the labour of others. And, deeply concerned though Chekhov undoubtedly was over the tribulations of the working masses during Russia's industrial revolution, he never writes of them primarily as a social reformer, being far more concerned to depict the paralysis of will which afflicts the bosses. These not only fail to use their power to improve conditions, but cannot even exploit their own privileges with intelligent selfishness in order to obtain some kind of personal satisfaction.

The predicament of Anne, in *A Woman's Kingdom*, is so well portrayed that the reader may be mesmerized into forgetting one latent element in the situation: that the wretched woman should either have rolled up her elegant sleeves, taken over her own factory and become a functioning iron-mistress, or else sold up the establishment there and then and gone to live in comfort somewhere else. However, if human beings invariably took sensible decisions, Chekhov would have found himself with nothing to write about.

Work or lack of work, career or lack of career—to frustrations in these areas is added the frustration in love also inevitable in Chekhov.

His women's unhappiness usually revolves round marriage. This may be because they do not achieve wedlock at all, such being the fate of the factory-owning Anne, and—we suspect—of Rashevich's daughters in *At a Country House*. Or marriage, if achieved, will provide its own tribulations. In *Three Years* a volte-face is executed whereby Chekhov has, in effect, turned the plot of Pushkin's *Eugene Onegin* on its head. There Tatyana's initial unrequited love for Onegin paves the way for a reversal of roles: the man ends up saddled with unrequited love for the woman whom he had originally spurned. *Three Years* more or less inverts the process, since Laptev initially falls in love with a Julia who does not love him, and induces her to marry him—but then falls out of love with her just as she is becoming enamoured of him.

The frustrations of *Three Years* are, by Chekhov's standards, considerably muted. At the end of the story he is suggesting that, if things are not so very good, neither are they so very bad. Living or partly living will continue very much as hitherto *du côté de chez* Laptev for the next thirteen or thirty years. The common pattern is also varied in that neither Julia nor Laptev is the victim of the other. Chekhov seems to sympathize with each of them in turn, but this even balance within a single work by no means represents his norm. Elsewhere he has a strong tendency to indicate, when portraying man–woman confrontations, that one party is the predator or persecutor, whether through indifference or malice, while the other is the innocent victim, whether through feebleness or bad luck.

Tanya Pesotsky, so sadistically ill-used by her insane husband in *The Black Monk*; Sophia Yagich in *The Two Volodyas*, so despised and ignored as a human being by both her husband and her lover; Martha of *Rothschild's Fiddle*, whom her coffin-making husband has always treated as an article of furniture—these figures, taken in conjunction with the concern for women's lot revealed in the portrayal of Anne of *A Woman's Kingdom* and of Julia in *Three Years*, might suggest that the Chekhov of 1893–5 had set himself up as a defender of women's rights and the scourge of a male-dominated world. He seems at times to be protesting against the limited range of activity open to the women of his age, perhaps agreeing with Sophia Yagich—'aghast to think that girls and women of her class had no resort but non-stop troika rides and living a lie, or taking the veil and mortifying the flesh'.

Outside the present volume, however, Chekhov's women include a fair share of harpies or predators to set against the innocent and pathetic victims. One has only to think of two remarkably vicious Olgas—those of *The Butterfly* (1892) and *His Wife* (1895)—of the heroine of *Ariadne* (1895), or of Natasha in *Three Sisters* (1901) to see that their creator was not *a priori* committed to vindicating or attacking either sex exclusively. Of course not. He was not that kind of person, for rarely has anyone been less prone to operate in facile preconceived categories and terms. Rather does he seem to suggest, over the years, that predator attracts victim and vice versa without sexual discrimination in either direction.

Even in the present volume, comparatively feminist in balance though it is, we do meet one female monster-in-potential, disguised as a vivacious young girl. She is Masha Shelestov of *The Russian Master*, perhaps the finest story of 1894 and one in which Chekhov develops his own special brand of anti-romanticism with the greatest subtlety. The history of the work's composition (outlined at greater length in Appendix vi, below) itself furnishes an ironical comment on Chekhov's irony. Having conceived, in 1889, a two-tier narrative—idyll and counter-idyll—Chekhov yielded to the pleas of his soft-hearted relatives by publishing the first half on its own as a self-contained work and by temporarily jettisoning the projected dénouement. He had, in fact, intended to 'blow to smithereens' the happiness of his hero and heroine, yet stayed his hand for five years before moving into the attack by writing the anti-sentimental Chapter Two which totally disrupts the sentimental Chapter One. Even then it was with gentle nudges, rather than sledgehammer blows, that he overturned his characters' happiness, for it is—as usual—on trivialities, not on some great passionate crisis, that the marriage of the young Nikitins begins to founder.

Masha's concern to conserve dairy products—her obsession with sour cream, milk and cheese—her confession of having 'eaten too much jam': these are signals of acute disapproval to those versed in the Chekhovian symbolism of consumables whereby his non-approved characters tend to be associated with food. But so restrained is Chekhov's demolition of the idyll that we need to read *The Russian Master* in the context of his work as a whole before we can feel the full force of Nikitin's farewell cry of despair. 'There is nothing more terrible, insulting and mortifying than the smiling, smug complacency of the second-rate. I must run away, I must escape this very day or I shall go out of my mind.'

Aged thirty-four at the time when he wrote *The Russian Master*,

Chekhov seemed to have become a confirmed bachelor. Though he did eventually succumb to wedlock seven years later, many of his stories contrive to display, through the attitudes of his characters, a marked distaste for amorous entanglements and domestic trivialities. Indeed, one can read sections of these works as the author's own apology for neglecting the duty, as his friends and family tended to see it, of taking a wife. As I wrote in the Introduction to volume vi of this edition, when discussing Gregory Orlov, hero of *An Anonymous Story*, 'Chekhov repeatedly chose to portray a vulgar, over-domesticated housewife dragging her husband and household down to the level of the kitchen, and even indulging in the extremely deprecated activity of making jam.' Orlov, by contrast, thought that 'a decent man's flat should be like a warship, containing nothing superfluous'.[1]

The exploiter, practically the discoverer, of triviality as a fictional theme, Chekhov again and again demonstrates the hold which it can obtain on potentially enterprising and worthwhile characters. So much did he make this theme his own, infusing it with his astringent brand of anti-sentimental poetry, that readers are apt to forget the occasions on which grander, more tragic, more spectacular concerns are invoked. Such a strong theme is the insanity and death of Kovrin, the sinister yet pitiable hero of *The Black Monk*. As Chekhov had already shown with *Ward Number Six* (1892), and as he was also to show with *Murder* (1895) and *In the Hollow* (1899), he could describe violent death and mental derangement with the same telling economic artistry with which he could portray the soul-destroying impact of trivialities and pin-pricks. Even here, however, it would be unwise to insist too heavily on the author's sympathy for the pathetic Tanya and on his antipathy for her monstrously cruel husband Kovrin. There was, it seems clear from Chekhov's work and record as a whole, more than a little latent under-tow in the opposite direction. Tanya had, after all, committed the crime of trying to domesticate Kovrin; and would, given the chance, have made him as much a prisoner of mindless domestication as the unfortunate Nikitin in *The Russian Master*. Not for nothing does *milk*—that non-approved fluid and emblem of domesticity—play a comparable role in the two stories, for the same dairy product which symbolizes Masha's ascendancy also becomes the symbol of Tanya's failure to attain comparable status. It is no accident that Kovrin's most vicious outburst against his wife occurs at the moment when she tells him that 'it must be time for your milk'. This provokes the magnificent tirade

[1] *The Oxford Chekhov*, vol. vi, pp. 11-12.

in which he asserts that even insanity is preferable to being submerged in domestic bliss.

'Why, oh why did you try to cure me? Bromides, idleness, warm baths, being watched, this craven fear of every mouthful, every step—it will turn me into a downright imbecile in the end. I was losing my mind, I had delusions of grandeur, but I was elated, I was even happy, I was attractive and original. Now I've become more reasonable and stable, but I'm just like everyone else— I'm a mediocrity, and I'm bored with life. Oh, how cruelly you have treated me!'

Once again, as in *Ward Number Six*, Chekhov has put his own protest against the tyranny of triviality and complacent mediocrity into the mouth of a lunatic. But to say this is not, of course, to claim Kovrin as an ideological hero and Tanya as the villain of the piece. Certainly not, for the general balance is very much the other way round. The author's ultimate sympathies are creatively elusive, and it is the tension between two opposing tugs, not the overwhelming of one current by another, which seems the most significant element. There is also the point that even *The Black Monk*, with its successfully developed strong theme, is also in the end one more denunciation of trivialization as an abiding menace to the human condition: one to which even death is preferable.

Though *The Russian Master* and *The Black Monk* are perhaps the finest stories in this volume, the claims of the comparatively neglected *At a Country House* should not be ignored. It demonstrates how skilfully Chekhov the supremely 'economical' master of understatement could on occasion venture into the area of creative overstatement. Like his superb farce *A Tragic Role* (1889), like the masterly *Dreary Story*, this work is almost all tirade. It consists largely of the outpourings of an elderly sufferer from logorrhoea—one so intoxicated with the exuberance of his own verbosity that he forgets his surroundings, deeply insults his guest and thereby deprives his two daughters of their only male companion and prospective suitor. The theme may seem slight and reminiscent of the early 'little stories', many of them highly facetious, which Chekhov had churned out in quantity in the early 1880s. But so deft is the handling, so richly realized the theme of mutual misunderstanding, that *At a Country House* must rate among the author's masterpieces. Students of his art will also note how, towards the end, he briefly flirts with the idea of rehabilitating the miserable Rashevich. He begins, but only begins, to evoke the reader's sympathy for the poor old boy; but ends—anti-sentimental to the last—on a note of strong condemnation.

In the first story of the present volume the Two Volodyas of the title, together with their victim Sophia and the chain-smoking Rita, all seem to incur the disapproval which Chekhov the fiction-writer (often more ascetic than Chekhov the man) so often bestows on the self-indulgent. *The Two Volodyas* therefore belongs, with *At a Country House*, to the category of works in which the author's sympathies and antipathies are clearly revealed, and without the recurrent element of ambivalence to which reference was made above. Visits to restaurants, brandy-swigging, chain-smoking, loud laughter, too much talking, casual fornication—these are some of the misdemeanours severally or individually attributed to the guilty quartet of the earlier story. How eloquent a contrast they offer to the clean, austere world of the well-scrubbed, modest, silent Olga and her convent. The colouring of Olga and her milieu is insistently monochrome, with all the emphasis on pallor and blackness—a feature typical of Chekhov's invocation of purity and self-denial in a naughty and unclean world. And by the end of the story even the misguided Sophia is at last beginning to assimilate Chekhov's message when, in the last paragraph, she is reported as weeping during her visits to the convent and as feeling (a sign of grace at last) 'as if she had brought something soiled, pathetic, worn-out into the cell with her'.

Though effectively portrayed, the nun Olga remains a pallid personage, figuratively as well as literally. And, as this aspect of *The Two Volodyas* reminds us, Chekhov—like almost all writers of fiction—was more effective when depicting 'negative', non-approved characters than when portraying those figures who seem to enjoy their creator's positive approval. He was effective, too, as a negative moralist: though it was rarely his primary purpose to purvey lessons in conduct, even the least perceptive of his readers can, if he wishes, draw from the works many a useful hint on how *not* to behave. Big Volodya, Small Volodya, Sophia and Rita from our first story; Lysevich, Rashevich and Panaurov from later items – these figures from the present volume are all admirable guides since, by scrupulously refraining from behaving like any of them, a reader would be likely to turn into a better human being. In the only work in this volume exclusively de-voted to lower-class life – *Rothschild's Fiddle* – the same negative moral may also be detected: only after many decades of marriage and his wife's death does the coffin-maker Jacob feel any stirrings of tenderness towards her. Here Chekhov reverts to a theme of 1885, as found in his story *Sorrow*, where 'an aged, drunken village turner speaks tenderly to his dying wife (whom he has beaten regularly during forty years of marriage) while conveying her to hospital by cart: only to discover that she has given up the ghost *en route*, too soon to appreciate this one and only expression of her husband's all-too-well concealed devotion'.[1]

Rothschild's Fiddle is reminiscent of the 'Tolstoyan' type of story of which Chekhov had written not a few in the late 1880s. But they were unusual in the sense that the author had temporarily and sporadically embraced ethical homiletics more directly than he generally permitted himself even at this early, more didactically inclined, stage of his career. The result was a small group of works designed to preach the virtues of love, forgiveness and the like somewhat in the manner of Leo Tolstoy's magnificent moralizing tales. But Chekhov's efforts in this area are aesthetically disappointing. We also note that, even when he assumes the role of teacher more directly, it still remains true that his impact is greater when that teaching is negative. It is so both in *Sorrow* and *Rothschild's Fiddle*, the latter being a particularly impressive sample of its author's art. In these works Chekhov preaches love (if he does) by holding up the bad example of those who have failed to generate it. When, in a sample of direct didacticism unique in his mature writings, he proceeds to the positively moralistic approach of *The Head Gardener's Story*, the result is less happy. Whatever may be the individual reader's attitude to the formula *love of man* there propagated (an admirable slogan for confidence-tricksters, some might feel), the fictional realization of that theme has given rise to what is, for Chekhov, an astonishingly ineffective story from any point of view.

Fortunately the same accusation cannot be levelled against *The Student*—once more a work exceptional in presenting a kind of fictional sermon, and one which might be mistaken by the untutored for the work of a fervent Christian believer. That the author was nothing of the sort we know from several forthright references in his letters. Still, to reject the dogmas and eschatological claims of the various Christian denominations is not necessarily to be wholly unsympathetic to the spirit of Christianity. Himself no believer, Chekhov nevertheless respected religious faith in others, always provided that they were not given to excessive proselytizing. He was also, in his somewhat patron-

---

[1] Hingley, *A New Life of Anton Chekhov*, pp. 58–9.

izing way, apt to feel that women in particular were less liable to get up to mischief if they subscribed to some form of religious belief.

All the same, it is not easy to see why Chekhov should have preferred this particular story to all his other works. He also invoked it as evidence that he possessed an optimistic outlook, and to the extent that he conveys an essential harmony among human beings of all kinds and ages, this claim is understandable—especially as disharmony is so much more commonly the burden of his muse. Be this as it may, *The Student* is impressive enough in its way, and it makes its simple point tellingly. Yet it comes nowhere near to the level of the best writing in the present volume. Such is my own opinion. But that such assessments are a matter of individual taste I am well aware; if some reader should agree with Chekhov that *The Student* is the finest story here presented my equanimity will not be shattered.

Optimist; pessimist; detailed chronicler of the Russian merchant milieu; moralist and atmosphere-evoker; sentimentalist and anti-sentimentalist; inflater and deflater of illusions; apostle of asceticism; champion of modesty, sensitivity and unassertiveness; scourge of domesticity, vulgarity and triviality; hounder of eaters, drinkers, talkers, card-players, fornicators—the Chekhov of the present volume passes before our eyes in these and many other guises. No one of these elements is the true Chekhov, yet all are important in varying degree and at varying times to the work of one who, as man and writer, has tempted endless enthusiasts, critics and reviewers (especially those who know him least) into the trap of summing him up.

THE TWO VOLODYAS

[*Володя большой и Володя маленький*]

(1893)

THE TWO VOLODYAS

'LET GO of me, I want to drive, I'm going to sit by the driver,' shouted Sophia. 'Wait, driver, I'm coming on the box with you.'

She was standing in the sledge while her husband Volodya and her childhood friend, another Volodya, both held her arms to stop her falling. On rushed the troika.

'I told you not to give her brandy,' whispered her husband irritably to the other Volodya. 'It really was rather naughty of you.'

With women like his wife Sophia, rowdy and somewhat tipsy high spirits usually presaged hysterical laughter and then tears—the Colonel knew that from experience, and he dreaded having to fuss with compresses and medicines when they got home, instead of going to bed.

'Whoa there,' shouted Sophia. 'I want to drive.'

She was truly happy and jubilant. During the two months since her wedding she had been nagged by the thought of having married Colonel Yagich for his money and 'out of frustration'. But at the out-of-town restaurant this evening she had at last convinced herself that she loved him passionately. He was so trim, so spry, so lithe despite his fifty-four years, he was so charming when he joked and hummed an accompaniment to the gipsy girls' music. Older men are a thousand times more attractive than young ones nowadays, that's a fact, as if age and youth had exchanged roles. The Colonel was two years older than her father, but what did that matter when he was far, far more dynamic, high-spirited and vivacious, quite honestly, than she was herself? And she was only twenty-three.

'Oh my darling,' she thought. 'You splendid man.'

She had also decided at the restaurant that no spark of her old feelings for the other Volodya remained in her heart. To that childhood friend whom, only yesterday, she had loved to distraction and despair, she now felt utterly indifferent. He had seemed such an apathetic, drowsy, unattractive nonentity all evening. His casual habit of dodging payment in restaurants had outraged her this time, and she had nearly told him to stay at home if he was so poor. The Colonel had paid for everything.

Perhaps it was the trees, telegraph poles and snow-drifts flitting past her eyes which prompted such a variety of thoughts. The restaurant bill had come to a hundred and twenty roubles, she reflected, the gipsies had been paid a hundred, and she could throw away a whole thousand tomorrow if she liked, whereas before her wedding two months ago she had had less than three roubles to call her own. She had had to go to her father for every little thing. How her life had changed!

Her thoughts were muddled, and she remembered when she had been about ten—how Colonel Yagich, now her husband, had flirted with her aunt, how everyone at home had said that he had 'ruined' Aunt, how Aunt indeed had often come down to dinner with her eyes red from crying, how she was always going off somewhere, how people had said that the poor creature didn't know what to do with herself. He had been very handsome then, famous all over town for his fantastic success with women, and was said to visit his lady admirers daily like a doctor on his rounds. Even now, for all the grey hair, wrinkles and spectacles, his lean face sometimes looked very handsome, especially in profile.

Sophia's father was an army doctor who had once served in Yagich's regiment. The other Volodya's father was a medical officer, and had served in the same regiment too. Despite amorous adventures often highly complex and hectic, the younger Volodya had been a brilliant student. After graduating with honours he had chosen to specialize in foreign literature, and was said to be writing a thesis. He lived in barracks with his father the medical officer, and had no money of his own though he was now thirty. As children he and Sophia had lived in different flats in the same building, he had often come and played with her, they had been taught dancing and French together. But when he had grown into a slender, very handsome youth she had begun to feel shy with him, and had then fallen madly in love with him. And in love with him she had remained until her recent marriage. He too had had remarkable success with women, pretty well from the age of fourteen, and the ladies who deceived their husbands with him would excuse themselves by saying that Volodya was so 'little'. There was a recent account of him as a student living in rooms near the university—every time you knocked you'd hear his step on the other side of the door and the low-voiced apology, '*Pardon, je ne suis pas seul.*' He was a great joy to Yagich, who, like the old poet Derzhavin blessing the young Pushkin, expected great things of him, and was obviously devoted to him. They would play billiards or piquet for hours in silence. If Yagich went troika-riding he would take Volodya with him, and only Yagich was privy to the secrets of Volodya's thesis. Earlier, in the Colonel's younger days, they had often found themselves in competition, but without jealousy. When they were in company together Yagich was called 'Big Volodya' and his friend 'Small Volodya'.

Besides Big Volodya, Small Volodya and Sophia, the sledge had another occupant, Sophia Yagich's cousin Rita—a spinster in her thirties, very pale with black eyebrows and pince-nez, who chain-smoked even in the freezing cold. She always had ash on the front of her dress and on her lap. She spoke through her nose, she drawled, she was undemonstrative, she could put back as many liqueurs and brandies as she liked without getting drunk, and she told *risqué* stories in a dull, tasteless way. At home she read the intellectual reviews morning, noon and night, scattering ash over them, or ate crystallized apples.

'Do stop fooling, Sophia,' she drawled. 'Don't be so silly, really.'

When the city gates came in view the troika slowed down, there were glimpses of houses and people, and Sophia subsided, cuddling up to her husband, utterly lost in thought. Small Volodya sat opposite her. Now gloomy notions began to tinge her happy, light-hearted reveries. The man opposite knew she had been in love with him, she supposed, and he must have believed this talk about her marrying the Colonel 'out of frustration'. She had never told him she loved him, she had no wish for him to know about it, she had hidden her feelings, but his expression showed that he understood her perfectly—and her pride suffered. But most humiliating of all, given her situation, was that Small Volodya had suddenly started taking notice of her after her marriage, which had never happened before. He would sit with her for hours in silence or idly chatting, and now in the sledge he was gently pressing her leg and massaging her hand without talking to her. He had only been waiting for her to get married, obviously. No less obviously, he despised her. She aroused in him only interest of a certain kind, as if she was a loose woman. And it was this combination of jubilant love for her husband with humiliation and injured pride that made her feel so thoroughly mischievous, made her want to sit on the driver's box, shout and whistle.

They were just passing the convent when a great clanging came from the huge twenty-ton bell. Rita made the sign of the cross.

'That's where Olga is,' said Sophia, also crossing herself and shuddering.

'What made her take the veil?' the Colonel asked.

'Sheer frustration,' answered Rita angrily, with an obvious allusion to the marriage of Sophia and Yagich. 'That sort of thing is all the rage now. It's a challenge to society as a whole. A jolly girl she was, a terrific flirt who cared only for dances and dancing partners. And then, suddenly, this business! What a surprise.'

'That's not true,' said Small Volodya, lowering the collar of his fur coat and revealing his handsome face. 'It wasn't just frustration, I'm very sorry, it was something utterly horrible. Her brother Dmitry was sentenced to hard labour in Siberia, and now no one knows where he is. Her mother died of a broken heart.'

He raised his collar again.

'Olga did the right thing,' he added tonelessly. 'To be a foster-child, and in our precious Sophia's home at that—it's enough to give you pause.'

Sophia heard the sneer in his voice and wanted to pay him back in kind, but said nothing. Then, feeling that mischievous urge again, she stood up.

'I want to go to the service,' she shouted tearfully. 'Turn back, driver, I want to see Olga.'

They turned back. The tolling of the convent bell was deafening, and there was something in it reminiscent of Olga and her life, Sophia felt. Other church bells also started ringing. When the driver halted Sophia jumped from the sledge and rushed to the gate unescorted.

'Do please hurry,' shouted her husband. 'It's late.'

She went through the dark gate and along the path to the main church. Snow crunched under her feet and the tolling resounded right above her head, seeming to penetrate her whole being. She came to the church door, the three steps down and the porch with frescoes of saints on both sides. There was a smell of juniper and incense. Then came another door which a dark figure opened with a low bow.

In church the service had not yet started. One nun was attending to the icon screen and lighting the candles in their massive holders, another was lighting a chandelier. Here and there by the columns and side-altars stood unmoving black figures.

'They'll just stand where they are till morning,' thought Sophia. How dark, cold and depressing this was, she felt—worse than a grave-yard. Feeling bored, she looked at the still, frozen figures, and suddenly her heart missed a beat. Somehow she had recognized one of the nuns—short, with thin shoulders and a black shawl on her head—as Olga, though Olga had been a buxom lass and rather taller when she had entered the convent. Hesitant and mightily agitated for some reason, Sophia went up to the novice, looked into her face over her shoulder and recognized Olga.

'Olga!' She threw up her arms, too moved to say more.

The nun knew her at once. She raised her eyebrows in amazement, and her pale, freshly washed, clean face glowed with pleasure—as did also, apparently, the white kerchief visible under her shawl.

'The Lord has wrought a miracle.' She too threw up her hands, which were thin and pale.

Sophia embraced her firmly and kissed her, afraid as she did so that she must smell of brandy.

'We were just driving past and thought of you,' she gasped, as if she had been walking too fast. 'Lord, how pale you are. I, er, I'm very glad to see you. Well, how are things, how are you, are you bored?'

Sophia looked round at the other nuns. 'We've had so many changes,' she went on quietly. 'I married Volodya Yagich, you know, I'm sure you remember him. I'm very happy with him.'

'The Lord be praised. And is your father well?'

'Yes, he often remembers you. But you should come and see us during the holiday, Olga. How about it?'

Olga laughed. 'Very well, I'll come the day after tomorrow.'

Without knowing why, Sophia burst into tears, wept silently for a minute, then wiped her eyes.

'Rita will be so sorry to have missed you,' she said. 'She's with us too. Small Volodya's here as well. They're at the gate. They'd be so pleased to see you. Let's go out to them—the service hasn't begun, has it?'

'All right then,' agreed Olga. She crossed herself three times and went out with Sophia.

'You're happy then, are you, Sophia?' Olga asked when they were outside the gate.

'Yes, very.'

'Thank God.'

When Big Volodya and Small Volodya saw the nun they got off the sledge and greeted her respectfully, both obviously touched by the pallor of her face and her black habit, both pleased that she remembered them and had come to greet them. To shield her from the cold Sophia wrapped her in a rug and covered her with a flap of her fur coat. Her recent tears had relieved and purged her spirits, and she was glad that this rowdy, turbulent and essentially sullied night had unexpectedly come to so pure and gentle an end. To keep Olga near her longer she suggested taking her for a ride.

'Get in, Olga, we'll go for a bit of a spin.'

The men expected the nun to refuse since the religious don't gad around in troikas, but to their surprise she assented and mounted the sledge. As the three-horse team whisked them off towards the city gates all were silent, concerned only for her comfort and warmth, each comparing her former with her present state. Her expression was neutral, rather impassive, frigid, pale and transparent as though she had water rather than blood flowing through her veins. Two or three years ago she had been a buxom, rosy-cheeked girl, always talking about young men and laughing uproariously at the slightest pretext.

The sledge turned back at the town gate. About ten minutes later they halted at the convent and Olga got out. A medley of peals now rang from the belfry.

'May the Lord preserve you.' Olga gave a low nun-like bow.

'You will visit us, won't you, Olga?'

'Yes, yes, of course.'

She moved off quickly and soon disappeared through the dark gateway. Then the sledge bowled off again, and they all somehow felt terribly sad. Nobody spoke. Sophia felt weak all over and her spirits fell. To have got a nun into a sledge and taken her for a troika ride in tipsy company—it now struck her as silly, tactless and rather sacrilegious. The desire for self-deception had left her along with her intoxication. She neither did nor could love her husband, she now realized, all that was arrant nonsense. She had married him for his money because he was what her schoolfriends had called 'madly rich', because she was terrified of being left on the shelf like Rita, because she was fed up with her doctor father, because she wanted to spite Small Volodya. Could she have imagined, when contemplating the marriage, that it would prove so ugly and unnerving an ordeal, nothing in the world would have induced her to consent to it. But things were past praying for now, she must put up with them.

They arrived home. Climbing into her warm, soft bed, pulling the quilt over her, Sophia remembered the dark porch, the smell of incense, the figures by the columns, and was aghast to think that those figures would stand there without moving all the time she would be asleep. Early mass would last a very long time, then there would be the Hours, then another mass and a prayer service.

'But God does exist, He certainly does, and I shall most certainly die, so sooner or later I must think about my soul and eternal life, as Olga does. Olga is saved now, she has solved all her problems. But what if there is no God? Then her life has been wasted. But what do I mean, "wasted"? Wasted how?'

A minute later another thought occurred.

'God exists, death will come without fail and one must think about one's soul. Should Olga face death this instant she would be unafraid, she is prepared. But the main thing is, she has made her own decision about life's problems. God exists, indeed. But is entering a convent really the only answer? To take the veil—why, that means renouncing life, destroying it.'

Sophia felt rather terrified and hid her head beneath her pillow. 'I mustn't, mustn't think about that,' she whispered.

Yagich was pacing the carpet in the next room, his spurs gently jingling. He was pondering.

It struck Sophia that the man was near and dear to her only in this, that he too was called Volodya. She sat up in bed.

'Volodya,' she called tenderly.

'What do you want?' her husband responded.

'Oh, nothing.'

She lay down again. There was a tolling, perhaps from that same convent bell, and she again remembered the porch and the dark figures. Thoughts about God and the inevitability of death drifted through her mind, and she pulled the quilt over her head to shut out the bells. She reckoned that she had a long, long life ahead of her before old age and death. Day in day out she would have to cope with the proximity of this man whom she didn't love, who had just come into the bedroom and was getting into bed, and she would have to suppress her hopeless love of another man—young, charming, somehow special. She looked at her husband and wanted to say good night, but suddenly burst into tears instead. She was annoyed with herself.

'Here we go again,' said Yagich.

She did calm down, but later—towards ten in the morning. She had stopped crying and shivering all over, but had acquired an acute head-ache instead. Yagich was hurrying off to late mass and was in the next room grumbling at the batman who was helping him dress. He came into the bedroom once, his spurs faintly jingling, and fetched something, then came in a second time—now wearing his epaulettes and decora-tions, limping a bit because of his rheumatism. He vaguely impressed Sophia as prowling and lurking like a beast of prey.

Then she heard him on the telephone.

'Put me through to the Vasilyevsky Barracks, please.' There was a short pause. 'Vasilyevsky Barracks? Kindly call Dr. Salimovich to the telephone.' Another short pause. 'Who's that speaking? Volodya? Good. Then ask your father to call round here straight away, there's a good fellow. Fact is, my lady wife has come considerably unstuck after last night's business. He's out, eh? Ah, well. Many thanks, that's fine— I'll be most obliged. *Merci*.'

Yagich came into the bedroom for the third time, bent over his wife, made the sign of the cross over her, gave her his hand to kiss—the women who loved him used to kiss his hand, and he expected it—and said he would be back for dinner. He left.

Towards noon the maid announced Small Volodya. Swaying with fatigue and her headache, Sophia swiftly donned her splendid new lilac-coloured négligé with the fur trimmings and hurriedly did something to her hair. She felt inexpressibly tender, trembling both with joy and the fear that he might leave. She only wanted to look at him.

Small Volodya had arrived in formal visiting style—tail-coat and white tie. When Sophia came into the drawing-room he kissed her hand and said how truly sorry he was that she was unwell. When they had sat down he praised her négligé.

'I was put out by meeting Olga last night,' she said. 'It rather unnerved me at first, but I envy her now. She's as firm as a rock, there's no budging her. But was there really no other resort, Volodya? Can you really solve life's problems by burying yourself alive? That's death, isn't it—not life?'

At the mention of Olga, Small Volodya's face expressed tender concern.

'Now you're a clever man, Volodya,' said Sophia. 'So show me how I can best follow her example. I'm not a believer, of course, and couldn't take the veil, but I could do something equivalent, couldn't I? My life isn't easy,' she went on after a short pause. 'You teach me, then. Tell me something that will convince me. Say but one word.'

'One word? All right then. Ta-ra-ra-boomdeay.'

'Why do you despise me, Volodya?' she asked impetuously. 'You talk to me in some special—forgive me—caddish language. No one talks to their friends or to decent women like that. You're a successful scholar, you love academic work, but why, oh why do you never speak to me of that? Am I unworthy?'

'Whence this sudden yearning for scholarship?' Small Volodya frowned irritatedly. 'Perhaps you yearn for constitutional government? Or perhaps you'd prefer sturgeon with horseradish?'

'Oh, all right, I'm an insignificant, worthless, immoral, half-witted woman. I've made masses and masses of mistakes, I'm a nervous wreck, I'm corrupt and so I deserve contempt. But you're ten years older than me, Volodya, aren't you? And my husband's thirty years older. You watched me grow up, and if you'd wanted you could have made anything of me you liked—an angel, even. But you'—her voice trembled—'you treat me terribly. Yagich married me in his old age, and you——'

'Oh really, do give over.' Volodya moved nearer to her and kissed both her hands. 'Let us permit the Schopenhauers to philosophize and argue to their hearts' content, while we just kiss these dear little hands.'

'You despise me—oh, if you only knew what suffering that causes me,' she faltered, knowing in advance that he would not believe her. 'But I so much want to change, to turn over a new leaf, did you but know. I think of it with such joy,' she added, and tears of joy actually came to her eyes. 'To be a good, honourable, decent person, not to lie, to have a purpose in life——'

'Oh, for heaven's sake drop the play-acting, I dislike it.' Volodya's face assumed a petulant expression. 'It's so melodramatic, honestly. Let's behave like real people.'

To prevent him from leaving in a huff she began justifying herself, forcing a smile to please him, and again spoke of Olga, and of wanting to solve her problems in life and become a real person.

'Ta-ra-ra-boomdeay, ta-ra-ra-boomdeay,' he sang softly, spacing out the syllables.

Then he suddenly seized her waist. She, not knowing what she was doing, put her hands on his shoulders and for a minute gazed enraptured and entranced at his clever, ironical face, his forehead, his eyes, his handsome beard.

'As you have known for some time, I love you,' she confessed, blushing painfully and feeling her very lips twisted in a spasm of embarrassment. 'I love you. So why torture me?'

She closed her eyes and kissed him firmly on the lips. For a long time, perhaps a whole minute, she could not bring the kiss to an end, though she knew that it was improper, that he himself might think badly of her, that one of the servants might come in.

'Oh, how you torture me,' she said.

Half an hour later, when he had had what he wanted, he was eating a snack in the dining-room while she knelt before him, gazing passionately into his face, and he said that she was like a little dog waiting to

be thrown a piece of ham. Then he sat her on one knee, rocked her
like a child and sang.

'Ta-ra-ra-boomdeay.'

When he was ready to leave she asked him in a voice choked with
passion when they could meet next. 'Later today? Where?'

She held out both hands to his mouth, as if wanting to catch the
answer in them.

'I don't think today's convenient,' he said after some thought. 'We
might manage tomorrow.'

They parted. Before lunch Sophia went to see Olga at the convent,
but was told that she was reading the Psalter in memory of someone
who had died. From the convent she went to see her father, but he was
out too. Then she took a different cab and drove aimlessly up and down
streets broad and narrow, continuing thus until evening fell. Meanwhile
she somehow kept remembering the aunt with the eyes red from crying
and without a place in life.

That night they went troika-riding again and heard the gipsy singers
at the out-of-town restaurant. As they were driving past the convent
again Sophia remembered Olga, and was aghast to think that girls and
women of her class had no resort but non-stop troika rides and living
a lie, or taking the veil and mortifying the flesh.

Next day she had a rendezvous with her lover, after which she took
another lonely cab drive and again remembered her aunt.

A week later he dropped her, and then life resumed its former
routine, being just as dull, painful—just as agonizing, sometimes—as
ever. The Colonel and Small Volodya played billiards and piquet for
hours, Rita limply told insipid anecdotes, Sophia kept going for cab
drives and asking her husband to take her on troika trips.

Calling at the convent almost daily, she bored Olga with complaints
about her unbearable sufferings. And she wept, feeling as if she had
brought something soiled, pathetic, worn-out into the cell with her.
But Olga told her in the wooden voice of one repeating a lesson that
none of it mattered, it would all pass, God would forgive her.

THE BLACK MONK

[*Черный монах*]

(1894)

THE BLACK MONK

I

ANDREW KOVRIN M.A. was exhausted and distraught, but instead of seeking regular medical treatment he had a casual word over a bottle of wine with a doctor friend who advised him to spend spring and summer in the country. This coincided with a long letter from Tanya Pesotsky inviting him to stay at Borisovka. So he decided that he really did need the trip.

First he went to his own family estate, Kovrinka, in April and spent three weeks there on his own. Then, after waiting till the roads were passable, he set off by carriage to see his former guardian and mentor Pesotsky, a horticulturalist of national repute. From Kovrinka to the Pesotskys' place at Borisovka was reckoned about fifty miles, and it was sheer joy, that spring day, to drive on the soft surface in a well-sprung carriage.

Pesotsky's house was huge, with its columns, its peeling plaster lions, its frock-coated footman at the front door. The old-fashioned park, bleak and forbidding, was laid out in English style, extending nearly a thousand yards from house to river and ending in a precipitous clay cliff sprouting pines with exposed roots like hairy paws. Down below the water gleamed uninvitingly, sandpipers swooped and squeaked piteously. The atmosphere was always positively elegiac. But near the house—in the gardens, orchards and nursery beds occupying some eighty acres altogether—it was bright and cheerful even in bad weather. Nowhere had Kovrin seen such superb roses, lilies, camellias and tulips in all conceivable hues from snow-white to soot-black, such a general profusion of blooms, as at Pesotsky's. Spring was only beginning, and the true glory of the flower-beds still lurked in hot-houses. But what was already in bloom along the paths, and here and there in the beds—it sufficed to transport you, as you strolled about, to a realm of delectable colours, especially in the early morning when dew gleamed on every petal.

This ornamental part of the garden, which Pesotsky himself dismissed as mere frippery, had been sheer magic to Kovrin as a boy. What curiosities, what grotesque freaks, what travesties of nature were here! There were espaliered fruit trees, a pear formed like a Lombardy poplar, globose oaks and limes, an umbrella-shaped apple-tree, arches, letter designs, candelabra, and even an '1862'—the year of Pesotsky's horticultural début—in plums. There were also fine, graceful saplings with firm, straight stems like palms, and only a close look showed that these saplings were gooseberries or currants. But the most exhilarating and stimulating aspect of the garden was the constant bustle. From dawn to dusk near trees and shrubs, on paths and flower-beds, gardeners swarmed ant-like with their barrows, mattocks, watering cans.

Reaching the Pesotskys' house towards ten in the evening, Kovrin found Tanya and her father Yegor in a great pother. The clear, starry sky and the thermometer presaged frost by morning, but the head gardener Ivan Karlych had gone to town and there was no one dependable left. They talked of nothing but this frost over supper, and it was decided that Tanya would patrol the orchard after midnight instead of going to bed, to keep an eye on things, and that her father would rise at three or even earlier.

Kovrin sat with Tanya all evening and went into the garden with her after midnight. It was cold outside, there was a strong smell of burning. In the large 'commercial' orchard—it earned Pesotsky several thousand roubles' annual profit—thick, black, acrid smoke was settling on the ground and enveloping the trees, protecting all that money from frost. The trees stood like pieces on a draughts board, their rows as straight and even as soldiers on parade. This strict, meticulous precision, combined with the trees' identical height and their absolutely uniform crowns and trunks—it made a monotonous, depressing picture. Walking down the files, where bonfires of dung, straw and mixed rubbish smouldered, Kovrin and Tanya met occasional labourers drifting wraith-like through the smoke. The only trees in bloom were cherries, plums and certain varieties of apple, but the whole orchard swam in smoke. Not till they reached the nursery beds did Kovrin draw a deep breath.

'The smoke used to make me sneeze as a boy.' He shrugged. 'But I still don't see how smoke protects from frost.'

'It replaces the clouds when the sky's clear,' Tanya answered.

'But what do the clouds do?'

'You don't get frost in dull, cloudy weather.'

'So that's it.'

He laughed and took her arm. Her broad, very serious-looking, chilled face, her thin black eyebrows, the raised overcoat collar impeding the movements of her head, her whole slender, graceful presence, her dress hitched up because of the dew—it all moved him.

'Heavens, how we have grown up,' he said. 'When I last left here five years ago you were still a child. You were thin, long-legged, bareheaded in your short little dress. I used to tease you—called you "the heron". How time changes things!'

'Yes, it's five years.' Tanya sighed. 'A lot of water has flowed under the bridge since then. Tell me honestly, Andrew.' She spoke vivaciously, looking into his face. 'Have you grown away from us? Why do I ask, though? You're a man, you live your own fascinating life, you're a somebody. It's only natural we should feel strangers. Still, I'd like you to think of us as family, Andrew—we've earned that.'

'And so I do, Tanya.'

'Word of honour?'

'Yes indeed.'

'Yesterday you were surprised that we had so many photographs of you. But Father idolizes you, you know. Sometimes I think he's fonder of you than me. He's so proud of you. You're a scholar, a distinguished man, you've made a brilliant career, and he's certain you turned out that way only because he brought you up. I don't try to stop him thinking that, why shouldn't he?'

Dawn was breaking, as was particularly evident from the clarity with which smoke puffs and tree-tops were outlined in the air. Nightingales sang, the quails' call wafted in from the fields.

'Well, it's time for bed—it's cold too.' Tanya took his arm. 'Thanks for coming, Andrew. The people we know are dull and there are so few of them. With us it's garden, garden, garden and nothing else.' She laughed. 'Standard, half-standard, pippins, rennets, codlings, budding, grafting. Our whole life's gone into this garden. All I dream of is apples and pears. It's all very well of course, it's useful, but you do want a change sometimes. I remember you coming over for the holidays or just on a visit, and how the house felt fresher and brighter, as if the dustcovers had been taken off the chandelier and furniture. I was only a child, but I understood.'

She spoke at length, ardently, and it suddenly struck him that he might grow fond of this small, frail, voluble creature during the summer—be attracted, fall in love. Given their situation it would be so possible and natural. The idea moved and amused him. Bending down to that dear, worried face, he sang softly.

'Onegin, I cannot deny
I'll love my Tanya till I die.'

When they returned to the house Pesotsky was already out of bed. Not feeling sleepy, Kovrin got talking to the old man, and went back to the garden with him. Pesotsky was tall, broad-shouldered, large-paunched and short-winded, but always walked so fast that it was hard to keep up with him. He had a most preoccupied look, and was for ever hurrying as if expecting total disaster should he ever be one minute late.

'Now, here's an odd thing, dear boy.' He paused for breath. 'It's below zero at ground level, as you see. But you put a thermometer on a stick and lift it a dozen feet in the air, and it's warm. Now, why?'

'I really don't know.' Kovrin laughed.

'Humph. One can't know everything of course. However capacious the brain, it can't hold everything. You're more on the philosophical side, aren't you?'

'Yes. I lecture in psychology, but I study general philosophy.'

'And don't you get bored?'

'Far from it, it's all I live for.'

'Then may God bless you.' Pesotsky thoughtfully stroked his grey side-whiskers. 'Good luck to you. I'm delighted for you, delighted, dear boy——'

But then he suddenly cocked his ears, grimaced horribly, ran to one side, swiftly disappeared behind the trees in clouds of smoke.

'Who tied a horse to that apple-tree?' the desperate, blood-curdling shout was heard. 'What bastard, what swine dared tie a horse to an apple-tree? God, God, they've ruined, frozen, befouled and mucked everything up! The garden's ruined—ye gods, it's wrecked!'

When Pesotsky returned he had a worn-out, aggrieved look.

'What in hell can one do with these bloody yokels?' he asked tearfully, waving his arms. 'Stepka was carting dung last night and tied his horse to an apple-tree. He twisted the reins as tight as could be, the blackguard, and so the bark has been chafed in three places. What do you say to that? I spoke to him and he just stood there blinking, the imbecile. Hanging's too good for him.'

Calming down, he embraced Kovrin and kissed his cheek.

'Ah well, God bless you,' he muttered. 'I'm so glad you came—more than I can say. Thanks.'

Then, with that same swift gait and preoccupied look, he toured the whole garden, showing his former ward all the greenhouses, conservatories, cold houses and two rows of beehives which he called the wonder of the age.

As they walked the sun rose and brightly lit the garden. It grew warm. Foreseeing a fine, happy, long day, Kovrin recalled that this was only early May after all, and that the whole summer lay ahead—a summer which would be just as bright, happy and long, and there suddenly stirred within him a joyous, youthful feeling such as he had experienced when running about this orchard as a boy. He embraced the old man, kissed him tenderly. Much moved, both went into the house and drank tea out of old-fashioned porcelain cups with cream and rich, plump pastries. These small details again reminded Kovrin of his childhood and youth. The marvellous present, the newly-awakened impressions of the past—they blended together, making him feel fine, yet hemmed in.

He waited for Tanya to wake, had coffee with her, took a stroll, then went to his room and sat down to work. He read attentively, he made notes, occasionally raising his eyes to glance at the open windows or fresh flowers which stood, still wet with dew, in vases on the table, then again lowered his eyes to his book, feeling all his veins throbbing and vibrating with pleasure.

II

In the country he continued to lead a life no less febrile and restless than in town. He read a lot, he wrote, he studied Italian. When strolling he enjoyed thinking that he would soon be back at his desk again. Everyone was surprised that he slept so little. If he chanced to doze for half an hour during the day he would lie awake all that night, and this sleepless vigil would leave him as buoyant and cheerful as ever.

He talked a lot, drank wine, smoked expensive cigars.

The Pesotskys were visited almost daily by young ladies of the locality who played the piano and sang with Tanya. A young man, a neighbour and an excellent violinist, sometimes came over too. Kovrin listened to the playing and singing so avidly that he became exhausted, the symptoms being eyes that seemed glued shut and a head lolling to one side.

One afternoon he was sitting reading on the balcony after tea. Meanwhile Tanya, a soprano, with one of the young ladies, a contralto, and the young violinist were practising Braga's famous *Serenade* in the drawing-room. Kovrin hung on the words—it was in Russian—but just couldn't understand them. At last, putting his book aside and concentrating, he did understand. In a garden at night a morbidly imaginative girl hears mysterious sounds so weird and wondrous that

she is compelled to acknowledge them as divine harmony which soars
back aloft to the heavens, being incomprehensible to us mortals.
Kovrin's eyelids grew heavy. He rose, he wearily paced the drawing-
room and then the ballroom. When the singing ended he took Tanya's
arm and they went out on the balcony.

'I've been obsessed with a certain legend since this morning,' said he.
'I don't know whether I read it or heard it somewhere, but it's an odd,
incongruous sort of story. It's not remarkably lucid, for a start. A
thousand years ago a black-garbed monk was walking through some
Syrian or Arabian desert. A few miles away fishermen saw another
black monk moving slowly over the surface of a lake. This second
monk was a mirage. Now forget all the laws of optics seemingly
ignored by the legend, and hear the next bit. The mirage generates
another mirage. The second generates a third, and so the black monk's
image is endlessly transmitted from one atmospheric stratum to
another. He is seen, now in Africa, now in Spain, now in India, now in
the far north. Having left the earth's atmosphere behind at last, he now
wanders through the entire universe, never encountering conditions
which would enable him to fade away. Perhaps he's to be seen on Mars
somewhere, now, or on some star of the Southern Cross. But the
legend's very kernel and essence is this, my dear. Exactly a thousand
years after that monk walked in the desert the mirage will return to the
earth's atmosphere and manifest itself to men. The thousand years is
said to be just about up, so we can expect the black monk any day now
according to the legend.'

'An odd sort of mirage.' Tanya disliked the legend.

'But I just can't remember where I got it all from, that's what baffles
me.' Kovrin laughed. 'Did I read it somewhere? Was I told it? Can I
have dreamt of the black monk? I swear to God I don't remember.
But the tale obsesses me, I've thought of it all day.'

Leaving Tanya to her guests, he went out and strolled pensively near
the flower-beds. The sun was setting, and the newly watered flowers
gave off a tantalizing damp scent. Singing had started in the house
again, the distant fiddle sounding like a human voice. Where had he
heard or read the legend? Racking his brains, Kovrin wandered into
the park and found himself by the river.

Descending the path down a steep bank past bare roots to the water,
he disturbed the sandpipers and put up a brace of ducks. The last rays
of the setting sun still gleamed here and there on the grim pines, but on
the river's surface evening had fully set in. Kovrin crossed the foot-

bridge to the other side. Before him lay a broad field of young rye not yet in ear. No abode of man, no living soul was out there, and the path looked as if it led to that unknown, mysterious spot where the sun had just gone down, and where its setting rays flamed so broadly and majestically.

'What a sense of space, of peace, of freedom,' Kovrin thought as he walked along the path. 'The whole world seems to gaze at me, holding its breath, waiting for me to grasp its meaning.'

But then the rye rippled and a gentle evening breeze softly brushed his bare head. Soon afterwards came another more powerful gust, the rye rustled and he heard the pines' muffled murmur behind him. Kovrin halted in amazement. On the horizon a tall, black column like a whirlwind or sand-storm had risen from earth to sky. Though the outlines were blurred it was not standing still, but moving with awesome speed—that was immediately obvious. It was coming straight at Kovrin, growing smaller and clearer the nearer it came. Plunging into the rye on one side to make way, he was only just in time.

Arms crossed on chest, bare feet not touching the ground, the black-garbed, grey-haired, black-browed monk hurtled past.

Rushing on another half dozen yards, he looked back at Kovrin, nodded, gave a friendly yet knowing grin. Oh, what a white, a ghastly white, thin face. Swelling again, he skimmed the river, crashed soundlessly into clay cliff and pines, went straight through them and vanished into thin air.

'Well, well,' muttered Kovrin. 'So the legend was true.'

Without trying to explain this weird apparition, satisfied just to have got such a near, clear view, not only of the black robes but even of the monk's face and eyes, Kovrin returned home agreeably excited.

There were people strolling calmly in the park and garden, there was piano-playing in the house—only he had seen the monk, then. He longed to tell Tanya and Pesotsky all about it, but realized that they would certainly think he was raving and panic. Better say nothing. He laughed aloud, he sang, he danced a mazurka, he was in great form. Everyone—Tanya, her guests—found that he had a special, somehow radiantly inspired look about him this evening, and that he was quite fascinating.

III

When the guests had left after supper he went to his room and lay on the sofa, wanting to think about the monk. But soon afterwards Tanya came in.

'Here, Andrew, have a look at Father's articles.' She handed him a bundle of pamphlets and offprints. 'They're very good, he does write beautifully.'

'Now, that's going too far.' Pesotsky had followed her in with a forced laugh, feeling embarrassed. 'Don't listen to her please, and don't read them. Oh, all right, do read them if you need something to send you to sleep. They're an excellent soporific.'

'I think they're superb.' Tanya spoke with deep conviction. 'You read them, Andrew, and persuade Father to write more often. He could produce an entire course in horticulture.'

Pesotsky gave a forced guffaw, blushed and uttered the phrases commonly spoken by bashful authors. In the end he yielded.

'Then you must read Gaucher's piece first, and these articles in Russian,' he muttered, running his trembling fingers through the pamphlets. 'Otherwise you won't understand. Before reading my objections you must know what I'm objecting to. But it's all such nonsense, so boring. Besides, I think it's bedtime.'

Tanya went out. Sitting on the sofa beside Kovrin, Pesotsky sighed deeply.

'Yes, dear boy,' he said after a short pause. 'Yes indeed, my academic friend. Here am I writing my articles, exhibiting at shows, winning medals. "Pesotsky's apples are big as your head," they'll tell you. "Pesotsky has made his fortune with his orchard," say they. Pesotsky's king of his own little castle, in other words. What's it all for, though, that's the problem? The garden really is splendid, it's a show-piece. It's less a garden than an institution vital to the state—one which marks, as it were, a step towards a new era in Russian economics and industry. But to what purpose, what's it all in aid of?'

'It speaks for itself.'

'That's not my point. What will become of the garden when I die, that's what I want to know. Without me it won't last one month as you now see it. The key to its success isn't that it's a big garden with lots of gardeners, it's my love of the work, don't you see? Perhaps I love it more than I love myself. See here, I do everything myself. I work from dawn to dusk. All the grafting, all the pruning, all the planting—I do it, the whole lot. When anyone helps I grow so jealous and annoyed that I'm rude. The key to it all is love. I mean the keen eye and hands of a man handling his own property. I mean how you feel when you're away visiting someone for an hour, and you sit down but you aren't really there. You're not yourself because you're afraid of something happening to your garden. But who'll look after it when I die? Who'll do the work? My head gardener? My under-gardeners? What do you think? Now, I'll tell you something, friend. The worst enemy isn't hares, cockchafers or frost in this business, it's man—the man whose heart's not in it.'

'But what about Tanya?' Kovrin laughed. 'She can't possibly do more damage than the hares. She loves gardening, she understands it.'

'Indeed she does. If the garden goes to her after I'm dead, if she runs it, then that's ideal of course. But what if she marries, God forbid?' Pesotsky whispered with a scared glance at Kovrin. 'That's just the point. If she marries and has children she'll have no time to think of the garden. What I most fear is her marrying some greedy young coxcomb who'll let the place out to market-women, and it will go to rack and ruin in a year. Women—they're all hell let loose in this business.'

Sighing, Pesotsky paused for a while.

'I may be selfish, but I don't want Tanya to marry, quite honestly. There's that popinjay with the fiddle who visits us. I know Tanya won't marry him, I'm sure of that. But I can't stand the sight of him. Altogether I'm rather a crank, dear boy, I confess it.'

Pesotsky stood up and paced the room excitedly, obviously wanting to say something crucial but not venturing.

'I'm very fond of you indeed and I'm going to be frank.' He had steeled himself at last, thrusting his hands into his pockets. 'On certain ticklish questions I'm quite blunt, I don't beat about the bush. And I can't stand what's called minding one's own business. So I tell you straight, you're the one man I wouldn't fear marrying my daughter to. You're intelligent, you're good-hearted, you wouldn't let my labour of love perish. But above all I love you as a son, I'm proud of you. If you and Tanya should hit it off together, well, I'd be all for it. I'd be glad. I'd be happy, even. I tell you straight with no trimmings, as an honest man.'

Kovrin laughed. Pesotsky opened the door to go out, paused on the threshold.

'If you and Tanya had a son I'd make him a gardener,' he said thoughtfully. 'Anyway, that's all idle dreaming. Good night.'

Left to himself, Kovrin settled down more comfortably and tackled the articles. One was entitled 'Catch-Cropping', another 'Observations on Mr. Z's Remarks on Double Trenching the Soil of a New Garden'. A third was 'Grafting with Dormant Buds, Continued'. It was all like that. But what a neurotic, uneasy tone. What frenzied, almost clinical zeal. One article had what seemed a most inoffensive title and uncontroversial subject, being about the golden rennet apple. But Pesotsky began and ended it with *audiatur altera pars* and *sapienti sat*, sandwiching between these tags a spate of mixed venomous adjurations on 'the ignorant pedantry of our high and mighty horticultural pundits who gaze down on nature from their ivory towers', or on M. Gaucher, 'whose reputation has been created by ignoramuses and amateurs'. At this point there was an out-of-context, strained, bogus-sounding expression of regret that peasants could no longer be birched for damaging trees while stealing fruit.

'Gardening's a fine, nice, healthy pursuit,' thought Kovrin. 'Yet even here passions rage. It must be because intellectuals are neurotic and hyper-sensitive in every walk of life. Perhaps it can't be helped.'

He remembered how keen Tanya was on her father's articles. Short, pale, so thin that her shoulder-blades stuck out, with dilated, dark, intelligent eyes, she was always peering and questing. She walked like her father, with short, brisk steps. She spoke a lot, she liked arguing, and when doing so would mimic and gesticulate an accompaniment to every sentence, even the least important. She must be excessively sensitive.

Kovrin read on, but could take nothing in and gave it up. A pleasant excitement, the feeling with which he had just danced the mazurka and listened to the music, now weighed him down, evoking a host of thoughts. He stood up and paced the room, thinking of the black monk. It struck him that if no one else had seen that strange phantom, then he himself must be ill and had reached the stage of seeing things. The idea frightened him, but not for long.

'But I feel all right, don't I? I'm not hurting anyone. So there's no harm in my hallucinations,' he thought, and was reassured.

He sat on the sofa, clutching his head to contain the joy passing understanding which filled his whole being, then paced the room again and sat down to work. But the ideas which he found in his book did not satisfy him. He wanted something colossal, vast, shattering. Towards dawn he undressed and went reluctantly to bed. He must get some sleep, after all.

Hearing Pesotsky walk out into the garden, Kovrin rang for a servant and ordered wine. He enjoyed several glasses of claret and then covered himself up. His consciousness became dimmed, he fell asleep.

IV

Pesotsky and Tanya often quarrelled and abused each other.

One morning Tanya burst into tears after some squabble and went to her room. She did not come out for lunch or tea. At first Pesotsky walked around looking pompous and sulky, as if trying to show that justice and order were the most important things in life, but he soon flagged and lost heart. He drifted sadly through the park, sighing 'Oh, God, God, God', he ate not a crumb for dinner. At last, guilty and remorseful, he knocked on her locked door and timidly called her name.

The response from behind the door was a faint voice, exhausted by crying, yet resolute. 'Kindly leave me alone.'

The master's and mistress's distress was reflected by the whole household, even the gardeners. Kovrin too, deep in some fascinating work, felt depressed and embarrassed in the end. Hoping somehow to dispel the general low spirits, he decided to intervene, and knocked on Tanya's door in the late afternoon. He was admitted.

'Come, come, you should be ashamed,' he joked, looking in amazement at Tanya's tear-stained, grief-stricken face covered with red blotches. 'Is it really so serious? Come, now.'

'How he torments me, did you but know.' Tears, hot and profuse, spurted from her large eyes. 'He's made my life a misery.' She wrung her hands. 'I didn't say anything to him, not a thing. All I said was that there's no need to keep extra gardeners if—if you can hire them by the day when you need them. Why, our—our gardeners have been idle all this week. That's all I—I said, but he yelled at me and made a lot of insulting, deeply offensive remarks. What for?'

'That's quite enough of that.' Kovrin patted her hair. 'You've had your quarrel and your little cry, and that will do. You mustn't be angry any more. It won't do, especially as he loves you so very, very much.'

'He has ruined my—my whole life,' sobbed Tanya. 'All I hear from him is taunts and—and insults. He thinks I don't belong in this house. Very well then, he's right. I'll leave here tomorrow and get a job as a telegraph clerk. I don't care.'

'Come, come. Don't cry, Tanya. Don't, dear. Both of you are

quick-tempered and highly-strung, and you're both in the wrong. Come along, I'll help heal the breach.'

Kovrin spoke kindly and persuasively, but she still cried, her shoulders quivering, her fists clenched as if she had been genuinely overtaken by some dire calamity. He pitied her all the more because, though her grief was not serious, she yet suffered deeply. How little was needed to make this creature unhappy for a whole day, perhaps for a whole lifetime. While soothing her, Kovrin reflected that he could search the entire face of the globe in vain without finding anyone who loved him as dearly as this girl and her father. He had lost his own father and mother in early childhood, and but for these two would perhaps never have known true affection until his dying day—never have known that innocent, selfless love only possible with someone very dear and close. This weeping, trembling girl's nerves responded, he felt, to his own half-sick, overwrought nerves as iron to a magnet. He, who could never have loved a healthy, strong, rosy-cheeked girl, was attracted by pale, frail, unhappy Tanya.

He gladly stroked her hair and shoulders, pressed her hands, wiped her tears.

Then she at last stopped crying. She went on complaining for some time—about her father and her intolerably hard life in that house, begging Kovrin to see things her way. Then she gradually began to smile, sighing that God had given her such a bad character. In the end she laughed aloud, called herself an idiot and ran from the room.

A little later, when Kovrin went into the garden, Pesotsky and Tanya were walking side by side down a path just as if nothing had happened, eating rye bread and salt because they were both famished.

V

Pleased to have proved so successful a peacemaker, Kovrin went into the park. He sat on a bench pondering, and heard the rattle of carriages and women's laughter as guests arrived. While evening's shadows fell across the garden he vaguely heard a fiddle and singers' voices, which reminded him of the black monk. Where, in what clime, on what planet was that optical incongruity now floating?

Barely had he recalled the legend, conjuring up in fancy the dark phantom seen in the rye field, when without the faintest rustle there silently emerged from behind the pine tree exactly opposite a man of medium height, his grey head uncovered, garbed all in black, barefoot, like a beggar. On his deathly white face black eyebrows stood out sharply. With a friendly nod the beggar or pilgrim silently approached the bench and sat down. Kovrin recognized the black monk. For a moment each gazed at the other—Kovrin with amazement, the monk amiably and with his old, rather sly, knowing look.

'But you're a mirage, you know,' Kovrin said. 'So why are you here, why are you sitting still? It doesn't fit the legend.'

'No matter,' the monk answered quietly after a short pause, turning to face Kovrin. 'Legend, mirage, I myself—these are all figments of your overheated imagination. I am an apparition.'

'So you don't exist then?' Kovrin asked.

'Think as you choose.' The monk gave a slight smile. 'I exist in your imagination, and your imagination is part of nature. Therefore I exist in nature too.'

'You have a very mature, intelligent, highly expressive face, as if you really had lived more than a thousand years,' said Kovrin. 'I had no idea that my imagination could create such phenomena. But why do you look at me so delightedly? Do you like me?'

'Yes. You are one of those few justly called the Elect of God. You serve Eternal Truth. Your ideas, your purposes, your outstanding scholarship, your whole life—all bear the divine, celestial stamp, being dedicated to the Rational and the Beautiful, that is to the Eternal.'

'You speak of Eternal Truth. But can men attain that, do they need it, if there is no life after death?'

'But there is,' said the monk.

'You believe in eternal life, then?'

'Of course. You human beings have a great and glorious future. And the more men there are like you on earth the quicker will that future be attained. Without you—you who serve the highest principles, who live consciously and freely—humanity would be nothing. In the normal course of events it would have had to wait a long time for the consummation of its terrestrial evolution. But you will lead it to the Kingdom of Eternal Truth several thousand years ahead of time. Herein lies your high merit. You are the incarnation of God's blessing immanent in mankind.'

'But what purpose has eternal life?' Kovrin asked.

'The same as any other life. Pleasure. True pleasure is knowledge, and eternal life will offer sources of knowledge infinite and inexhaustible. That's what "in my Father's house are many mansions" means.'

'It's so nice hearing you talk, did you but know.' Kovrin rubbed his hands delightedly.

'I'm so glad.'

'But when you've gone I know I shall worry about whether you exist or not. You're a ghost, a hallucination. Does that mean I'm mentally ill, insane?'

'Suppose you are. Why let it bother you? You're sick because you're overworked, you've worn yourself out. You have sacrificed your health to the Ideal, in other words, and ere long you'll sacrifice your very life to it. What could be better? Such is the goal of all lofty natures endowed with superior gifts.'

'But if I know I'm insane how can I have faith in myself?'

'Now, why assume that men of genius, those in whom all mankind has faith, haven't also seen visions? Genius is akin to madness, scientists now tell us. Only mediocrities, only the common herd are healthy and normal, my friend. Talk about the neurosis of the age, overwork, degeneracy and so on can seriously disturb only those who see life's goal in the present—the common herd, that is.'

'The Romans spoke of *mens sana in corpore sano*.'

'Not everything the Romans and Greeks said is true. Heightened consciousness, excitement, ecstasy, all that distinguishes prophets, poets and martyrs to the Ideal from common folk—it's all inimical to man's animal nature, that is to his physical health. I repeat, if you want to be healthy and normal, join the herd.'

'It's funny how you say things that often occur to me independently,' said Kovrin. 'It's as if you had spied and eavesdropped on my secret thoughts. But let's not talk about me. What do you mean by eternal truth?'

The monk gave no answer. Kovrin glanced at him, but could not make out his face, the features being hazy and blurred. Then the monk's head and hands began to disappear. His body merged with the bench and the evening twilight until he had vanished entirely.

'The hallucination is over.' Kovrin laughed. 'What a pity.'

He went back to the house in the best of spirits. It had not been his vanity, it had been the very core of his being which the monk's few words had flattered. To be one of the Elect, to serve Eternal Truth, to join ranks with those who will make man worthy of God's Kingdom several thousand years ahead of time, saving him from several millennia of unnecessary struggle, sin and suffering, to sacrifice youth, strength, health and all else to the Ideal, to be ready to die for the common weal

—how lofty, how beatific a destiny! His own past—so pure, so chaste, so industrious—flashed through his mind. He remembered what he had learnt, what he had taught others, and decided that the monk had not exaggerated.

Tanya was coming towards him through the park. She had changed her dress.

'So you're here,' she said. 'We've been looking for you everywhere. But what's the matter?' she wondered, glancing at his radiant, beaming face and tear-filled eyes. 'Andrew, how strange you seem.'

'I am contented, Tanya.' Kovrin put his hands on her shoulders. 'More than that, I am happy. Tanya, dear Tanya, you're such a nice creature. Dear Tanya, I am so very, very glad.' He fervently kissed both her hands. 'I have just experienced such wonderful, bright, celestial moments. But I can't tell you all of it because you'd say I was mad or disbelieve me. Let's talk about you. Lovely, marvellous Tanya! I love you and that love is now part of me. To have you near me, to meet you a dozen times a day—it has become a spiritual necessity. I don't know how I'll do without you when I go home.'

'Oh, really.' Tanya laughed. 'You'll forget us in a couple of days. We're nobodies and you're a great man.'

'No, we must be serious,' he said. 'I'll take you with me, Tanya. How about it—will you come. Will you be mine?'

'Oh, really.' Tanya tried to laugh again, but the laugh would not come and red blotches appeared on her face.

She was breathing fast and walked quicker and quicker, not towards the house but further into the park.

'I never thought of that, never.' She clenched her hands as if in despair.

Kovrin followed her, talking and still wearing that radiant, beatific expression.

'I want a love to possess me entirely, and only you can give me such love, Tanya. Oh, I'm so happy.'

Dumbfounded, she stooped—shivering, seeming ten years older. But he found her beautiful, loudly and joyfully exclaiming how lovely she was.

VI

Having learnt from Kovrin that the two had not only 'hit it off together', but that there was even to be a wedding, Pesotsky paced his room for a while, trying to hide his excitement. His hands shook, his neck swelled and turned crimson, he gave orders for his trap to be harnessed and he drove off. Tanya, seeing him whip the horses and pull his cap hard down almost on to his ears, understood his mood, locked herself in her room and spent the day crying.

Peaches and plums were already ripe in the greenhouses. The packing and despatch to Moscow of this delicate, sensitive freight required much care, labour and fuss. So hot and dry had the summer been that every tree had needed watering, a very time-consuming procedure for the gardeners. And swarms of caterpillars had appeared, which the gardeners and even—to Kovrin's great disgust—Pesotsky and Tanya would squash with their fingers. Meanwhile they also had to take orders for fruit and trees in the autumn, and to conduct a large correspondence.

Then, just at crisis point, when no one seemed to have a free moment, harvesting began and robbed the garden of more than half the labour force. Very sunburnt, dead tired, bad-tempered, Pesotsky kept dashing off into garden or fields, shouting that he was being torn limb from limb and would put a bullet in his brain.

Then came fuss over the trousseau, to which the Pesotskys attached no small importance. The snipping of scissors, the rattle of sewing-machines, the fume of flat-irons, the tantrums of the dressmaker, a neurotic, touchy lady—these things had everyone in the house in a daze. As if to make things worse, guests came every day and had to be amused, fed and even put up for the night. But all this drudgery was as nothing, it passed unnoticed. Tanya felt as if love and happiness had caught her unawares, though she had been certain, somehow, since the age of fourteen that Kovrin would marry her and no one else. She was stunned and bewildered, she could not believe it all.

Now such joy would suddenly overwhelm her that she felt like soaring into the clouds and giving thanks to God, now she would suddenly remember that she would have to leave her beloved home and part from her father in August. Or the idea would strike her from God knows where that she was a trivial nonentity unworthy of a great man like Kovrin, and off to her room she would go, lock herself in and weep bitterly for several hours. When they had guests Kovrin would suddenly impress her as strikingly handsome—she thought all the women were in love with him and jealous of her. Her heart would swell with exultant pride as if she had vanquished the whole world. But let him so much as smile a welcome to some young lady and she would shake with jealousy. Off to her room she would go, and there would be more tears. These new emotions obsessed her, she helped her father like an automaton, not noticing the peaches, the caterpillars, the workmen or the swift passage of time.

Pesotsky's evolution was much the same. He worked from dawn to dusk, he was always dashing off somewhere, flaring up, losing his temper, but all in an enchanted daze. There might have been two of him. One was the real Pesotsky listening to the head gardener Ivan Karlych reporting mishaps, waxing indignant, clutching his head in despair. The other was an impostor, a semi-intoxicated creature who suddenly broke off business conversations in mid-sentence and patted the head gardener's shoulder.

'Say what you like, but breeding does count,' he would mutter. 'His mother was a marvellous, admirable, brilliant woman. To look at her kind, clear, pure, angelic face—it was a real joy. She drew beautifully, wrote verse, spoke five foreign languages, sang. The poor woman died of consumption, may she rest in peace.'

'When he was a little boy and grew up in my house,' Unreal Pesotsky would sigh a little later, 'he had just such an angelic, clean-cut kind face. His glance, his movements, his conversation were gentle and elegant like his mother's. As for brains, he always astounded us with his intelligence. He wasn't, incidentally, made an M.A. for nothing, indeed he was not! But you just wait and see what he'll be like in ten years' time, Ivan Karlych. There will be no touching him.'

But then Real Pesotsky would take over, grimace fearfully, clutch his head, shout.

'Bastards! They've messed it, mucked it, frozen it all to hell! The garden's gone to rack and ruin!'

Meanwhile Kovrin was working with his former zeal, not noticing all the fuss. Love only added fuel to the flames. After every meeting with Tanya he would go to his room happy and elated, would take up book or manuscript as passionately as he had just kissed Tanya and told her that he loved her. What the black monk had said about the Elect of God, Eternal Truth, the brilliant future of mankind and the rest of it—all that conferred outstanding significance on his work, filling his heart with pride and a consciousness of his own superiority. He met the black monk once or twice a week in the park or at home, and had a long conversation. But this did not so much frighten as delight him, for he was absolutely convinced by now that such visions visit only the élite of distinguished men consecrated to the service of the Ideal.

The monk once appeared at dinner time and sat by the dining-room window. Overjoyed, Kovrin most adroitly struck up a conversation with Pesotsky and Tanya on a subject likely to interest the black guest, who listened, nodding affably. Pesotsky and Tanya also listened— merrily smiling and without suspecting that Kovrin was speaking to a figment of his imagination, not to them.

The Fast of the Assumption arrived unnoticed, and soon after that came the wedding—celebrated 'with a splash' at Pesotsky's insistence, that is, with senseless revels lasting forty-eight hours. Some three thousand roubles' eating and drinking were done, but what with the wretched hired band, the rowdy toasts and the waiters' bustle, what with the din and the crowd, the expensive wines and remarkable viands ordered from Moscow went unappreciated.

VII

On a long winter's night Kovrin lay in bed reading a French novel. Poor Tanya, whose head ached in the evenings because she wasn't used to town life, had long been asleep and was uttering occasional incoherent sentences.

It struck three. Kovrin put out his candle and lay down. He lay with eyes closed for a while but could not sleep, probably because the bedroom was too hot and Tanya was talking in her sleep. At half-past four he relit his candle and saw the black monk sitting in the armchair by his bed.

'Greetings.' The monk paused. 'What are you thinking about now?'

'Fame,' Kovrin answered. 'I've just been reading a French novel about a young scholar who behaves foolishly and pines away because he yearns to be famous. I don't understand that yearning.'

'That's because you have too much sense. You don't care for fame, it's a toy which doesn't interest you.'

'True enough.'

'Repute does not attract you. What's flattering, amusing or edifying about having your name carved on your tombstone only to be erased, gilt and all, by the passage of time? Anyway, there are too many of you, luckily, for mankind's feeble memory to retain your names.'

'Quite so,' Kovrin agreed. 'Besides, what need to remember them? But let's discuss something else. Happiness, for instance. What is happiness?'

When five o'clock struck he was sitting on the bed, feet dangling on the carpet. He addressed the monk.

'In ancient times there was a happy man who ended up scared of his own happiness, so great was it. So he sacrificed his favourite ring to the gods in order to appease them. Now, do you know, I'm getting a bit worried about my own happiness, just as Polycrates was. I find it odd to experience bliss unalloyed from dawn to dusk. It obsesses me, it swamps all other feelings. Sadness, grief, boredom—I don't know what they are. Here I am unable to sleep, I have insomnia, but I'm not bored. It's beginning to puzzle me, quite seriously.'

'Now, why?' the monk was astonished. 'Is joy so unnatural a feeling? Shouldn't it be man's normal lot? The loftier his intellectual and moral development, the freer he is, the more pleasure does life afford him. Socrates, Diogenes and Marcus Aurelius felt joy, not grief. And the Apostle says "Rejoice evermore". So do rejoice, then, and be happy.'

Kovrin laughed. 'But what if the gods wax angry?' he jested. 'If they remove my comforts, make me cold and famished, I doubt if that will suit me.'

Meanwhile Tanya had woken up and was staring at her husband in horror and amazement. There he was talking, addressing the armchair, gesticulating and laughing. His eyes gleamed, and there was something odd about that laugh.

'Who are you talking to, Andrew?' She clutched the hand which he had stretched towards the monk. 'Who is it, dear?'

'Eh?' Kovrin was taken aback. 'Who, you ask? Why, with him sitting over there.' He pointed at the black monk.

'There's no one there, no one at all. You're ill, Andrew.'

Tanya embraced her husband. She clung to him as if she was protecting him from apparitions, covering his eyes with her hand.

'You're ill,' she sobbed, trembling all over. 'Forgive me, my dearest darling, but I've noticed something amiss with you for some time. Your mind is sick, my dear.'

Infected by her trembling, he again glanced at the armchair, now empty, felt a sudden weakness of the arms and legs. Scared, he started dressing.

'It's nothing, Tanya, nothing,' he muttered, quivering. 'Actually, I am a bit unwell, it's time to admit it.'

'I noticed it ages ago, and so did Father.' She tried to force back her sobs. 'You talk to yourself, you smile oddly, you don't sleep. God,

God, save us,' she said in horror. 'But don't be afraid, dear. Never fear, for God's sake don't be afraid.'

She started dressing too. Only as he looked at her now did Kovrin take in the full danger of his position—the meaning of the black monk and the conversations with him. Now he knew that he had lost his reason.

Not understanding why, both dressed and went into the ballroom—she leading, he following. And there, woken by the sobbing, in his dressing-gown, candle in hand, stood Pesotsky, who was staying with them.

'Never fear, my dear,' said Tanya, shaking like one in fever. 'Don't be afraid. This will all pass, Father, it will be all right.'

Kovrin was too upset to speak. He wanted to make a jocular remark to his father-in-law. 'You must congratulate me, I think I've gone off my head.' But he only moved his lips, smiling bitterly.

At nine o'clock that morning they put on his greatcoat and his furs, wrapped a shawl round him, and took him to the doctor by carriage. He began to receive treatment.

VIII

It was summer again, and the doctor had ordered him to go to the country. Kovrin was better now, he no longer saw the black monk, he needed only to get fit. Living with his father-in-law in the country, he drank a lot of milk, worked only two hours a day, took no wine, did not smoke.

On St. Elias' Eve at the end of July a service was held in the house. When the clerk handed the priest the censer the huge old ballroom smelt like a graveyard. Kovrin was bored. He went into the garden. Ignoring the gorgeous flowers, he drifted about, sat on a bench, strolled through the park. Reaching the river, he climbed down and stood there, pensively contemplating the water. Those grim pines with their matted roots which had seen him here so young, so merry, so high-spirited last year—they no longer whispered, but stood still and dumb as if not recognizing him. And in fact his head was cropped, he no longer had his beautiful long hair, his walk was listless, he was fuller in the face and paler than last summer.

He crossed the footbridge to the far bank. Rows of cut oats stood where rye had grown last year. The sun had set, and a broad red glow burned on the horizon, presaging wind next day. It was quiet. Gazing towards where the black monk had first appeared last year, Kovrin stood for about twenty minutes until the sunset had faded.

When he reached home again, weary and discontented, the service was over. Pesotsky and Tanya were having tea on the terrace steps. They were talking, but when they saw Kovrin they stopped abruptly and he concluded from their expressions that they had been discussing him.

'It must be time for your milk,' Tanya told her husband.

'No it's not.' He sat on the lowest step. 'Drink it yourself, I don't want it.'

Tanya exchanged an alarmed glance with her father. 'You yourself say the milk does you good,' she said apologetically.

'Oh yes, lots and lots of good,' Kovrin sneered. 'I congratulate you. Since Friday I have put on another pound.' He clutched his head tightly in his hands and spoke in anguish. 'Why, oh why did you try to cure me? Bromides, idleness, warm baths, being watched, this craven fear of every mouthful, every step—it will turn me into a downright imbecile in the end. I was losing my mind, I had delusions of grandeur, but I was elated, I was even happy, I was attractive and original. Now I've become more reasonable and stable, but I'm just like everyone else—I'm a mediocrity, and I'm bored with life. Oh, how cruelly you have treated me! I saw visions, but what harm did they do anyone, I'd like to know?'

Pesotsky sighed. 'God knows what you're on about, it makes tedious listening.'

'Then don't listen.'

Other people's presence, Pesotsky's in particular, now riled Kovrin, who would answer drily and coldly—rudely, even—never looking at the other without a sneer of hatred, much to Pesotsky's distress as he coughed, apologetically but not feeling in the least to blame. Not understanding why their affectionate, friendly relations had so abruptly changed, Tanya would cling to her father and gaze anxiously into his eyes. She wanted to understand but could not. All she knew was that relations were deteriorating daily, that her father looked much older of late, while her husband had become irritable, moody, cantankerous, unattractive. No longer could she laugh and sing, she left her meals untouched, she lay awake all night with terrible forebodings. Such were her torments that she once spent the time from lunch till evening in a dead faint. Her father had seemed to be weeping during the service, and now, as the three of them sat on the terrace, she strove to put it from her mind.

'How lucky Buddha, Mahomet and Shakespeare were that their kind relatives and doctors did not treat them for ecstasy and inspiration,' said Kovrin. 'Had Mahomet taken potassium bromide for his nerves, worked only two hours a day and drunk milk, that remarkable man would have left as little trace behind him as his dog. It's the doctors and the well-meaning relatives who will cretinize mankind in the end. Mediocrity will rate as genius, civilization will perish. I'm so, so grateful to you, did you but know it,' Kovrin added irritably.

He felt so exasperated that he stood up quickly and went indoors to stop himself saying more. It was quiet, the smell of tobacco flowers and jalap drifted in from the garden through the open windows. In the huge, dark ballroom flecks of green moonlight lay on the floor and the grand piano. Kovrin remembered the ecstasies of the previous summer with this same scent of jalap and the moon shining in through the windows. To recreate his previous year's mood, he hurried to his study, lit a strong cigar and told a servant to bring wine. But the cigar left a disgustingly bitter taste in his mouth, and the wine too had a different taste from last year's. And such were the effects of abstinence that the cigar and two gulps of wine made his head spin and his heart pound so that he had to take potassium bromide.

'Father idolizes you,' Tanya told him before going to bed. 'You have some grudge against him, and it's killing him—one sees him ageing by the hour. I implore you, Andrew, for God's sake, for your own dead father's sake, for the sake of my peace of mind—do be nice to him.'

'I neither can nor will.'

'But why not, why ever not?' Tanya trembled all over.

'Because I dislike him and that's that,' said Kovrin casually, shrugging his shoulders. 'But don't let's talk about him, he's *your* father.'

'I simply fail to understand.' Tanya clutched her temples and stared fixedly. 'Something mysterious and horrible is happening in this house. You've changed, you're not yourself. You, a rational, distinguished man, lose your temper over trifles, involve yourself in squabbles. Such little things upset you—one's so amazed sometimes, one can't believe it's you. All right, all right, don't be angry, please,' she went on, fearing her own words and kissing his hands. 'You're an intelligent, amiable, decent man. You'll be fair to my father, he's so kind-hearted.'

'He's not kind-hearted, he's just complacent. These farcical buffoons like your father, with their smug, fat faces, these dear old hail-fellow-well-met cranks—I once found them touching and amusing in fiction, in music-hall turns and in life too. But now they just disgust me. All they think of is self, self, self. And what disgusts me most is their smugness. They're like oxen or pigs, complacent down to their very guts.'

Tanya sat on the bed, laid her head on the pillow.

'This is sheer torture.' Her voice betrayed her utter exhaustion and difficulty in speaking. 'Not a moment's peace since winter. God, it's so dreadful, it's agony.'

'Oh yes, we all know I'm the wicked ogre, and you and daddy dear are the babes in the wood. Naturally!'

Tanya found his face ugly and disagreeable. The hatred, the sneering did not suit him. She had, indeed, noticed previously that there was something missing from his face, as if that too had changed since he had had his hair cut short. She wanted to say something wounding but, at once detecting this hostile impulse, took fright and left the bedroom.

IX

Kovrin was appointed to a university chair. His inaugural lecture was scheduled for the second of December and a notice to that effect had been posted in the university corridor, but on the date in question he wired the registrar that he was too ill to lecture.

He was bringing up blood. He would spit blood, and had sizeable haemorrhages twice a month, when he would feel exceptionally weak and drowsy. The illness did not particularly alarm him because he knew that his mother, now dead, had survived ten or more years of the same disease. His doctors told him there was no danger, only advising him not to get excited, to lead a regular life and talk less.

In January the lecture was again cancelled for the same reason, and by February it was too late to start the course. He had to postpone it until the following year.

He no longer lived with Tanya, but with another woman two years older than himself, who looked after him like a baby. His mood was calm and submissive. He readily yielded, and when Barbara—such was his companion's name—proposed taking him to the Crimea, he agreed, though foreseeing no good outcome to the trip.

They reached Sevastopol one evening and put up at an hotel to rest before going on to Yalta next day. Both were tired after their journey. Barbara had some tea, went to bed and was soon asleep. But Kovrin stayed up. Before leaving home—an hour before driving to the station—he had received from Tanya a letter which he had not dared open and which was now in his coat pocket. The thought of it worried him. In his heart of hearts he now believed that his marriage to Tanya had been a mistake, he was glad to have broken with her finally. The memory of this woman who had ended as a walking skeleton, in whom everything seemed to have died but those large, staring, intelligent eyes—that memory evoked in him only pity and annoyance with himself. The handwriting on the envelope reminded him how unfair and cruel he had been two years ago, how he had taken revenge on completely innocent people for his own spiritual emptiness, boredom, loneliness and discontent. He also, incidentally, remembered tearing his thesis, and all the articles written during his illness, into small pieces, throwing them out of the window, and seeing the scraps of paper fluttering in the breeze and lodging in trees and flowers. In every line he saw strange, utterly unfounded pretensions, militant frivolity, impudence and delusions of grandeur. It had made him feel as if he was reading a description of his own vices. But when the last notebook had been torn up and thrown out of the window he had suddenly felt bitterly distressed, had gone to his wife and made a lot of disagreeable remarks. God, how he had tormented her. He had once said, wanting to hurt her, that her father had played an invidious role in their relationship by asking him to marry her. Chancing to overhear, Pesotsky had burst into the room in speechless despair, capable only of stamping his feet and uttering a sort of bellow like a man without a tongue, while Tanya had looked at her father, given a heart-rending shriek and fainted. It had been an ugly scene.

All this came to mind when Kovrin looked at the familiar handwriting. He went out on to the balcony. The weather was fine and warm, he could smell the sea. The glorious bay reflected the moon and the lights, and had an indefinable colour—a delicate, soft medley of dark blue and green. Here the water had the dark blue tint of vitriol, there the moonbeams seemed to have congealed and filled the bay in place of water. The general impression was a symphony of hues, an atmosphere peaceful, calm and elevating.

The ground-floor windows under the balcony must have been open because women's voices and laughter were clearly heard. Someone must be giving a party.

Kovrin forced himself to open the letter. He went back into his room and read as follows.

'My father has just died. I have you to thank for that, for you killed him. Our garden is going to ruin, strangers have the run of it—just what poor Father feared. For that too I have you to thank. I hate you from the bottom of my heart, I hope you'll soon be dead. Oh, how I do suffer—an unbearable pain is burning inside me. I curse you. I thought you were an outstanding man, a genius. I loved you, but you turned out to be a maniac.'

Unable to read on, Kovrin tore up the letter and threw it away. Anxiety—panic, almost—seized him. Barbara was asleep behind a screen, he could hear her breathing. Women's voices and laughter came up from the floor below, yet he felt as if there was no living soul in the hotel besides himself. That the unhappy, broken-hearted Tanya had cursed him in her letter, that she wanted him dead—it unnerved him. He glanced briefly at the door, as if fearing that the unknown force, that force which had wrought such havoc in his own life and in the lives of those dear to him in the last two years, might enter the room and possess him again.

That the best cure for jangled nerves is work he knew from experience. You must sit at your desk and at all costs make yourself concentrate on a single idea. From his red briefcase he took a notebook containing a draft scheme for a short work which he had thought of compiling if he got bored doing nothing in the Crimea. Sitting at the table, he tackled this plan, and felt as if his calm, resigned, detached mood was returning. The notebook and the project even made him think of the vanity of things earthly. How much life does exact in return for those insignificant or very ordinary benefits which it can bestow on man, he thought. To be given a university chair in one's late thirties, to be a conventional professor, expounding in listless, bored, ponderous language commonplace thoughts not even your own—to attain, in short, the status of a second-rate scholar—he, Kovrin, had had to study fifteen years, to work day and night, to suffer serious mental disorder, to experience a broken marriage and to commit various stupid, unjust acts better forgotten. That he was a mediocrity he now clearly realized, accepting the fact gladly since everyone ought, in his view, to be satisfied with what he is.

The draft project would have soothed him, but the torn letter, gleaming white on the floor, prevented him from concentrating. He got up from the table, collected the scraps of paper and threw them out of the window, but a light breeze blew in from the sea and scattered the bits of the paper about the window-sill. Once again anxiety akin to panic seized him, and he felt as if he was the only living soul in the whole hotel.

He went out on the balcony. The bay gazed at him like a living thing with its masses of azure, dark blue, turquoise and red eyes. It seemed to beckon him. Indeed, as it was hot and stuffy, a bathe might be a good idea.

On the ground floor beneath the balcony a violin suddenly struck up, and two female voices sweetly sang something familiar. That song from down below—it was about a deranged girl who heard mysterious sounds one night in a garden and decided that this was sacred harmony incomprehensible to us mortals.

Kovrin caught his breath, sadness seemed to make his heart miss a beat, and a wondrous, sweet, long-forgotten joy quivered in his breast.

On the far shore of the bay appeared a tall black column like a whirlwind or sand-storm. It swooped over the bay towards the hotel with terrifying speed, becoming ever smaller and darker. Barely had Kovrin time to make way.

The grey-haired, bareheaded, black-browed monk, barefooted, arms crossed on his breast, swept past and stopped in the middle of the room.

'Why did you not trust me?' he reproached Kovrin, gazing at him affectionately. 'Had you only trusted me when I told you you were a genius, you would not have spent two such miserable and sterile years.'

Now believing himself the Elect of God and a genius, Kovrin vividly recalled all his previous conversations with the black monk, and tried to speak, but blood was spurting straight out of his throat on to his chest. Not knowing what to do, he moved his hands over his chest, and his cuffs became soaked with blood. Wanting to call Barbara, who was asleep behind the screen, he made an effort.

'Tanya,' he called.

He fell on the ground and raised himself on his arms.

'Tanya,' he called again.

He called on Tanya, he called on the great garden with its gorgeous, dew-sprinkled flowers, he called on the park, he called on the pines with their matted roots, the rye field, his brilliant research work, his youth, his daring, his joy, he called on life which had been so beautiful. Seeing a great pool of blood on the floor near his face, he was too weak, now, to utter a word, but bliss, boundless and ineffable, suffused his whole being. While a serenade was played beneath the balcony the black monk whispered to him that he was a genius—that he was dying only because his weak human body had lost its equilibrium and could no longer serve as the frame for a genius.

When Barbara woke and emerged from behind the screen Kovrin was dead with a frozen smile of ecstasy on his face.

A WOMAN'S KINGDOM

[Бабье царство]

(1894)

A WOMAN'S KINGDOM

I

On the Eve

THERE was a thick wad of banknotes from the manager of Anne's timber plantations who had written enclosing fifteen hundred roubles, the proceeds of winning a court case on appeal. She disliked and feared such words as 'proceeds', 'winning' and 'case'. That legal proceedings were necessary she knew, but whenever her works manager Nazarych or her timber bailiff—great litigants, those two—won her a case, she always felt abashed and rather guilty. Now too she was embarrassed and ill at ease, wanting to put these fifteen hundred roubles away from her and not see them.

Other women of her age—twenty-five—were busy looking after homes, she wistfully reflected. They were tired, they would sleep soundly, they would wake up in the best of holiday spirits tomorrow. Many were long since married and had children. She alone was somehow obliged to pore over these letters like some old crone, to jot notes on them, to write answers, and then to do nothing all evening until midnight but wait until she felt sleepy. Tomorrow people would be wishing her happy Christmas and asking favours of her all day, and the day after tomorrow there was bound to be trouble at the works—someone beaten up, someone who had drunk himself to death—which would somehow make her suffer pangs of conscience. After the holidays Nazarych would dismiss a score of workers for absenteeism, and all twenty would huddle, bare-headed, at her porch. She would be too embarrassed to go out to them, and they would be driven off like dogs. Then everyone she knew would tittle-tattle behind her back and write anonymous letters about her being a millionairess—an exploiter who ruined people's lives and trod the workers into the dust.

Here, on one side, was a bundle of letters which she had read and set apart—begging letters. They were hungry, drunken people, these, burdened with large families, ill, humiliated, unrecognized.

Anne had already noted on each letter that three roubles were to go to one man and five to another. These letters would go to the office today, and tomorrow the distribution of relief—what her clerks called 'feeding time at the zoo'—would take place there.

They would also distribute four hundred and seventy roubles in dribs and drabs—interest on the capital willed to the poor and needy by her late father. There would be ugly jostling. A queue, a long line of people of a sort—alien, with bestial faces, ragged, cold, hungry, already drunk—would stretch from works gates to office door, hoarsely invoking their mother, their patroness Miss Glagolev and her parents. Those at the back would shove those in front, those in front would curse and swear. Tiring of the noise, the oaths, the keenings, the office clerk would leap out and cuff someone's ear to the general satisfaction. But her own people—the workers who had received nothing for the holiday beyond their wages, and had already spent the last copeck of those—would stand in the middle of the yard, look and laugh, some enviously, others ironically.

'Factory owners, especially women, prefer their beggars to their workpeople,' thought Anne. 'That's always the way.'

Her glance fell on the wad of money. It would be a good idea to distribute this unneeded, odious lucre to the workers tomorrow, but you couldn't give a worker something for nothing, or else he would ask you for more later. And what did these fifteen hundred roubles add up to anyway seeing that there were over eighteen hundred workers at the factory, not counting wives and children? Perhaps one might single out the author of one of these begging letters, some miserable creature who had long lost hope of a better life, and give him the whole lot. The poor fellow would be thunderstruck at getting the money, he might feel happy for the first time in his life. The idea struck Anne as original, amusing, entertaining. She pulled one letter out of the pile at random and read it. Some clerk called Chalikov had been out of work for a long time. He was ill, and he was living in the house belonging to one Gushchin. He had a consumptive wife and five young daughters. This four-storey tenement where he lived—Gushchin's—was well known to Anne. And a nasty, rotten, unhealthy building it was too.

'I'll give this Chalikov the money,' she decided. 'But I won't send it, I'd better take it myself to avoid unnecessary fuss. Yes,' she reasoned, putting the fifteen hundred in her pocket, 'I'll have a look, and perhaps fix up something for the little girls too.'

She cheered up, rang the bell and asked for her sledge to be brought round.

It was nearly seven in the evening when she got into her sledge. The windows of all the works buildings were brightly lit, which made it seem very dark in the huge compound. By the gate and in the far part of the yard, near the stores and the workers' barracks, electric lights glowed.

Anne disliked and feared these dark, grim blocks, these store-sheds and the barracks where the workers lived. She had only been inside the main factory building once since her father's death. High ceilings with iron girders, masses of huge, swiftly turning wheels, transmission belts and levers, the piercing hiss, the shriek of steel, the clattering of trollies, the harsh breath of steam, the faces pale, crimson or black with coal dust, the shirts wet with sweat, the gleam of steel, copper and fire, the smell of oil and coal, and the wind, now very hot, now cold—it all seemed sheer hell. She felt as if the wheels, the levers, the hot, hissing cylinders were striving to break loose from their couplings and annihilate people, while worried-looking men ran about, not hearing each other, bustling round the machines, trying to halt their terrible movement. They had shown Anne some object, explained it respectfully. She remembered them drawing a piece of white-hot iron out of the furnace in the forging shop, and how an old man with a strap on his head and another—young, in a dark-blue blouse with a chain on his chest, angry-looking, presumably a charge-hand—struck a piece of iron with hammers, how golden sparks scattered in all directions, how a little later they clattered a huge piece of sheet iron in front of her. The old man stood to attention, smiling, while the young one wiped his wet face with his sleeve and explained something to her. She still remembered, too, a one-eyed old man sawing a piece of iron in another workshop with a scatter of filings, and a red-haired man in dark glasses with holes in his shirt working a lathe, making something out of a piece of steel. The lathe roared, shrieked, whistled—a noise which made Anne feel sick, she felt as if something was boring into her ears. She looked, listened, understood nothing, smiled condescendingly, felt ashamed. To live off work you don't understand and can't like, to receive hundreds of thousands of roubles from it—how odd.

Not once had she visited the workers' barracks, reputedly an abode of bed-bugs, damp, debauchery and chaos. Astonishingly enough, thousands of roubles were spent yearly on the amenities of those barracks, but the workers' plight worsened every year, to judge from the anonymous letters.

'There was more system in Father's time,' thought Anne, driving out of the yard. 'That was because he'd been a worker himself, and knew what was needed. But I know nothing and get everything wrong.'

She again felt depressed, no longer glad to have embarked on this excursion. No longer was she intrigued and amused to think of the lucky creature on whose head the fifteen hundred roubles would suddenly alight like manna from heaven. To visit this Chalikov person while a business worth millions gradually disintegrated at home, while the workers in their barracks lived worse than convicts—that was stupid behaviour, it meant trying to cheat one's conscience.

Along the metalled road and across the field beside it workers from the neighbouring cotton and paper mills were thronging towards the lights of the city. Laughter and cheerful conversation hung in the frosty air. Looking at the women and youngsters, Anne suddenly felt a need for their simplicity, the crudeness, the jostling. She clearly pictured the distant past when she had been little Annie sharing a blanket with her mother—while their tenant, a washerwoman, was laundering in the next room. From adjoining apartments the sound of laughter, swearing, children's crying, an accordion, the buzz of lathes and sewing-machines had penetrated the thin walls, while her father Akim, that jack-of-all-trades, would ignore the cramped conditions and the noise as he soldered away at the stove, drew plans, used his plane. And she longed to wash and iron clothes, and run errands to shop and tavern, as she had every day when living with her mother. She would rather be a worker than an owner. Her huge house with its chandeliers and pictures, her butler Misha complete with tail-coat and velvety moustache, the imposing Barbara, the sycophantic Agatha, the young persons of both sexes who came begging for money almost daily and who always made her feel rather guilty, the officials, the doctors, the ladies who dispensed charity on her behalf, flattering her while secretly despising her lowly origins—how it all bored her, how alien it was.

She reached the level-crossing and barrier. Houses alternated with allotments. And here at last was the wide street where the legendary Gushchin tenement stood. As it was Christmas Eve there was a lot of coming and going in this usually quiet street. The taverns and alehouses were rowdy. If someone not of the locality, some resident of the town centre, had driven past, he would have noticed only dirty, drunken, swearing people. But Anne, having lived in these regions since child-hood, seemed to see her late father, her mother, her uncle in the crowd.

Her father had been an easy-going, vague character. Carefree and frivolous, a bit of a dreamer, he had had no hankering for money, status or power. He would say that a working man had no time to bother with holidays and church-going. But for his wife he might never have kept the fasts, he would have eaten forbidden food in Lent. Now, her uncle Ivan, by contrast, had been hard as nails. In matters religious, political and moral he had been stern and inflexible, not only keeping himself up to the mark, but all his servants and acquaintances as well. God help anyone who had entered his room without making the sign of the cross. The sumptuous chambers where Anne now lived —he had kept them locked up, opening them only on special occasions for important guests, while living in the small icon-festooned room which was his office. He had leaned to the Old Religion, constantly receiving bishops and priests of that persuasion, though he had been christened and married, and had buried his wife, by Reformed Orthodox rites. He had disliked his brother Akim, his only heir, for his easy-going attitude, which he called simple-minded and foolish, and for his indifference to religion. He had treated Akim shabbily, like one of his workers, paying him sixteen roubles a month. Always addressing his brother rather formally, Akim would take his whole family and do obeisance to him at Shrovetide. But then, three years before his death, Ivan had made himself more approachable. He had forgiven Akim and told him to hire a governess for Anne.

The gates to the Gushchin tenement were dark, deep-set and stinking, there was the sound of men coughing by the walls. Leaving her sledge in the street, Anne went into the yard and asked the way to the clerk Chalikov's flat, Number Forty-Six. She was directed to the last door on the right on the second floor. Near that last door, in the yard, and even on the stairway, there was the same foul smell as at the gate. Anne had lived in houses like this as a child, when her father had been an ordinary worker. Then, after her circumstances had changed, she had often visited them on charitable errands. The narrow stone staircase with its high steps, dirty, with its landing on each floor, the greasy lamp in the well, the stink, the bins by the doors on the landings, pots, rags—she had known it all from time immemorial.

Through one door, which was open, she saw some Jewish tailors sitting on a table wearing their caps and sewing. She passed people on the staircase, but it did not occur to her that they might harm her. She feared workers and peasants, sober or drunk, as little as she feared her intellectual friends.

Flat Forty-Six had no hall, but opened straight into the kitchen. In factory-hands' and craftsmen's quarters there is usually a smell of varnish, tar, leather or smoke, depending on the occupant's job, but the quarters of impoverished gentlefolk and clerks are distinguished by a dank, rather acrid stench. No sooner had Anne crossed the threshold than this disgusting stink enveloped her. In one corner a man in a black frock-coat sat at a table, his back to the door. That must be Chalikov himself, and there were five little girls with him. The eldest, broad-faced and thin, with a comb in her hair, looked about fifteen, while the youngest was a plump little thing with hair like a hedgehog, no more than three years old. All six were eating. Near the stove, cooking tongs in hand, stood a small, very thin, yellow-faced woman in a skirt and white blouse. She was pregnant.

'I never thought you'd be so disobedient, Liza,' said the man reproachfully. 'You should be ashamed, dear me you should. So you want Daddy to whip you, do you?'

Seeing an unknown lady on the threshold, the emaciated woman quivered and put down her tongs.

'Vasily,' she called after a while in a hollow voice, as if not believing her eyes.

The man looked round and jumped up. He was a bony, narrow-shouldered person with sunken temples and a flat chest. His eyes were small, deep-set and dark-rimmed, his nose was long, beaky and somewhat twisted to the right, his mouth was wide. With his forked beard and clean-shaven upper lip he looked more like a footman than an official.

'Does Mr. Chalikov live here?' Anne asked.

'Yes indeed, ma'am,' Chalikov answered sternly, but then recognized Anne.

'Miss Glagolev, Miss Anne!' he shouted, then suddenly choked and threw up his arms as if scared out of his wits. 'My guardian angel!'

He ran towards her, groaning like one suffering a stroke. There was cabbage in his beard, he smelt of vodka. Laying his forehead on her muff, he appeared to swoon.

'Your hand, your precious hand!' he gasped. 'This must be a dream, a wonderful dream. Wake me up, children.'

He turned to the table. 'Providence has hearkened to us,' he sobbed, waving his fists. 'Our rescuer, our angel is here. We're saved! On your knees, children, on your knees.'

For some reason Mrs. Chalikov and all the girls except the youngest began tidying the table.

'You wrote that your wife was very ill.' Anne felt ashamed and annoyed. 'I shan't give him that fifteen hundred,' she thought.

'Here my wife is.' Chalikov spoke in a thin little voice like a woman's, sounding as if he was fighting back his tears. 'Here she is, poor creature, with her one foot in the grave. But we don't complain, ma'am. Better death than such a life. Die, poor woman, die!'

Why was the man so affected wondered Anne with annoyance. 'He's been used to dealing with merchants, that's obvious.'

'Please talk to me sensibly,' she said. 'I don't like play-acting.'

'Yes, ma'am. Five orphan children by their mother's coffin with the funeral candles burning, and you call that play-acting. Ah me!' said Chalikov bitterly, and turned away.

'You shut up,' whispered his wife, pulling him by his sleeve and turning to Anne. 'The place is untidy, ma'am. You must excuse us, you know how it is with families. Cramped we may be, but our hearts are in the right place.'

'I shan't give them that fifteen hundred,' thought Anne again.

To be quickly rid of these people and the sour smell, she took out her purse, deciding to leave twenty-five roubles, no more, but then suddenly felt ashamed at having driven so far and troubled them for nothing.

'If you'll give me paper and ink I'll write to a doctor now, one I know well, and ask him to call.' She blushed. 'He's a very good doctor. And I'll leave money for medicine.'

Mrs. Chalikov rushed to wipe the table.

'It's dirty here, what do you think you're doing?' hissed Chalikov, looking at her angrily. 'Take her to the lodger's room.' He addressed Anne. 'Come into the lodger's room, ma'am, I venture to request. It's clean there.'

'Mr. Pimenov asked us not to go into his room,' said one of the little girls sternly.

But they had already taken Anne out of the kitchen through a narrow corridor-room, between two beds. From the way the beds were placed it was clear that two people slept lengthways on one, and three crossways on the other. The next room, the lodger's, really was clean. There was a neat bed with a red woollen quilt, a pillow in a white pillow-case, and even a special watch-holder. On a table covered with a linen tablecloth were a cream inkwell, pens, paper, framed photographs, all tidily arranged, and there was a second, black table with watch-making instruments and dismantled watches in orderly array. About the walls hung hammers, pincers, augers, chisels, pliers and so on, and three wall clocks, all ticking, hung there too—one of them huge with fat pendulum weights such as you see in taverns.

As she started writing the letter Anne saw on the table before her a portrait of her father and one of herself. Surprised, she asked who the room's occupant was.

'The lodger, ma'am—Pimenov. He works at your factory.'

'Oh? I thought it must be a watch-maker.'

'He works on watches privately, in his spare time. It's his hobby, ma'am.'

After a pause, during which only the clocks' ticking and the squeaking of pen on paper could be heard, Chalikov sighed and spoke with sardonic resentment.

'Being a gentleman, a white-collar worker—these things don't make your fortune, that's sure enough. For all your badges of office and status you may still have nothing to eat. If one of the lower orders helps the poor he's a much finer gentleman, say I, than one of your Chalikovs sunk in poverty and vice.'

To flatter Anne he added one or two more sentences disparaging his social position, obviously demeaning himself because he thought himself above her. Meanwhile she had finished the letter and sealed it. Her letter would be thrown away, the money would not be used for medical treatment—that she knew, but she still left twenty-five roubles on the table and then, after some thought, added two more red, ten-rouble notes. Mrs. Chalikov's thin yellow hand flashed before her eyes like a hen's claw and clutched the money.

'You've graciously given us money for medicines,' Chalikov quavered. 'But now hold out a helping hand to me too, and to my children.' He sobbed. 'My unhappy children—it's not myself I fear for, it's my daughters. I fear the Hydra of Debauchery!'

Trying to open her purse, which had jammed shut, Anne felt embarrassed, and blushed. She was ashamed to have people standing before her looking at her hands, waiting and probably laughing at her to themselves. Meanwhile someone had come into the kitchen and stamped his feet to shake off the snow.

'It's the lodger,' said Mrs. Chalikov.

Anne felt still more embarrassed, not wanting any of her work-people to find her in this ludicrous position. And then of course the lodger had to enter his room just as she had finally broken open the catch of her purse and was handing some banknotes to Chalikov, while that same Chalikov bellowed like one suffering a stroke, working his lips as if looking for a part of her to kiss. In the lodger she recognized the workman who had once banged that iron sheet in front of her in the foundry and given her those explanations. He had come straight from work, obviously. His face was black with smoke and near his nose one cheek had a smear of soot. His hands were quite black, his unbelted shirt shone with greasy dirt. He was a black-haired, broad-shouldered man of about thirty, of medium height, obviously very strong. One glance told her that he was a charge-hand on at least thirty-five roubles a month. Here was a tough, loud-mouthed fellow, one to bash his men's teeth in—you could tell that from the way he stood, from the posture which he suddenly and automatically assumed on seeing a lady in his room, and above all from his wearing his trousers outside his boots, from the pockets on his shirt, from the well-groomed pointed beard. Her late father Akim, brother to the owner though he had been, had yet feared charge-hands like this lodger, and had tried to keep on the right side of them.

'I'm sorry, we've rather taken over here while you were out,' said Anne.

The workman looked at her with surprise and an embarrassed smile, but said nothing.

'Speak a little louder, ma'am,' said Chalikov quietly. 'Mr. Pimenov's a bit hard of hearing when he gets home from work of an evening.'

But Anne, relieved to have nothing more to do here, nodded and quickly left. Pimenov saw her out.

'Have you been with us long?' she asked in a loud voice, not facing him.

'Since I was nine. I got my job in your uncle's day.'

'That's quite some time ago. Uncle and Father knew all the workers, but I know hardly any. I've seen you before, but I didn't know your name was Pimenov.'

Anne felt an urge to justify herself by pretending that she hadn't been serious, that she had been joking, when giving them that money just now.

'What a thing poverty is,' she sighed. 'We do our good deeds day in day out, but it makes no sense. I see no point in helping the Chalikovs of this world.'

'Of course not,' Pimenov agreed. 'What you give him will all go on drink. Now husband and wife will spend all night quarrelling and trying to get that money off each other,' he added with a laugh.

'Yes, our charity's useless, boring and ridiculous, admittedly. But then, one can't just ignore things either, can one? One must do something. What, for instance, can one do about the Chalikovs?'

She turned towards Pimenov and halted, waiting for his answer. He halted too, slowly and silently shrugging his shoulders. He obviously did know what to do about the Chalikovs, but it was something so crude and inhumane that he did not even venture to say it. So dull and unimportant were the Chalikovs to him that he had forgotten all about them a second later. Gazing into Anne's eyes, he smiled his pleasure, looking like someone who has had a delightful dream. Only now that she stood near to him could Anne see from his face, especially the eyes, how worn out and tired he was.

'This is the one I should give the fifteen hundred to,' she thought, but found the idea vaguely out of place and insulting to Pimenov.

'You must be aching all over after your day's work, but you insist on seeing me out,' she said on the way downstairs. 'Do go back.'

But he heard nothing. When they emerged in the street he ran ahead, unbuttoned the apron of the sledge and wished Anne a happy Christmas as he helped her into her seat.

II

Morning

'The bells stopped long ago. Everyone will be leaving church by the time you arrive, Lord help us. Do get up.'

'Two horses running, running,' said Anne as she woke up. Her maid, red-haired Masha, stood before her carrying a candle. 'What is it? What do you want?'

'The service is already over,' said Masha desperately. 'This is the third time I've tried to wake you. Sleep till evening for all I care, but it was you told me you wanted to be called.'

Anne raised herself on an elbow and looked out of the window. It was still quite dark outside, except that the bottom edge of the window frame was white with snow. The low, full-toned tolling of bells was heard, but that was some way off in another parish. The clock on the small table showed three minutes past six.

'All right, Masha, just a couple of minutes,' entreated Anne, pulling the quilt over her head.

She pictured the snow by the porch, the sledge, the dark sky, the congregation in church and the smell of juniper, which was all rather forbidding, but she was still determined to get up straight away and go to early service. Enjoying the warm bed, fighting off sleep—it has a way of being most delightful just when one is told to wake up—and picturing, now a huge garden on a hill, now the Gushchin place, she was irked all the time at having to get up that instant and drive to church.

When Anne did get up it was quite light and the clock said half-past nine. Masses of new snow had piled up overnight, the trees were robed in white, the air was extraordinarily bright, transparent and limpid, so that when she looked through the window she at first felt like giving a huge sigh. But, as she was washing herself, a residual childhood memory of joy that it was Christmas Day suddenly stirred within her, after which she felt relaxed, free and pure-hearted as if her very soul had been washed or plunged in white snow. In came Masha—tightly corseted, in her best clothes—and wished Anne Happy Christmas before doing her hair and helping her to dress, which took some time. The smell, the feel of her gorgeous, splendid new dress, its slight rustle and the whiff of fresh scent—all excited Anne.

'So Christmas has come,' she cheerfully remarked to Masha. 'Now we'll tell our fortunes.'

'Last year it came out as I was to marry an old man. Three times it came out that way.'

'Never mind, God is merciful.'

'I don't know, though, ma'am. Rather than be at sixes and sevens all the time I might do better marrying an old man, it seems to me.' Masha sighed sadly. 'I'm gone twenty, it's no laughing matter.'

Everyone in the house knew that red-haired Masha loved the butler Misha with a deep yet hopeless passion which had now lasted three years.

'Oh, don't talk such nonsense,' said Anne, attempting to console her. 'I'll soon be thirty and I still mean to marry a young man.'

While the mistress was dressing, Misha paced the ballroom and drawing-room in his new tail-coat and lacquered boots, waiting for her to come out so that he could offer her the compliments of the season. He had a special walk, always treading softly and delicately. Looking at his legs, his arms and the tilt of his head, you might have thought that he wasn't just walking but learning to dance the first figure of the quadrille. Despite his thin, velvety moustache, despite his handsome, not to say caddish exterior, he was as dignified, judicious and pious as an old man. He always bowed low when praying, and liked burning incense in his room. Respecting and venerating the rich and well-connected, he scorned the poor and suppliants of any kind with the full force of his chaste flunkey's soul. Under his starched shirt he wore a flannel vest, winter and summer, setting great store by his health. He kept his ears plugged with cotton-wool.

When Anne and Masha crossed the ballroom he inclined his head downwards, slightly to one side, and spoke in his pleasant, honeyed voice. 'Madam, I have the honour to wish you all happiness on the solemn occasion of Our Lord's Nativity.'

Anne gave him five roubles and poor Masha nearly fainted. His festive air, his posture, his voice, his words pierced her with their beauty and elegance. She continued to follow her mistress, her mind a blank, seeing nothing, only smiling—now blissfully, now bitterly.

The upper storey of the house was called 'the best rooms', 'above stairs' or 'the chambers', while the lower floor, where Aunt Tatyana officiated, was 'the tradesmen's', 'the old folks'' or simply 'the women's' quarters. In the former they received the quality and educated persons, in the latter humbler folk and Aunt's own friends.

Beautiful, buxom, healthy, young, fresh, radiantly conscious of her gorgeous dress, Anne went down to the ground floor. There she met reproaches. 'Here are you, an educated woman, forgetting God, sleeping through morning service, and not coming down to break your fast.' They all threw up their hands and fervently told her that she was a remarkably good-looking woman. Not doubting that they meant what they said, she laughed, kissed them, and gave them one, three or—as the case might be—five roubles. She liked it down here. On all sides were icon-cases, icons, icon-lamps, portraits of men of the cloth. It smelt of monks. There was a clattering of knives in the kitchen, a whiff of something rich and succulent swept through the place. The yellow-stained floors shone, and from the doors to the corners with their icons were narrow carpet runners with bright blue stripes. The sun's rays slashed through the windows.

In the dining-room sat some old women—strangers. There were old women in Barbara's room too, and a deaf-and-dumb girl who seemed vaguely embarrassed and kept mumbling incoherently. Two thin little girls, invited over from the children's home for the holidays, came up to kiss Anne's hand, but stopped in front of her, stunned by the richness of her dress. One girl was a bit cross-eyed, Anne noticed, feeling a sudden pang, for all the relaxed Christmassy mood, to think that the child would be neglected by suitors and never get married. In Agatha's, the cook's, room half a dozen enormous peasants in new shirts were sitting over the samovar—not factory-hands, these, but relatives of the kitchen staff. Seeing Anne, they jumped up and stopped chewing out of politeness though all had their mouths full. Her chef Stephen came in from the kitchen in his white hat, carrying a knife, and wished her happy Christmas. Felt-booted yardmen came in and did the same. A water-hauler peered in with icicles on his beard, but dared not enter.

Anne walked from room to room with the whole lot tagging behind —her Aunt, Barbara, Nikandrovna, the seamstress Martha, 'Downstairs' Masha. Barbara—a thin, slim, tall woman, the tallest person in the house—was all in black, smelling of cypress-wood and coffee. She crossed herself and bowed to the icons in each room. The sight somehow reminded one that she had prepared a shroud for her own funeral, and also that she kept her lottery certificates in a trunk along with that shroud.

'Now, let's see some Christmas spirit, Annie dear.' Barbara opened the kitchen door. 'Do forgive the wretch—such nuisances these people are.'

In the middle of the kitchen knelt the coachman Panteley, dismissed for drunkenness back in November. Though a kindly man, he was prone to violence in his cups, when he couldn't sleep but haunted the works, shouting menacingly that he knew 'all the goings-on'. That he had been drinking non-stop between November and Christmas was obvious from his jowly, puffy face and bloodshot eyes.

'Forgive me, Miss Anne,' he wheezed, banging his head on the ground and displaying a neck like a bull's.

'My aunt it was dismissed you, so you'd better ask her.'

'What's this about your aunt?' asked her aunt, puffing her way into the kitchen. She was so fat that you could have rested a samovar and tray of cups on her bust. 'What's this aunt business? You're mistress here, so you deal with it. These scallywags can all go to blazes for all I care. Oh, stand up, you great ox!' she shouted at Panteley, losing her temper. 'Get out of my sight! This is the last time I'll forgive you—if it happens again you can expect no mercy.'

They went to the dining-room for coffee. But hardly were they

seated at table when Downstairs Masha hurtled in, uttered the horror-
struck announcement 'carol singers', and ran out again. There was a
noise of people blowing their noses, of a deep bass cough and of footsteps, as if shod horses were being brought into the vestibule by the
ballroom. Then, after half a minute's silence, the singers suddenly
emitted so loud a shriek that everyone jumped. While they were
singing the almshouse priest arrived with his verger and sexton.
Donning his stole, the priest slowly averred that it had snowed that
night while the bells were ringing for early service, but it had not been
cold, whereas a sharp frost had come on by morning, dash it, and it
must now be about twenty degrees below.

'There are, however, those who claim that winter is healthier than
summer,' said the verger, but at once assumed a stern expression and
sang after the priest: 'Thy Nativity, O Christ, our God——'

Soon afterwards the priest from the works hospital arrived with his
sexton, followed by nuns from the Red Cross and children from the
local home. Singing went on almost without a break. They sang, they
ate, they departed.

Members of the works staff, about a score of them, came to offer the
compliments of the season. These were all senior people—engineers,
their assistants, pattern-makers, the accountant and so on—all respectable in their new black frock-coats. They were a fine body of men, an
élite, and each knew his worth—if he lost his job today he'd be gladly
taken on at another factory tomorrow. That they liked Anne's aunt
was obvious because they relaxed with her and even smoked, and the
accountant put his arm round her broad waist as they all crowded over
to the buffet. One reason why they felt so much at ease was perhaps
that Barbara—the all-powerful supervisor of staff morals in the old
man's day—now counted for nothing in the house. And perhaps
another reason was that many of them still remembered the days when
Aunt Tatyana, treated strictly by the brothers, had dressed like an
ordinary peasant such as Agatha, and when Miss Anne herself had run
round the yard near the works buildings and everyone had called her
little Annie.

The staff ate, smoked and gazed dumbfounded at Anne. How she had
grown up, how pretty she had become. Yet this elegant girl, reared by
governesses and tutors, was to them a stranger and an enigma, and so
they involuntarily gravitated to her aunt, who spoke to them more
intimately, who kept pressing them to eat and drink, who clinked
glasses with them and had already drunk two rowanberry gins. Anne

was always scared of being thought proud, an upstart, a crow decked in peacock's feathers. Now, as the staff crowded round the food, she stayed in the dining-room and joined in the talk. She asked Pimenov, whom she had met on the previous day, why he had so many watches and clocks in his room.

'I do repairs,' he answered. 'I do them in my spare time, on holidays, or when I can't sleep.'

Anne laughed. 'So if my watch goes wrong I can bring it to you for repair?'

'Certainly, I'll be glad to,' said Pimenov. And when, not knowing why, she unhooked the magnificent watch from her corsage and gave it to him, he looked quite overcome with emotion. He examined it silently and gave it back. 'Certainly, I'll be glad to,' he repeated. 'I don't mend pocket watches any more. I have bad eyesight, and the doctor has told me not to do close work. But I can make an exception for you.'

'All doctors are liars,' said the accountant, and everyone laughed. 'Don't you believe them,' he went on, flattered by the laughter. 'In Lent last year a cog flew out of a drum and caught old Kalmykov on the head. You could actually see his brains, and the doctor said he was going to die. He's still alive and working, though, only he now has a stutter through this business.'

'Doctors do talk nonsense, indeed they do, but not all that much,' sighed Aunt. 'Peter Andreyevich lost his sight, God rest his soul. He worked all day in the factory near a hot furnace like you, and he went blind. Heat's bad for the eyes. Anyway, why talk about it?' She shook herself. 'Let's go and have a drink. Happy Christmas to you all, dears. I don't usually drink, but I'll have one with you, may I be forgiven. Cheers!'

Anne sensed that Pimenov despised her as a dispenser of charity after yesterday's business, but was entranced by her as a woman. She noticed that he was really behaving quite nicely, and was presentably dressed. True, his frock-coat sleeves were a bit short, the waist seemed too high, and the trousers were not of the fashionable broad cut, but his cravat was tied with tasteful nonchalance, nor was it as loud as the others'. And he must be good-natured, for he submissively ate everything that her aunt put on his plate. She remembered how black, how sleepy he had been yesterday—a rather touching recollection.

When the staff were ready to leave, Anne held out her hand to Pimenov and felt like asking him to call on her some time, but was unable to. Somehow her tongue would not obey her. And, in case anyone might suppose that she found Pimenov attractive, she shook hands with his colleagues too.

The next arrivals were boys from the school where she was Visitor. All had short hair and wore grey smocks in uniform style. Their schoolmaster—a tall, whiskerless, obviously nervous youth with red blotches on his face—paraded them in rows. The boys started singing in harmony, but with harsh, disagreeable voices. The works manager Nazarych—a bald, sharp-eyed Nonconformist—never had got on with schoolteachers, but this one with his fussy arm-waving he despised and hated without even knowing why. He treated him arrogantly and rudely, he withheld his salary, he interfered with the teaching. In order to get rid of the man once and for all, Nazarych had, a fortnight before Christmas, appointed a distant relative by marriage to the post of school caretaker, a drunken oaf who disobeyed the teacher and was impertinent to him in his pupils' presence.

Anne knew all this, but could not help, being scared of Nazarych herself. Now she at least wanted to be kind to the schoolteacher and tell him that she was very satisfied with him, but when the singing was over and he embarked on some highly embarrassed apology, and after her aunt, speaking to him as one of the family, had casually dragged him off to the table, she felt depressed and ill at ease. Ordering that the children should be given presents, she went upstairs to her own quarters.

'There's a lot of cruelty about these Christmas arrangements really,' she said aloud a little later, looking out of the window at the boys flocking from the house to the gate and putting on their furs and over-coats as they went, shivering from cold. 'On holidays you want to rest and stay at home with your family, but the poor boys, the master and the staff are somehow obliged to go out in the cold, wish you happy Christmas, convey their respects, suffer embarrassment.'

Misha, standing just by the ballroom door, heard all this.

'We didn't start it and it won't end with us. Of course, I'm not an educated man, madam, but to my way of thinking the poor must always respect the rich. God puts his mark on a scoundrel, 'tis said. Gaols, doss-houses, taverns—they're always full of the poor, while decent people are always rich, mark my words. Deep calls to deep, that's what they say of the rich.'

'You're rather given to such boring, incomprehensible talk, Misha.' Anne crossed to the other side of the room.

It was just turned eleven o'clock. The calm of the vast rooms, broken only now and then by singing wafted up from the ground floor, was enough to make you yawn. The bronzes, the albums, the pictures on the wall—seascapes with little boats, a meadow with cows, views of the River Rhine—were so unoriginal that one's eyes slid over them seeing nothing. The Christmas spirit had already begun to pall. Anne still felt beautiful, kind, admirable, but now sensed that these qualities were of no use to anyone. For whom had she put on this expensive dress? Why? She had no idea. As always on festive occasions, she began to suffer from loneliness, obsessed with the thought that her beauty, her health, her riches were only a sham, that she was a misfit on this earth, that no one needed or loved her. She walked through all her rooms, humming and glancing through the windows. Pausing in the ballroom, she could not help addressing Misha.

'I don't know who you think you are, Misha.' She sighed. 'Truly, God will punish you for this.'

'For what, madam?'

'You know perfectly well. I'm sorry to meddle in your private affairs, but I think you're ruining your life out of sheer obstinacy. You're just the age to marry, now, aren't you? And she's a fine, a most deserving girl. You'll never find a better, she's beautiful, clever, gentle, devoted. And her looks! If she was one of our set, or in high society, men would love her for her marvellous red hair alone. Look how her hair sets off her complexion. Oh God, you understand nothing, you don't know what you need yourself,' Anne added bitterly, and tears came to her eyes. 'Poor child, I'm so sorry for her. I know you want to marry someone with money, but I've told you I'll give Masha a dowry.'

Misha could picture his future wife only as a tall, buxom, stately, respectable-looking woman, strutting like a peahen, always wearing a long shawl on her shoulders for some reason, whereas Masha was thin, slight, corseted, and walked with a modest gait. Above all she was too seductive, and sometimes strongly attracted Misha. But he thought that sort of thing went with impropriety, and not at all with marriage. When Anne has promised the dowry he had weakened for a time. But then a poor student, with a brown top-coat over his uniform, had brought Anne a letter, and had been so taken with Masha that he couldn't resist embracing her near the coat-hooks downstairs, and she had given a little cry. Misha had seen this from the staircase above them, and had been rather put off by Masha ever since. A poor student! Had she been kissed by a rich student or an officer the result might have been different, who knows?

'Why don't you?' Anne asked. 'What more could you want?'

Eyebrows raised, Misha stared silently at an armchair.

'Do you love anyone else?'

No answer. Masha of the red hair came in with letters and visiting cards on a tray. Guessing that they had been talking about her, she blushed till she nearly cried.

'The postmen are here,' she muttered. 'And a clerk, a Chalikov or something, has come and is waiting downstairs. He says you asked him here today for some reason.'

'What impudence.' Anne was angry. 'I never asked him at all. Say he's to clear out, I'm not at home.'

There was a ring at the door. This was their own parish priests, who were always received in the best rooms—upstairs, that is. After the priests the works manager Nazarych and then the works doctor called. Then Misha announced the inspector of elementary schools. The reception of visitors had begun.

Whenever she had a free moment Anne sat in a deep armchair in the drawing-room, closed her eyes and reflected that her loneliness was entirely natural since she had not married and never would. But it was not her fault. From ordinary working-class surroundings—where, if memory served, she had been so comfortable, so much at ease—fate itself had cast her into these huge rooms. What was she to do with herself? She couldn't think. Why did all these people keep coming and going? She hadn't the faintest idea. The present proceedings seemed trivial and otiose since they neither did not could give her a minute's happiness.

'Oh, to fall in love.' She stretched herself, and the mere idea warmed her heart. 'And I should get rid of the factory,' she mused, imagining all those ponderous buildings, those barracks and that school being lifted from her conscience.

Then she remembered her father, reflecting that he would surely have married her to some working man like Pimenov if he had lived longer. He would have told her to marry, and that would have been that. It would have been all right too, for then the factory would have fallen into the right hands.

She pictured the curly head, the bold profile, the thin, mocking lips, the strength, the terrible strength of his shoulders, arms and chest, and the rapture with which he had examined her watch today.

'Why not?' she said. 'It would be all right, I'd marry him.'

'Miss Anne,' called Misha, coming silently into the dining-room.

'How you did frighten me.' She trembled all over. 'What do you want?'

'Miss Anne,' he repeated, laying his hand on his heart and raising his eyebrows. 'You are my employer and benefactress, no one but you can tell me who to marry, seeing that you are a mother to me. But do ask them not to laugh at me and tease me below stairs. They won't let me alone.'

'And what form does this teasing take?'

'Masha's Misha, they call me.'

'Ugh, how idiotic.' Anne was outraged. 'You're all so stupid—you too, Misha. Oh, you do bore me so, I can't bear the sight of you.'

III

Dinner

As in the previous year, Anne's last visitors to arrive were Krylin, a senior civil servant, and the well-known lawyer Lysevich. They came as dusk was falling.

Old Krylin, in his sixties, wide-mouthed and lynx-faced with white dundrearies round his ears, wore uniform, a St. Anne ribbon and white trousers. He held Anne's hand in both his own for some time, staring into her face, moving his lips.

'I respected your uncle and your father, and they were favourably disposed towards me,' he brought out at last, all on one note, carefully articulating each syllable. 'Now, as you see, I consider it my pleasant duty to convey the compliments of the season to their respected lady successor, despite my infirmity and the considerable distance. And very glad I am to see you in good health.'

The barrister Lysevich—tall, handsome, fair-haired, with a touch of grey about temples and beard—was notable for extreme elegance of manner. He would waltz into the room, bow with apparent reluctance, wriggle his shoulders as he spoke—all with the lazy grace of a spoilt horse in need of exercise. He was sleek, rich, remarkably healthy. Once he had even won forty thousand roubles in a lottery, but had concealed this from his friends. He liked good food, especially cheese, truffles, shredded horse-radish in hempseed oil, and claimed to have eaten uncleaned giblets, fried, in Paris. He spoke smoothly, evenly, without

hesitation, permitting himself the occasional coy pause and flick of the
fingers as if at a loss for a word. He had long ceased believing what he
had to say in court. Or perhaps he did believe it, but attached no value
to it. All that stuff was so old hat, out-of-date, trite.

He believed only in the unusual and the recondite. Hackneyed
moralizing could move him to tears, if expressed with originality. His
two notebooks were bescribbled with out-of-the-way expressions
culled from various authors, and when at a loss for a phrase he would
nervously rummage in both books and usually fail to find it. Old Akim
had once light-heartedly taken him on as works lawyer to lend tone to
the place, at a retainer of twelve thousand roubles. But the factory's
entire legal activity consisted only of a few minor suits which Lysevich
left to his assistants.

Anne knew that there was no work for him at the factory. But she
could not bring herself to dismiss him, lacking the courage and liking
him. He called himself her 'legal adviser', referring to his retainer, for
which he applied regularly on the first of the month, as 'this boring
necessity'. When Anne's woods had been sold for railway sleepers after
her father's death, Lysevich had fiddled more than fifteen thousand on
the deal and shared it with Nazarych, as she knew. She had wept bitterly
on learning of the fraud, but had then come to accept it.

Having wished her a happy Christmas and kissed both her hands,
Lysevich looked her up and down, and frowned.

'Don't!' he said with sincere regret. 'I've told you not to, dear
lady.'

'Don't what, Victor?'

'I've told you not to put on weight. Your family all have this unfortunate tendency to stoutness. Don't do it,' he pleaded, kissing her hand.
'You're such a fine, splendid woman.' He turned to Krylin. 'Here she
is, my dear sir. Permit me to present—the only woman in the world
I have ever really loved.'

'That doesn't surprise me. To know Miss Glagolev at your age and
not love her would be impossible.'

'I adore her,' the lawyer went on with complete sincerity but with
his usual lazy grace. 'I love her, but not because I'm a man and she's a
woman. When I'm with her I feel as if she belonged to some third sex
and I to a fourth, as if we were soaring off together to a domain of the
most subtle hues, and there blending into a spectrum. Such relationships
are defined best of all by Leconte de Lisle. He has one marvellous passage, truly remarkable.'

Rummaging in one notebook and then in the other, Lysevich calmed down on failing to find the dictum. They talked of the weather, of the opera, of Duse's imminent tour. Anne recalled Lysevich and, she thought, Krylin dining with her on the previous Christmas Day, and as they were about to leave she urgently submitted that they must stay to dinner as they had no more visits to make. After some hesitation the guests agreed.

Besides the ordinary meal of cabbage stew, sucking pig, goose with apples and so on, a 'French' or 'chef's' dinner would be prepared in the kitchen on major festive occasions in case any first-floor guests should wish to partake. When the clattering of crockery began in the dining-room Lysevich evinced obvious excitement. He rubbed his hands, wriggled his shoulders, frowned, movingly described the dinners that the old men had once given, and said what a superb turbot soup Anne's chef made—more of a divine inspiration than a *bouillabaisse*. He was looking forward to the meal, he was already eating and enjoying it in his imagination. When Anne took his arm and led him to the dining-room, when he had at last drunk a glass of vodka and put a piece of salmon in his mouth, he was actually purring with pleasure. He chewed loudly and revoltingly, making noises through his nose, his eyes greasy and voracious.

The *hors-d'œuvre* were lavish, including fresh mushrooms in sour cream and *sauce provençale* with fried oysters and crayfish tails well primed with sour pickles. The main part of the meal consisted of exquisite dishes specially cooked for the festivities, and the wines were excellent. Misha served like one in a trance. Placing a new dish on the table, removing the lid of a gleaming tureen, pouring the wine, he was solemn as a professor of the black art. From his face, from his walk like the first figure in the quadrille, the lawyer several times concluded that the man was a fool.

After the third course Lysevich turned to Anne.

'A *fin de siècle* woman—I mean a young one and, of course, a rich one—must be independent, clever, elegant, intelligent, bold. And a shade immoral. I say a shade immoral, immoral within limits, because you'll agree that everything is exhausting in excess. You mustn't vegetate, dear lady, you mustn't live like all the rest, you must savour life, and a touch of immorality is the very spice of existence. Plunge into flowers with a reek that drugs the senses, choke in musk, eat hashish. Above all love, love, love. If I were you I'd start off with seven men, one for each day of the week, and I'd call one Monday, the next Tuesday, the third Wednesday and so on. Let each know his own day.'

His talk unnerved Anne. She ate nothing, drank only one glass of wine, and told him that he must for goodness' sake let her speak.

'To me personally love makes no sense without a family,' she said. 'I'm lonely—lonely as the moon in the sky, and the waning moon at that. Say what you like, but I know, I feel that this void can only be filled by love in its ordinary sense. Such a love will define my duties, my work, enlighten my view of life, I feel. From love I want peace of mind, calmness. I want to get as far as possible from musk and all your *fin de siècle* mumbo-jumbo. In other words,' she said with embarrassment, 'I want a husband and children.'

'You want to marry? Why not? That too is possible,' agreed Lysevich. 'You should try everything—marriage, jealousy, the sweetness of your first adultery, children even. But hurry up and enjoy life, dear lady, hurry—time's passing, it won't wait.'

'All right, I jolly well will marry.' She looked angrily at his sleek, complacent face. 'I'll marry in the most conventional, commonplace way, I'll radiate happiness. And, believe it or not, I'll marry an ordinary working man, a mechanic, a draughtsman or something.'

'Not a bad idea either. Princess falls in love with swineherd. That's all right, seeing that she's a princess. It's all right for you too because you're exceptional. If you want to love some Negro or blackamoor, dear lady, go ahead and send for a Negro. Deny yourself nothing. Be bold as your own desires, don't tag along behind them.'

'Am I really so hard to understand?' Anne was outraged, tears gleamed in her eyes. 'Can't you see I have a huge business on my hands, two thousand workers for whom I must answer before God? Men go blind and deaf working for me. Life frightens me, scares me stiff. And, while I suffer, you have the cruelty to bring up these wretched Negroes. And—and you grin.' Anne banged her fist on the table. 'To go on living as I am now, to marry someone as idle and incompetent as myself—that would just be a crime. I can't go on like this,' she said fiercely. 'I can't cope.'

'How pretty she is!' Lysevich was entranced. 'What a devilish handsome woman. But why so angry, dear lady? I may be quite wrong, but what if you do make yourself miserable and renounce the joys of life in the name of ideals which I, incidentally, deeply respect? What good will that do the workers? None. No, it's immorality for you, debauchery,' he said decisively. 'Be corrupt, it's your duty—get that well and truly into your head, dear lady.'

Glad to have had her say, Anne cheered up. She was pleased to have spoken so well, pleased to be reasoning so honestly and stylishly. She was also certain that if Pimenov, say, should fall in love with her she would be delighted to marry him.

Misha poured champagne.

'You provoke me, Victor.' She clinked glasses with the lawyer. 'You annoy me by giving advice when you know nothing of life yourself. A mechanic or draughtsman—to you he's a country bumpkin. But they're such clever people, they're quite outstanding.'

'I knew and respected, er, your father and uncle,' Krylin enunciated. He was stretched out like an effigy, and had been eating non-stop. 'Those were men of considerable intellect and, er, high spiritual qualities.'

'Oh, we've heard quite enough about those qualities,' muttered the lawyer, and asked permission to smoke.

After dinner Krylin was led off for his nap. Lysevich finished his cigar and followed Anne to her study, waddling because he had eaten too much. Disliking secluded nooks full of photographs, fans on the wall, the inevitable pink or blue lamp in the middle of the ceiling, he thought them expressions of a feeble, unoriginal mind. Moreover, memories of certain romantic affairs, of which he was now ashamed, were associated with such a lamp. But he much liked Anne's study with its bare walls and characterless furniture. He felt easy and relaxed on the sofa, glancing at Anne who usually sat on the carpet in front of the hearth, knees clasped in her hands as she gazed meditatively at the flames while giving him the impression that her Nonconformist peasant instincts were aroused.

When coffee and liqueurs were served after dinner he would perk up and tell her bits of literary news. He spoke in the flamboyant, exalted style of one transported by his own rhetoric, while she listened, reflecting as ever that such enjoyment was worth his twelve thousand roubles three times over, and forgave all she disliked in him. Sometimes he described the plots of short stories or even novels, and a couple of hours would pass unnoticed like so many minutes. Now he began in a rather sentimental, feeble voice, eyes closed.

'It's ages since I read anything, dear lady,' he said when she asked him to talk. 'Though I do sometimes read Jules Verne.'

'And I thought you were going to tell me something new.'

'Humph. Something new,' Lysevich muttered sleepily and settled back still further into the corner of the sofa. 'Modern literature doesn't suit the likes of you and me, dear lady. It can't help being what it is, of course, and to reject it would be to reject the natural order of things, so I do accept it, but——'

Lysevich seemed to have fallen asleep, but a little later his voice was heard again. 'Modern literature's all like the autumn wind in the chimney, for ever groaning and moaning. "Oh, oh, oh, you're so unhappy, your life is like prison, and a dark, damp prison at that. Alas, you're doomed, there's no hope for you." That's all very well, but I'd rather have a literature which teaches you to escape from prison. Maupassant is the only modern writer I occasionally read.' Lysevich opened his eyes. 'He's a good writer, a fine writer.' Lysevich stirred on the sofa. 'He's a remarkable artist, a terrifying, monstrous, supernatural artist.' Lysevich got up from the sofa, raised his right hand. 'Maupassant!' said he in ecstasy. 'Read Maupassant, dear lady. One page will give you more than all the riches of this earth. Every line contains a new horizon. The most delicate and tender spiritual motions alternate with mighty tempestuous sensations, your soul seems subjected to a forty-thousandfold atmospheric pressure, and turns into an insignificant speck of an indeterminate pinkish substance—if you could put it on your tongue it would have a bitter, sensuous taste, I think. What a frenzy of transitions, motifs, melodies. You are resting on lilies-of-the-valley and roses when suddenly an idea—awful, wonderful, irresistible —unexpectedly swoops on you like a railway train, swamps you with hot steam, deafens you with its whistle. Read, read, read Maupassant. I demand it, dear lady.'

Lysevich brandished his arms and paced the room in a great pother.

'No, it cannot be,' he said, as if in despair. 'His last work exhausted, intoxicated me. But I'm afraid you won't react to it at all. If it is to sweep you off your feet you must savour it, slowly squeeze the juice out of each line and drink it. Yes, drink it!'

After a long exordium containing many expressions like 'demoniac passion', 'tissue of nervous ganglia', 'sand-storm', 'crystal' and so on, he at last began to explain the plot. Now speaking in less high-flown style and in great detail, he quoted by heart whole descriptions and conversations. The characters enchanted him, and as he retailed them he assumed poses, changing his voice and facial expression like a real actor. He gave exulting cachinnations—now low-pitched, now thin and reedy—he threw up his hands, he clutched his head as if it was about to burst. Anne had read the book, yet listened with fascination, finding the lawyer's account far finer and more complex than the original. He directed her attention to the various subtleties, he emphasized the felicitous expressions and profound ideas, while she saw it all as if it was actually happening, with herself as one of the characters. She cheered up, she too laughed aloud and threw up her hands, reflecting that an existence like hers was impossible—why live badly when one could live well? She remembered what she had said and thought at dinner, gloried in it. And when Pimenov suddenly came to mind she felt happy and wanted him to love her.

His recital concluded, Lysevich sank exhausted on the sofa.

'You're a wonderful, splendid woman,' he said a little later in a feeble, sick voice. 'I'm so happy with you, dear lady. But why must I be forty-two and not thirty? My tastes and yours don't coincide. You need immorality, whereas I went through that phase ages ago and want a most subtle love, insubstantial as a sunbeam—to a woman of your age, in other words, I'm no damn use.'

He reckoned to like Turgenev, that bard of first love, purity, youth and melancholy Russian landscapes. Yet there was nothing that touched him closely in this passion for 'virgin' love, it was just something he had heard of, something abstract and divorced from reality. He was now telling himself that his love for Anne was platonic and idealistic. What that meant he didn't know, but he felt relaxed, at ease, warm. Anne seemed enchantingly eccentric, and he mistook the euphoria aroused in him by this ambience for his 'platonic' love.

He pressed his cheek to her hand. 'Why have you punished me, dearest?' he asked in the voice with which people coax infants.

'How? When?'

'You haven't sent me my Christmas bonus.'

Never having heard of lawyers receiving Christmas bonuses, Anne was embarrassed at not knowing how much to give him. And something she must give him because he obviously expected it even as he gazed at her with love-lorn eyes.

'Nazarych must have forgotten, but it's not too late to be mended,' she said.

Then she suddenly remembered yesterday's fifteen hundred roubles, now on her bedroom dressing-table. Fetching that distasteful sum, she gave it to the lawyer, who stuck it in his coat pocket with his lazy elegance. It all went off rather charmingly and naturally. The unexpected reminder of the bonus, the fifteen hundred roubles—it was pure Lysevich, all this.

'*Merci.*' He kissed her finger.

In came Krylin with a beatific, sleepy air, having taken off his decorations.

He and Lysevich sat on a bit longer, drank their glass of tea, prepared to leave. Anne was rather put out, having quite forgotten where Krylin worked. Should she give him money too? And, if so, should she give it now or send it in an envelope?

'Where does he work?' she whispered to Lysevich.

'Damned if I know,' muttered the yawning lawyer.

She reflected that Krylin would not have paid his respects to her uncle and father for no return. He had obviously been their agent in good works, serving in some charitable institution, so she thrust three hundred roubles in his hand as she said good-bye. He seemed astounded. For a time he looked at her silently, eyes glazed, but then seemed to understand.

'But you can't have a receipt before the new year, dear madam.'

Now completely limp, Lysevich slumped and tottered as Misha helped him into his furs. On his way downstairs he looked utterly debilitated, and would obviously fall fast asleep the moment he got into his sledge.

'Have you, sir, ever felt,' he languidly asked Krylin, pausing on the staircase, 'as if some invisible force was stretching you out until you got longer and longer and ended up as a length of the finest wire? The feeling is, subjectively speaking, peculiarly and quite incomparably sensual.'

Standing on the upper level, Anne saw both give Misha a banknote.

'Good-bye, don't forget me,' she shouted, and ran to her bedroom.

She quickly threw off her dress, which now bored her, put on her négligé and ran downstairs, laughing and clattering her feet like an urchin. She felt very skittish.

IV

Evening

Aunt in her loose cotton blouse, Barbara and a couple of old women were having supper in the dining-room. Before them on the table was a hunk of salt-beef, a ham and various salted foods, and from the very fat, tasty-looking salt-beef steam rose to the ceiling. They did not drink wine down here, but had a great variety of spirits and cordials. The cook Agatha—buxom, fair-haired, stocky—stood by the door, arms crossed, talking to the old women while the dishes were taken and served by Downstairs Masha with a crimson ribbon in her dark hair. The old women had been stuffing themselves since morning, and had had tea with a rich pie only an hour before supper, so they were now forcing themselves to eat as if it were a duty.

'Oh dear,' gasped Anne's aunt when Anne suddenly ran into the dining-room and sat on the chair next to her. 'You nearly scared me to death.'

The household liked Anne being cheerful and frolicsome, which always reminded them that the old men had died, that the old women no longer held sway in the house, and that they could all do as they liked without fear of being kept up to the mark. Only the two old women unknown to Anne looked askance at her, amazed that she was singing to herself, for singing at table is a sin.

'She's pretty as a picture, is Madam,' drooled Agatha in her sing-song voice. 'A pearl beyond price she is. And oh what a lot of nice people came to see our princess today, Lord love us. Generals, officers, fine gentlemen. I kept a-looking through the window and a-counting of 'em, and then I gave up.'

'Let them stay at home, the scallywags,' said Aunt. She looked sadly at her niece, adding that they had only 'wasted the poor child's time'.

Having eaten nothing since morning, Anne was famished. They poured her a very dry cordial which she drank, eating salt-beef and mustard and finding it all most tasty. Then Downstairs Masha served turkey, soused apples and gooseberries, which Anne also liked. Only one thing irked her—waves of heat came from the tiled stove, it was stuffy and everyone's cheeks glowed. After supper they took off the tablecloth and served bowls of mint cakes, nuts and raisins.

'Now, you sit with us too, come on,' Aunt told the cook.

Agatha sighed and sat down at table. Masha set a cordial glass before her too, and Anne felt as if the heat proceeded equally from the stove and Agatha's white neck. They all said how hard it was to get married these days. At one time men had at least been attracted by money if not by beauty, whereas there was no telling what they wanted now. Once only the lame and the hunchbacks had been left on the shelf, but even beauty and riches were spurned nowadays. It was all because they were immoral and didn't fear the Lord, Aunt began saying, but then suddenly remembered that her brother Ivan and Barbara had both been righteous-living, God-fearing people, yet had had children on the wrong side of the blanket and sent them to a home. So she pulled herself up and changed the conversation to a former suitor of hers, a factory employee, and how she had loved him. But her brothers had made her marry a widowed icon-painter who had died two years later, thank God. Downstairs Masha also sat at table and enigmatically averred that a strange man—black-moustached, in an overcoat with an astrakhan collar—had taken to appearing in their yard every morning this week. He would come into the yard, look up at the mansion windows, then go on to the factory. He wasn't bad either—quite good-looking.

All this talk somehow made Anne suddenly long for marriage. She was seized by an urge akin to anguish, feeling ready to give half her life and all her possessions just to know that there was a man upstairs dearer to her than anyone on earth, one who really loved her and yearned for her. The idea of intimacy so inexpressibly entrancing moved her. Her healthy young woman's instincts flattered her with the lie that true romance lay ahead, even though it had not yet arrived. Convinced, she threw herself back in her chair, which made her hair fall down. She began laughing, and that set the others laughing too. For some time this spontaneous laughter rang through the dining-room.

It was announced that 'the Beetle' had arrived, and would stay the night—a small, thin, pious woman of about fifty called Pasha or Spiridonovna, in black dress and white kerchief, sharp-eyed, sharp-nosed, sharp-chinned. She had a sly, venomous look, and stared at you as if she could see through you. Her lips were heart-shaped, and her poisonous, misanthropic character had earned her the nickname Beetle in business people's houses.

She entered the dining-room, looking at no one, faced the icons and sang in an alto voice 'Thy Birth', 'A Maid This Day' and 'Christ is Born'. Then she turned and riveted them all with a glance.

'Happy Christmas.' She kissed Anne's shoulder. 'Such a trouble I did have getting here, kind ladies.' She kissed Aunt's shoulder too. 'I started off this morning, but on my way I called on some folk for a bit of a rest. "Do stay, do stay, Spiridonovna," said they. Aye, and evening came on before I noticed.'

As she did not eat meat they gave her caviare and salmon, which she ate while scowling at everyone, and she drank three glasses of spirits. Having had her fill, she said grace and bowed low to Anne.

As they had done last year and the year before that, they played Kings, while all the servants from both floors crowded at the door to watch the game. Anne seemed to notice Misha, complete with condescending smile, flash past a couple of times amid the thronging lower orders. The first to be King was the Beetle, and Anne—a Soldier—paid her a forfeit. Then Aunt became King and Anne was a Peasant or Bumpkin, much to everyone's delight, while Agatha became a Prince and felt positively guilty, she was so pleased. At the other end of the table a second game was made up by the two Mashas, Barbara and the seamstress Martha, whom they had woken up specially to play, and who looked sleepy and bad-tempered.

During the game their talk touched on men, on how hard it was to find a good husband these days, on whether it was better to be a spinster or a widow.

'You're a fine, healthy, strapping wench,' the Beetle told Anne. 'But who are you saving yourself for, girl? That's what I don't see.'

'But suppose no one will have me?'

'Happen you've sworn to stay unwed?' the Beetle went on as if she hadn't heard. 'All right then, don't you wed. Don't,' she repeated, looking attentively and venomously at her cards. 'Have it your own way, friend. But they come in different shapes and sizes, do spinsters— bless 'em.' She sighed and led a King. 'They ain't all the same, dear. There's some keeps themselves like nuns, as pure as pure can be, or if one of them does sin now and then the poor thing suffers such agonies you wouldn't have the heart to blame her. Then there's others that wears black and makes their own shrouds while secretly loving some rich old fellow. Yes, my pets, there's witches that puts spells on an old man. They enslaves the man, my poppets, that they do, they turns him this way and that, and once they've snaffled lots of his money and securities, then they bewitches him to death.'

To these hints Barbara responded only by sighing and looking at the icon, her face a picture of Christian humility.

'There's one girl I know what's my worst enemy,' continued the Beetle, looking exultantly at everyone. 'Oh yes, she'm always a-sighing and a-looking at the icons, the she-devil. When she had a certain old fellow under her thumb you'd visit her, belike, and she'd give you a bite to eat and order you to bow to the ground while she recited her "A virgin did give birth". She'd give you a bite of food on holidays, but on working days she'd give you a telling off. Well, I'm going to make fun of her now as much as I want, my darlings.'

Barbara again looked at the icon and crossed herself.

'But no one will have me, Spiridonovna.' Anne wanted to change the subject. 'It can't be helped.'

'It's your fault, girl. You expect a gentleman, someone educated like, when you should marry among businessfolk like yourself.'

'We want none of them, heaven forbid.' Aunt was much alarmed. 'A gentleman will squander your money, but at least he'll be nice to you, silly girl. But a merchant—he'll be so strict you'll never feel at home in your own house. While you want to cuddle up to him he'll be claiming the interest on your investments, and if you sit down to a meal with him the lout will blame you for eating him out of *your* house and home. You marry a gentleman.'

They all spoke at once, loudly interrupting each other, while Aunt banged the nutcrackers on the table.

'We don't want your merchants here, that we don't.' She was angry and red-faced. 'If you bring a merchant to this house I shall enter a nunnery.'

'Shush! Be quiet!' shouted the Beetle. When all were silent she screwed up one eye. 'Know what, Anne, my pet? There ain't no sense in your getting wed proper like other folks. You're rich, you're free, you're your own mistress. But it ain't quite right for you to stay an old maid either, child. Now, I'll find you—you know—some miserable little half-wit what you can marry for appearance' sake, and then you'll have the time of your life. Oh yes, you'll toss your husband his five or ten thousand and let him go back where he came from, and then you'll be your own mistress. Love whom you like, no one can say a thing. That way you can love your gentlemen, your educated men. You'll be on top of the world.' Beetle clicked her fingers and whistled. 'A high old time you'll have.'

'But that would be a sin,' said Aunt.

'Never mind the sinning,' laughed the Beetle. 'She's educated, she understands. To cut someone's throat, to put spells on an old man— that's a sin, no doubt of it. But to love your sweetheart—that ain't no sin, far from it. Oh, really, what *ever* next! There's no sin in that, it was all invented by pious old women to cheat simple folks. I'm always on about sinning myself, but I don't even know what I means by it.' The Beetle drank some cordial and cleared her throat. 'You really let yourself go,' she said, now evidently addressing herself. 'Thirty years I spent brooding on sin, girls, being scared of it, but now I see I missed me chance, let it pass me by. Oh, I'm a fool, such a fool.' She sighed.

'It's a short life a woman's is, and she should make the most of each little day. You're beautiful, Anne dear, very beautiful and you're rich, but when you're thirty-five or forty you'll be finished, that'll be the end. Don't you listen to anyone, my girl. You enjoy yourself, you have your fling until you're forty—plenty of time to pray about it after, plenty of time for doing penance and sewing your shroud. Give the devil his due, say I. You really let yourself go. Well, how about it—will you make some little man happy?'

'I will,' laughed Anne. 'I don't care now, I'd marry an ordinary worker.'

'That's right, and a good idea too. And you could have the pick of the bunch, by golly!' The Beetle frowned and shook her head. 'Not half you couldn't.'

'That's what I tell her,' said Aunt. 'If you can't find a gentleman, says I, then don't marry a merchant, but someone more common. At least we'd have a man about the house. And there's no lack of good folk. Take our own factory workers—sober, respectable lads, they are.'

'Not half they ain't,' agreed the Beetle. 'Fine fellers, they are. How about me marrying her to Basil Lebedinsky, Auntie?'

'But Basil's legs are too long,' said Aunt seriously. 'He's a dry stick and there's not much to his looks.'

The crowd near the door laughed.

'Well, there's Pimenov. Want to marry Pimenov?' the Beetle asked Anne.

'All right. Marry me to Pimenov.'

'You really mean it?'

'Yes I do,' said Anne resolutely, and banged the table. 'I'll marry him, I promise.'

'You mean it?'

Anne suddenly felt ashamed of her burning cheeks, of everyone staring at her. She jumbled the cards on the table, rushed from the room. Dashing upstairs, reaching the upper floor, sitting by the grand piano in the drawing-room, she heard a roar like the crashing of the sea from below. They were talking about her and Pimenov, probably, and perhaps the Beetle was exploiting her absence to insult Barbara, without of course scrupling to mince her words any longer.

On the whole upper floor there was only one lamp lit, in the ball-room, and its feeble light filtered through the door into the dark drawing-room. It was ten o'clock, no more. Anne played a waltz, then a second and a third without a pause. She looked into the dark corner behind the piano, she smiled, she felt as if she was appealing to someone, and it occurred to her to go to town and pay a visit—to Lysevich, say—and tell him about her feelings. She wanted to talk non-stop, to laugh, to play the fool, but the dark corner behind the grand piano was grimly silent, and all around her the entire upper storey was quiet and deserted.

She loved sentimental ballads, but as her voice was rough and untrained she only played accompaniments and sang barely audibly, under her breath. She sang in a whisper one song after another, all mostly about love, parting, hopes dashed. And she imagined herself stretching out her hands to him. 'Pimenov, take this burden from me,' she would beg him in tears. And then, as though her sins were forgiven, she would feel joy and peace of mind. A free and perhaps happy life would begin. Yearning and expectant, she bent over the keys. She fervently wanted a change to take place in her life there and then, straight away, and was scared to think that her present existence would still continue for a while. Then she again played the piano and sang under her breath, while all around was silence. No longer was the roar heard from below, they must all be asleep down there. It had struck ten some time ago. The long, lonely, boring night was upon her.

Anne paced all the rooms, lay on the sofa for a while, read some letters, delivered that evening, in her study. There were twelve letters wishing her a happy Christmas, and three anonymous unsigned ones. In one an ordinary worker complained in an atrocious, hardly legible hand that workers were sold rancid vegetable oil smelling of paraffin in her factory shop. In another someone respectfully denounced Nazarych for taking a thousand-rouble bribe when buying iron at the last auction. In a third she was abused for callousness.

Anne's excited, festive mood was now passing, and she tried to maintain it by sitting at the piano again and quietly playing one of the latest waltzes. Then she remembered how intelligently and straightforwardly she had reasoned and talked at dinner this evening. She looked around at the dark windows, at the walls with their pictures, at the feeble light which came from the ballroom—and then suddenly and unexpectedly burst into tears. She was distressed to feel so lonely, to have no one to talk to or consult. She tried to keep up her spirits by picturing Pimenov in her imagination, but nothing came of it.

The clock struck twelve. In came Misha in a jacket instead of his tail-coat, and silently lit two candles. Then he went out and came back a minute later with a cup of tea on a tray.

'Why do you laugh?' She had noticed a smile on his face.

'I heard you make that joke about Pimenov when I was downstairs.' He covered his laughing face with his hand. 'You should have asked him to dinner with Mr. Lysevich and Mr. Krylin just now. He'd have had the fright of his life.' Misha's shoulders shook with laughter. 'I bet he doesn't even know how to hold a fork.'

The flunkey's laughter, his words, his jacket and his little whiskers impressed Anne as unclean. To avoid seeing him, she covered her eyes and involuntarily imagined Pimenov dining with Lysevich and Krylin. And Pimenov's figure—so diffident, so unlike a professional man's—seemed pathetic and helpless, arousing her disgust. Only now did she clearly see for the first time that day that all her thoughts and words about Pimenov and marriage to an ordinary working man were foolish, unreasonable, wrong-headed. To prove the opposite, to conquer this disgust, she wanted to remember what she had said at dinner, but could not call it to mind. She was ashamed of her thoughts and deeds, scared that she might have spoken foolishly during the day, disgusted at her own feebleness. How very distressing it all was. She took a candle, rushed downstairs as if someone was chasing her, woke up Spiridonovna and assured her that it had all been a joke. Then she went to her bedroom. Red-haired Masha, who had been dozing in the armchair near the bed, jumped up to adjust the pillows. Her face was exhausted and sleepy, and her splendid hair was all over on one side.

'That clerk Chalikov was here again this evening,' she yawned. 'But I didn't dare tell you. He was very drunk, says he'll be back tomorrow.'

'What does he want with me?' Anne angrily flung her comb on the floor. 'I don't want to see him, I won't!'

There was nothing left to her in life but this Chalikov, she concluded, and he would never stop persecuting her—reminding her daily how dull and inane her existence was. What else was she capable of but helping the poor? Oh, how stupid it all was.

She lay down without taking off her clothes, and burst out sobbing from shame and boredom. The most aggravating and stupid thing seemed to her that today's thoughts about Pimenov had been decent, fine, honourable. Yet she felt at the same time that Lysevich and even Krylin were nearer to her than Pimenov and all her workers put together. Were it possible to portray the long day, now ended, in a picture, then everything rotten and cheap—the dinner, say, the lawyer's words, the game of Kings—would have been the truth, she now felt, while her dreams and the talk about Pimenov would have stood apart from it all as striking a false, jarring note. She also reflected that it was too late, now, for her to dream of happiness. Her whole life was in ruins, and it was impossible for her either to return to the days of sharing a bed with her mother or to devise some new, special mode of existence.

Red-haired Masha knelt in front of the bed looking at Anne sadly, with amazement. Then she too burst into tears and leant her face against Anne's hands. No words were needed to explain why the girl was so upset.

'We're such idiots, you and I,' said Anne, laughing and crying. 'Idiots, that's what we are.'

ROTHSCHILD'S FIDDLE

[*Скрипка Ротшильда*]

(1894)

ROTHSCHILD'S FIDDLE

It was a small town, more wretched than a village, and almost all the inhabitants were old folk with a depressingly low death rate. Nor were many coffins required at the hospital and gaol. In a word, business was bad. Had Jacob Ivanov been making coffins in a county town he would probably have owned a house and been called 'mister'. But in this dump he was plain Jacob, his street nickname was 'Bronze' for whatever reason, and he lived as miserably as any farm labourer in his little old one-roomed shack which housed himself, his Martha, a stove, a double bed, coffins, his work-bench and all his household goods.

Jacob made good solid coffins. For men—village and working-class folk—he made them to his own height, and never got them wrong because he was taller and stronger than anyone, even in the gaol, though now seventy years old. For the gentry, though, and for women he made them to measure, using an iron ruler. He was not at all keen on orders for children's coffins, which he would knock up contemptuously without measuring. And when paid for them he would say that he 'quite frankly set no store by such trifles'.

His fiddle brought him a small income on top of his trade. A Jewish band usually played at weddings in the town, conducted by the tinker Moses Shakhkes who took more than half the proceeds. And since Jacob was a fine fiddler, especially with Russian folk tunes, Shakhkes sometimes asked him to join the band for fifty copecks a day plus tips. Straight away it made his face sweat and turn crimson, did sitting in the band. It was hot, there was a stifling smell of garlic, his fiddle squeaked. By his right ear wheezed the double-bass, by his left sobbed the flute played by a red-haired, emaciated Jew with a network of red and blue veins on his face. He was known as Rothschild after the noted millionaire. Now, this bloody little Jew even contrived to play the merriest tunes in lachrymose style. For no obvious reason Jacob became more and more obsessed by hatred and contempt for Jews, and for Rothschild in particular. He started picking on him and swearing at him. Once he made to beat him, whereat Rothschild took umbrage.

'I respect your talent, otherwise I am long ago throwing you out of window,' he said with an enraged glare.

Then he burst into tears. This was why Bronze wasn't often asked to play in the band, but only in some dire crisis, when one of the Jews was unavailable.

Jacob was always in a bad mood because of the appalling waste of money he had to endure. For instance, it was a sin to work on a Sunday or a Saint's Day, while Mondays were unlucky, so that made two hundred odd days a year when you had to sit around idle. And that was all so much money wasted. If someone in town held a wedding without music, or Shakhkes didn't ask Jacob to play, that meant still more losses. The police superintendent had been ill for two years now. He was wasting away, and Jacob had waited impatiently for him to die, but the man had left for treatment in the county town, and damned if he didn't peg out there. Now, that was at least ten roubles down the drain, as his would have been an expensive coffin complete with brocade lining. Thoughts of these losses hounded Jacob mostly at night. He would put his fiddle on the bed beside him, and when some such tomfoolery preyed on his mind he would touch the strings and the fiddle would twang in the darkness. That made him feel better.

On the sixth of May in the previous year Martha had suddenly fallen ill. The old woman breathed heavily, drank a lot of water, was unsteady on her feet, but she would still do the stove herself of a morning, and even fetch the water. By evening, though, she would already be in bed. Jacob fiddled away all day. But when it was quite dark he took the book in which he listed his losses daily and began, out of sheer boredom, to add up the annual total. It came to more than a thousand roubles. This so shocked him that he flung his abacus on the floor and stamped his feet. Then he picked up the abacus and clicked away again for a while, sighing deep, heartfelt sighs. His face was purple and wet with sweat. He was thinking that if he had put that lost thousand in the bank he would have received at least forty roubles' interest a year. So that was forty more roubles down the drain. However hard you tried to wriggle out of it, everything was just a dead loss in fact.

Then he suddenly heard Martha call out. 'Jacob, I'm dying.'

He looked round at his wife. Her face was flushed in the heat, her expression was exceptionally bright and joyous. Accustomed to her pale face and timid, unhappy expression, Bronze was put out. She really did look as if she was dying, glad to be saying a permanent good-bye to hut, coffins and Jacob at long last.

Gazing at the ceiling and moving her lips, she looked happy, as if she could actually see her saviour Death and was whispering to him.

It was dawn and the first rays were seen through the window. As he looked at the old woman, it vaguely occurred to Jacob that for some reason he had never shown her any affection all his life. Never had he been kind to her, never had he thought of buying her a kerchief or bringing her sweetmeats from a wedding. All he had done was yell at her, blame her for his 'losses', threaten to punch her. True, he never had hit her. Still he had frightened her, she had always been petrified with fear. Yes, he had said she couldn't have tea because they had enough other expenses without that, so she only drank hot water. And now he knew why she looked so strangely joyous, and a chill went through him.

When it was fully light he borrowed a neighbour's horse and drove Martha to hospital. There were not many patients, so he did not have long to wait. Only about three hours. To his great joy the patients were not received on this occasion by the doctor, who was ill himself, but by his assistant Maxim, an old fellow said by everyone in town to be better than the doctor, drunken brawler though he was.

'I humbly greet you,' said Jacob, taking his old woman into the consulting-room. 'You must excuse us troubling you with our trifling affairs, sir. Now, as you see, guv'nor, my old woman has fallen sick. She's my better half in a manner of speaking, if you'll pardon the expression——'

Frowning, stroking his side-whiskers, the white-eyebrowed assistant examined the old woman, who sat hunched on a stool, wizened, sharp-nosed, open-mouthed, her profile like a thirsty bird's.

'Hurrumph. Well, yes,' the assistant slowly pronounced, and sighed. 'It's influenza, fever perhaps. There's typhus in town. Ah well, the old woman's lived her life, praise the Lord. How old is she?'

'Seventy come next year, guv'nor.'

'Ah well, her life's over. Time she was on her way.'

'It's true enough, what you just said, sir.' Jacob smiled out of politeness. 'And we thanks you most kindly for being so nice about it, like. But, if you'll pardon the expression, every insect wants to live.'

'Not half it does.' The assistant's tone suggested that it depended on him whether the old woman lived or died. 'Now then, my good man, you put a cold compress on her head and give her one of these powders twice a day. And now cheerio to you. A very bong jour.'

From his face Jacob could tell that it was all up, and that no powders would help now. Obviously Martha was going to die soon, either today or tomorrow. He gave the assistant's elbow a push and winked.

'We ought to cup her, Mr. Maxim sir,' he said in a low voice.

'Haven't the time, my good man. Take your old woman and be off with you. So long and all that.'

'Begging your kindness, sir,' implored Jacob. 'As you know, mister, if it was her guts or her innards, like, what was sick, then it's powders and drops she should have. But this here is a chill, and the great thing with chills is to bleed 'em, sir.'

But the assistant had already called for his next patient, and a village woman with a little boy had come into the consulting-room.

'Buzz off you, beat it!' The assistant frowned at Jacob. 'Don't hang around.'

'Then at least put some leeches to her. I'll be grateful to you all my life, I will.'

The assistant lost his temper.

'Don't you bandy words with me,' he yelled. 'D-damned oaf!'

Jacob lost his temper too, and turned completely crimson. But he grabbed Martha's arm without a single word and took her out of the room. Only when they were getting into their cart did he cast a stern, mocking look at that hospital.

'They're a high and mighty lot round here,' he said. 'He'd have cupped a rich man, I'll be bound, but for a poor one he grudges even a single leech. Bastards!'

They arrived home, and Martha, after entering the house, stood for about ten minutes gripping the stove. If she was to lie down Jacob would talk about all the money he'd lost and blame her for lolling about and not wanting to work—or so she thought. And Jacob looked at her miserably, remembering that tomorrow was St. John's Day, and the day after that was St. Nicholas's Day, after which came Sunday and Unlucky Monday. That made four days when he couldn't work. But Martha was sure to die on one of those days, so he must make the coffin today. He took his iron ruler, went up to the old woman and measured her. Then she lay down and he crossed himself and started on the coffin.

When the work was finished, Jacob put on his spectacles and wrote in his book.

'Martha Ivanov: to one coffin, 2 roubles 40 copecks.'

He sighed. The old woman lay there all the time silently, her eyes shut, but when it grew dark that evening she suddenly called the old man.

'Remember fifty years ago, Jacob?' She looked at him happily. 'God gave us a little fair-haired baby, remember? We were always sitting by the river, you and I, singing songs under the willow tree.' She laughed bitterly. 'The little girl died.'

Jacob cudgelled his brains, but could recall neither baby nor willow. 'You're imagining things.'

The priest came and gave the last rites, whereupon Martha mumbled something or other. By morning she was gone.

Old women neighbours washed her, dressed her, laid her in her coffin. So as not to waste money on the sexton, Jacob read the lesson himself, and he got the grave for nothing because the cemetery care-taker was a crony of his. Four peasants bore the coffin to the cemetery out of respect, not for money. It was followed by old women, beggars and two village idiots while people in the street crossed themselves piously. Jacob was delighted that it was all so right and seemly, that it didn't cost much or hurt anyone's feelings. As he said good-bye to Martha for the last time he touched the coffin.

'Good workmanship, that,' he thought.

But on his way back from the cemetery he was overcome by a great sorrow. He felt vaguely unwell. His breath came hot and heavy, his legs were weak, he felt thirsty. Then various thoughts began to prey on his mind. He again remembered that never in his life had he been kind to Martha or shown her affection. The fifty-two years of their life together in one hut—it seemed such a long, long time. But somehow he had never given her a thought in all that time, he had no more noticed her than a cat or dog. But she had made up the stove every day, hadn't she? She had cooked, baked, fetched water, cut wood, shared his bed. And when he came back from weddings drunk she would reverently hang his fiddle on the wall and put him to bed—all this in silence, looking scared and troubled.

Rothschild approached Jacob, smiling and bowing.

'I been looking for you, mister,' he said. 'Mister Moses sends his respects, says he vonts you at once.'

Jacob wasn't interested. He wanted to cry.

'Leave me alone.' He walked on.

'Vot are you doing?' Rothschild ran ahead, much alarmed. 'Mister Moses'll be offended. You're to come at once, said he.'

Out of breath, blinking, with all those red freckles, the Jew dis-gusted Jacob. The green frock-coat with the black patches, his whole frail, puny figure—what a loathsome sight.

'Keep out of my way, Garlick-breath,' shouted Jacob. 'You leave me alone.'

The Jew, angered, also shouted. 'You are being quiet please or I am throwing you over fence.'

'Out of my sight, you!' bellowed Jacob, pouncing on him with clenched fists. 'Proper poison, them greasy bastards are.'

Scared to death, Rothschild crouched down, waving his hands above his head as if warding off blows, then jumped up and scampered off as fast as he could, hopping about and flapping his arms as he ran. You could see the quaking of his long, thin back. At this the street urchins gleefully rushed after him shouting 'Dirty Yid!' Barking dogs chased him too. Someone roared with laughter and then whistled, the dogs barked louder and in closer harmony.

Then a dog must have bitten Rothschild, for a shout of pain and despair was heard.

Jacob walked on the common, then started off along the edge of the town without knowing where he was going. 'There's old Jake, there he goes,' shouted the boys. Then he came to the river. Here sand-pipers swooped and twittered, ducks quacked. The sun's heat beat down and the water sparkled till it hurt the eyes. Walking along the tow-path, Jacob saw a buxom, red-cheeked woman emerge from a bathing hut.

'Damn performing seal,' he thought.

Not far from the bathing hut boys were fishing for crayfish, using meat as bait. They saw him.

'Hey, there's old Jake,' they shouted nastily.

Then came the broad old willow tree with its huge hollow and crows' nests.

Suddenly Jacob's memory threw up a vivid image of that fair-haired baby and the willow that Martha had spoken of. Yes, it was the same willow—so green, so quiet, so sad.

How old it had grown, poor thing.

He sat beneath it and began remembering. On the other bank, now a water meadow, had been a silver-birch forest, and over there on that bare hill on the horizon the dark blue bulk of an ancient pine wood. Barges had plied up and down the river. But now it was all flat and bare with the one little silver birch on the near side, slim and youthful as a young girl. There were only ducks and geese on the river, and it was hard to think that barges had ever passed here. Even the geese seemed fewer. Jacob shut his eyes and pictured vast flocks of white geese swooping towards each other.

How was it, he wondered, that he had never been by the river in the last forty or fifty years of his life. Or, if he had, it had made no impression on him. Why, this was a proper river, not just any old stream. You could fish it, you could sell the fish to shopkeepers, clerks and the man who kept the station bar, you could put the money in the bank. You could sail a boat from one riverside estate to another playing your fiddle, and all manner of folk would pay you for it. You could try starting up the barges again—better than making coffins, that was. Then you could breed geese, slaughter them and send them to Moscow in winter. 'The down alone would fetch ten roubles a year, I'll be bound.' But he had let all this go by, he had done nothing about it. Oh, what a waste, what a waste of money! If you put it all together —fishing, fiddling, barging, goose-slaughtering—what a lot of money you'd have made. But none of it had happened, not even in your dreams. Life had flowed past without profit, without enjoyment— gone aimlessly, leaving nothing to show for it. The future was empty. And if you looked back there was only all the awful waste of money that sent shivers down your spine. Why couldn't a man live without all that loss and waste? And why, he wondered, had they cut down the birch forest? And the pine wood? Why wasn't that common put to use? Why do people always do the wrong things? Why had Jacob spent all his life cursing, bellowing, threatening people with his fists, ill-treating his wife? And what, oh what, was the point of scaring and insulting that Jew just now? Why are people generally such a nuisance to each other? After all, it's all such a waste of money, a terrible waste it is. Without the hate and malice folks could get a lot of profit out of each other.

That evening and night he had visions of baby, willow, fish, dead geese, of Martha with her thirsty bird's profile, and of Rothschild's wretched, pale face, while various other gargoyle-like faces advanced on him from all sides muttering about all the waste of money. He tossed and turned, he got out of bed half a dozen times to play his fiddle.

Next morning he forced himself to get up and went to the hospital. That same Maxim told him to put a cold compress on his head and gave him powders, but his look and tone made Jacob realize that it was all up and that no powders would help now. Later, on his way home, he reckoned that death would be pure gain to him. He wouldn't have to eat, drink, pay taxes or offend folk. And since a man lies in his grave not just one but hundreds and thousands of years, the profit would be colossal. Man's life is debit, his death credit. The argument was correct, of course, but painfully disagreeable too. Why are things so oddly arranged? You only live once, so why don't you get anything out of it?

He didn't mind dying, but when he got home and saw his fiddle his heart missed a beat and he felt sorry. He couldn't take his fiddle with him to the grave, so it would be orphaned and go the way of the birches and the pines. Nothing in this world has ever come to anything, nothing ever will. Jacob went out of the hut and sat in the doorway clasping the fiddle to his breast. Thinking of his wasted, profitless life, he started playing he knew not what, but it came out poignantly moving and tears coursed down his cheeks. The harder he thought the sadder grew the fiddle's song.

The latch squeaked twice and Rothschild appeared at the garden gate. He crossed half the yard boldly, but when he saw Jacob he suddenly stopped, cringed and—through fear, no doubt—gesticulated as if trying to indicate the time with his fingers.

'Come along then,' said Jacob kindly, beckoning him. 'It's all right.'

Looking at him mistrustfully and fearfully, Rothschild began to approach but stopped a few feet away.

'Don't hit me, I beg you.' He squatted down. 'It's Mister Moses has sent me again. Never fear, says he, you go to Jacob again—tell him we can't do without him, he says. There's a vedding on Vednesday. Aye, that there is. Mister Shapovalov is marrying his daughter to a fine young man. A rich folks' vedding this, and no mistake!' The Jew screwed up one eye.

'Can't be done.' Jacob breathed heavily. 'I'm ill, son.'

He again struck up, his tears spurting on to the fiddle. Rothschild listened carefully, standing sideways on, arms crossed on his breast. His scared, baffled look gradually gave way to a sorrowful, suffering expression. He rolled his eyes as if in anguished delight.

'A-a-ah!' he said as the tears crawled down his cheeks and splashed on his green frock-coat.

After that Jacob lay down all day, sick at heart. When the priest heard his confession that evening and asked whether he remembered committing any particular sin he exerted his failing memory and once more recalled Martha's unhappy face and the desperate yell of the Jew bitten by a dog.

'Give my fiddle to Rothschild,' he said in a voice barely audible.

'Very well,' the priest answered.

Now everyone in town wants to know where Rothschild got such a fine fiddle. Did he buy it, did he steal it? Or did someone leave it with him as a pledge? He only plays the fiddle now, having given up the flute long ago. From his bow there flow those same poignant strains which used to come from his flute. But when he tries to repeat the tune Jacob had played in his doorway the outcome is so sad and mournful that his listeners weep and he ends by rolling his eyes up with an 'A-a-ah!'

So popular is this new tune in town that merchants and officials are always asking Rothschild over and making him play it a dozen times.

THE STUDENT

[Студент]

(1894)

THE STUDENT

The weather was fine and calm at first. Thrushes were singing, and in the near-by swamps some creature droned piteously as if blowing into an empty bottle. A woodcock flew over and a shot reverberated merrily in the spring air. But when darkness fell on the wood an unwelcome, piercing cold wind blew up from the east and everything grew silent. Ice needles formed on the puddles and the wood seemed inhospitable, abandoned, empty. It smelt of winter.

Ivan Velikopolsky, a student at a theological college and a sexton's son, was returning home along the path through the water meadow after a day's shooting. His fingers were numb, his face burned in the wind. This sudden onset of cold seemed to have destroyed the order and harmony of things, striking dread into Nature herself and causing the shades of night to thicken faster than was needful. Everything was so abandoned, so very gloomy, somehow. Only in the widows' allotments near the river did a light gleam. But far around, where the village stood about three miles away, everything drowned in the dense evening mist. The student remembered that, when he had left the house, his mother had been sitting barefoot on the lobby floor cleaning the samovar, while his father lay coughing on the stove. There was no cooking at home because today was Good Friday, and he felt famished. Cringing in the cold, he reflected that just such a wind had blown in the days of Ryurik, Ivan the Terrible and Peter the Great. Their times had known just such ferocious poverty and hunger. There had been the same thatched roofs with the holes in them, the same ignorance and misery, the same desolation on all sides, the same gloom and sense of oppression. All these horrors had been, still were, and would continue to be, and the passing of another thousand years would make things no better. He did not feel like going home.

The allotments were called widows' because they were kept by two widows, a mother and daughter. A bonfire was burning briskly—crackling, lighting up the plough-land far around. Widow Vasilisa, a tall, plump old woman in a man's fur jacket, stood gazing pensively at the fire. Her short, pock-marked, stupid-looking daughter Lukerya sat on the ground washing a cooking pot and some spoons. They had just had supper, obviously. Men's voices were heard, some local labourers watering their horses by the river.

'So winter's come back,' said the student, approaching the fire. 'Good evening.'

Vasilisa shuddered, but then saw who it was and smiled a welcome.

'Goodness me, I didn't recognize you,' she said. 'That means you'll be rich one day.'

They talked. Vasilisa, a woman of some experience—having been wet-nurse to gentlefolk and then a nanny—spoke delicately, always smiling a gentle, dignified smile. But her daughter Lukerya, a peasant whose husband had beaten her, only screwed up her eyes at the student, saying nothing and wearing an odd look as if she was deaf and dumb.

'On a cold night like this the Apostle Peter warmed himself by a fire.' The student held out his hands towards the flames. 'So it must have been cold then. What a frightening night that was, Granny, what a very sorrowful, what a very long night.'

He looked at the darkness around and abruptly jerked his head. 'Were you in church yesterday for the Twelve Gospel Readings?'

'Yes,' Vasilisa answered.

'At the Last Supper, you'll remember, Peter said to Jesus, "Lord, I am ready to go with Thee, both into prison, and to death." And the Lord said, "I say unto thee, Peter, before the cock crow twice, thou shalt deny me thrice." After supper Jesus prayed in mortal agony in the garden, while poor Peter was weary in spirit, and enfeebled. His eyes were heavy, he couldn't fight off sleep and he slept. Then, as you have heard, Judas that night kissed Jesus and betrayed Him to the torturers. They bound Him, they took Him to the high priest, they smote Him, while Peter—worn, tormented, anguished, perturbed, you understand, not having slept properly, foreseeing some fearful happening on this earth—went after them. He loved Jesus passionately, to distraction, and now, afar, he saw Him being buffeted.'

Lukerya put down the spoons and stared at the student.

'They went to the high priest,' he continued. 'They put Jesus to the question, and meanwhile the workmen had kindled a fire in the midst of the hall, as it was cold, and were warming themselves. Peter stood with them near the fire—also warming himself, as I am now. A certain maid beheld him, and said, "This man was also with Jesus." In other words she was saying that he too should be taken for questioning. All the workmen round the fire must have looked at him suspiciously and sternly because he was confused and said, "I know him not." A little later someone recognized him as one of Jesus' disciples and said,

"Thou also wast with him." But he denied it again. And for the third time someone addressed him. "Did I not see thee in the garden with Him this day?" He denied Him for the third time. And after that the cock straightway crowed, and Peter, looking at Jesus from afar, remembered the words which He had said to him at supper. He remembered, his eyes were opened, and he went out of the hall and shed bitter tears. The Gospel says, "And he went out, and wept bitterly." I can imagine it was a very quiet, very dark garden and his hollow sobs could hardly be heard in the silence.'

The student sighed, plunged deep in thought. Still smiling, Vasilisa suddenly sobbed and tears, large and profuse, flowed down her cheeks. She shielded her face from the fire with her sleeve as if ashamed of the tears, while Lukerya, staring at the student, blushed and her expression became distressed and tense as if she was holding back a terrible pain.

The workmen returned from the river. One of them, on horseback, was already near and the light from the fire quivered on him. The student said good night to the widows and moved on. Again darkness came upon him, and his hands began to freeze. A cruel wind blew, it was real winter weather again, and it did not seem as if Easter Sunday could be only the day after tomorrow.

The student thought of Vasilisa. Her weeping meant that all that had happened to Peter on that terrible night had a particular meaning for her.

He looked back. The lonely fire quietly flickered in the darkness, no one could be seen near it. Again the student reflected that, if Vasilisa had wept and her daughter had been moved, then obviously what he had just told them about happenings nineteen centuries ago—it had a meaning for the present, for both women, and also probably for this God-forsaken village, for himself, for all people. It had not been his gift for poignant narrative that had made the old woman weep. It was because Peter was near to her, because she was bound up heart and soul with his innermost feelings.

Joy suddenly stirred within him. He even stopped for a moment to catch his breath.

'The past', thought he, 'is linked to the present by an unbroken chain of happenings, each flowing from the other.'

He felt as if he had just seen both ends of that chain. When he touched one end the other vibrated.

Crossing the river by ferry, and then climbing the hill, he looked at his home village and at the narrow strip of cold crimson sunset shining in the west. And he brooded on truth and beauty—how they had guided human life there in the garden and the high priest's palace, how they had continued without a break till the present day, always as the most important element in man's life and in earthly life in general. A sensation of youth, health, strength—he was only twenty-two years old—together with an anticipation, ineffably sweet, of happiness, strange, mysterious happiness, gradually came over him. And life seemed enchanting, miraculous, imbued with exalted significance.

THE RUSSIAN MASTER

[*Учитель словесности*]

(1894)

THE RUSSIAN MASTER

I

W ITH a clatter of hooves on the wooden floor three fine, expensive horses were brought out of the stable: Count Nulin, the black, and then the grey, Giant, with his sister Mayka. While saddling Giant old Shelestov spoke to his daughter Masha.

'Come on, Marie Godefroi, up you get and off with you!'

Masha Shelestov was the youngest in the family. She was eighteen, but they still thought of her as a child, calling her by the pet names Manya and Manyusya. And when the circus had come to town she had enjoyed it so much that they had nicknamed her Marie Godefroi after the famous equestrienne.

'Off we go!' she shouted, mounting Giant.

Her sister Varya got on Mayka, Nikitin on Count Nulin, the officers mounted their own horses, and the long, picturesque cavalcade ambled out of the yard in single file with a gleam of officers' white tunics and ladies' black riding habits.

As they mounted and rode into the street Nikitin noticed that Masha had eyes for him alone, looking anxiously at him and Count Nulin.

'Hold him tight, Mr. Nikitin. Don't let him shy, he's only playing up.'

Whether by accident or because her Giant was a great friend of his Count Nulin, she rode beside Nikitin all the time, as she had the day before and the day before that, while he looked at her small, graceful form as she sat the proud grey, at her fine profile and the wholly unbecoming chimney-pot hat which seemed to age her. Enchanted, enthralled, enraptured, he looked and listened without taking much in.

'I swear I'll pluck up my courage,' he told himself. 'I'll speak to her this very day, by God I will.'

It was after six in the evening, the hour when white acacias and lilacs smell so strongly that the air and the very trees seem to congeal in their own perfume. The band played in the town park. Horses' hooves rang on the road. Laughter, voices, banging gates were heard on all sides. Soldiers they met saluted the officers, schoolboys bowed to Nikitin. Strollers, and those hurrying to the park for the music, all obviously enjoyed looking at the riders. How warm it was and how soft the clouds looked, scattered at random about the sky, how gently soothing were the shadows of the poplars and acacias—shadows reaching right across the wide street to grasp the houses on the other side as high as their first floors and balconies.

They rode on out of town, trotting down the highway. Here was no more scent of acacia and lilac, nor band music—just the smell of fields and the bright green of young rye and wheat. Gophers squeaked, rooks cawed. Wherever one looked all was green apart from a few black melon-plots here and there, and a white streak of late apple-blossom in the graveyard far to their left.

They passed the slaughterhouses and brewery, they overtook a military band hurrying to the country park.

'Polyansky has a fine horse, I admit,' Masha told Nikitin with a glance at the officer riding beside Varya. 'But it does have its blemishes. The white patch on its left leg is wrong, and you'll notice it jibs. There's no way of training it now, so it'll go on jibbing till its dying day.'

Like her father, Masha was keen on horses. To see anyone else with a fine horse was agony to her, and she liked faulting other people's mounts. Nikitin knew nothing about horses, though. Reining or curbing, trotting or galloping—it was all one to him. He just felt he looked out of place, which was why he thought the officers must attract Masha more than he, being so much at home in the saddle. And so he was jealous of them.

As they rode past the country park someone suggested calling in for a glass of soda water. They did. The only trees in this park were oaks just coming into leaf, and through the young foliage the whole park could be seen—bandstand, tables, swings and crows' nests like huge fur caps. Dismounting near a table, the riders and their ladies ordered soda water. Friends strolling in the park came up, including an army medical officer in riding boots and the bandmaster awaiting his bandsmen. The doctor must have taken Nikitin for a student because he asked whether he had come over for the summer holidays.

'No, I live here,' Nikitin answered. 'I teach at the high school.'

'Really?' The doctor was surprised. 'So young and teaching already?'

'Young indeed! Good grief, I'm twenty-six!'

'You do have a beard and moustache, yet you don't seem more than twenty-two or three. You certainly do look young.'

'Oh, not again—what bloody cheek!' thought Nikitin. 'The fellow takes me for a whipper-snapper.'

It riled him when people said how young he looked, especially in women's or schoolboys' company. Ever since coming to town and taking this job he had found himself disliking his own youthful appearance. The boys were not afraid of him, old men called him 'young chap', and women would rather dance with him than listen to his long speeches. He would have given a lot to be ten years older.

From the park they rode on to the Shelestovs' farm, stopped at the gate and called for the bailiff's wife Praskovya to bring them fresh milk. But no one drank it—they just looked at each other, laughed and started cantering back. As they rode back the band was playing in the country park, the sun had sunk behind the graveyard, and half the sky was sunset-crimson.

Again Masha rode with Nikitin. He wanted to tell her he was madly in love with her—but said nothing, afraid of the officers and Varya hearing. Masha was silent too. Sensing why this was and why she rode beside him, he felt so happy that everything—earth, sky, town lights, the brewery's black silhouette—blended before his eyes into something delightfully soothing while Count Nulin seemed to float on air, wanting to climb the crimson sky.

They arrived home. A samovar hissed on the garden table at one edge of which old Shelestov sat with some friends, officers of the local assizes. As usual he was criticizing someone.

'It's the act of a bounder, an utter bounder—yes, of a bounder, sir.'

Since falling in love with Masha, Nikitin had found everything about the Shelestovs to his liking—their house, its garden, afternoon tea, wicker chairs, their old nanny and even the old man's favourite word, 'bounder'. He only disliked the horde of cats and dogs and the turtle-doves moaning lugubriously in their big cage on the terrace. There were so many dogs about house and yard that he had learnt to distinguish only two since meeting the family—Bluebottle and Fishface.

Bluebottle was a small, mangy, shaggy-muzzled, spiteful, spoilt little tyke. She hated Nikitin, and at sight of him would put her head on one side, bare her teeth and embark on a long, liquid, nasal-guttural snarl. Then she would sit under his chair, and give a great piercing peal of yelps when he tried to chase her away. 'Don't be afraid,' his hosts would say. 'She's a good little dog.'

Fishface was a huge, black, long-legged hound with a tail like a ramrod. During tea and dinner it usually stalked silently beneath the

table, banging that tail on boots and table-legs. This was a good-
natured, stupid hound, but Nikitin couldn't stand it because it would
put its muzzle on your lap at mealtimes and slobber on your trousers.
He had often tried hitting its large head with his knife handle, had
flicked its nose, cursed it, complained. But nothing saved his trousers
from spots.

Tea, jam, rusks and butter tasted good after the ride. Everyone
drank his first glass with silent relish, but by the second they were
already arguing. It was always Varya who began these mealtime
disputes. She was twenty-three. A good-looking girl, prettier than
Masha, she was considered the cleverest and most cultured person in
the household and she wore the responsible, severe air befitting an
older daughter who has taken the place of her dead mother. As mistress
of the house she felt entitled to wear a smock when she had guests, she
called the officers by their surnames, and she treated Masha as a child,
addressing her in schoolmistressy style. She called herself an old maid—
she was quite sure she was going to get married, in other words.

Every conversation, even on the weather, she needs must convert
into an argument. She was a great one for quibbling, detecting
inconsistencies, splitting hairs. Start talking to her and she would be
glaring into your face, suddenly interrupting with a 'now, just you look
here, Petrov, you were saying the exact opposite only the day before
yesterday'. Or she would smile sardonically with an 'ah, so now we're
advocating the principles of the secret police, are we? Hearty congratulations!' If you made a joke or pun she'd pitch in at once with her
'feeble' or 'dead as a door nail'. Or, should an officer jest, she would
give a scornful grimace and call it 'barrack-room wit', rolling her Rs
so impressively that Bluebottle would growl back from under a chair.

Today's teatime quarrel began with Nikitin talking about school
examinations and Varya interrupting.

'Now, you look here, Nikitin. You say the boys have a hard time.
And whose fault is that, pray? For instance you set the eighth form an
essay on Pushkin as a psychologist. Now, in the first place you
shouldn't set such difficult subjects. And secondly how can you call
Pushkin a psychologist? Shchedrin, now, or Dostoyevsky, say—that's
a different story. But Pushkin is a great poet and nothing more.'

'Shchedrin is one thing, Pushkin is something else,' Nikitin sulkily
rejoined.

'I know Shchedrin isn't on your syllabus, but that's beside the point.
Just you explain what makes Pushkin a psychologist.'

'But it's plain as a pikestaff. Very well, then, I'll give examples.'

He recited some passages of *Eugene Onegin* and then of *Boris Godunov*.

'I see no psychology there,' sighed Varya. 'A psychologist delves into the crannies of the human soul. Those are fine verses, nothing more.'

Nikitin was offended. 'I know your sort of psychology. You want somebody to saw my finger with a blunt saw while I yell my head off, that's your idea of psychology.'

'Feeble! And you still haven't proved that Pushkin's a psychologist.'

When Nikitin found himself arguing against views which he thought hackneyed, conventional and the like, he usually jumped out of his seat, clutched his head in both hands, and ran up and down the room groaning—which is what he did now. He jumped up, he clutched his head, he walked round the table groaning, and then sat away from it.

The officers took his part. Captain Polyansky assured Varya that Pushkin really was a psychologist, citing two lines of Lermontov to prove it, and Lieutenant Gernet said that Pushkin wouldn't have had a statue erected to him in Moscow had he not been a psychologist.

'It's the act of a bounder,' was heard from the other end of the table. 'I said as much to the Governor. "It's the act of a bounder, sir," I told him.'

'I shan't argue any more!' shouted Nikitin. 'This could go on till doomsday, I've had enough. Oh, clear off, you bloody dog!' he shouted at Fishface who had put his head and paw on his lap.

A guttural snarl came from under his chair.

'Admit you're in the wrong!' Varya shouted. 'Own up!'

But some young ladies came in, and the dispute died a natural death. They all went into the drawing-room, where Varya sat at the grand piano and played dances. They danced a waltz, a polka and a quadrille with a grand chain led through the whole house by Captain Polyansky, after which they waltzed again.

Watching the youngsters in the drawing-room, the older folk sat out the dances and smoked, among them the municipal bank manager Shebaldin, renowned for his love of literature and dramatic art. He had founded the local music and drama group, taking part in performances himself, but for some reason only playing comic footmen or intoning Alexis Tolstoy's poem 'The Sinful Woman'. He had been nicknamed 'the Mummy' in town because he was tall, emaciated and sinewy with a fixed, solemn expression and dull, glazed eyes. So sincere was his love of the theatre that he even shaved his moustache and beard, which made him look still more like a mummy.

After the grand chain he shuffled up sideways to Nikitin.

'I had the pleasure of being present at the argument during tea,' he remarked, coughing. 'And I fully share your opinion. We're fellow-spirits, you and I, and I'd much welcome a chat. Now, have you read Lessing's *Hamburgische Dramaturgie*?'

'No.'

Shebaldin looked horrified, waved his hands as if he had burnt his fingers, and backed away from Nikitin without a word. The man's figure, his question, his surprise—all seemed absurd to Nikitin, who yet wondered whether it wasn't 'really rather embarrassing. Here I am teaching literature, and I still haven't read Lessing. I shall have to.'

Before supper everyone, young and old, sat down to play forfeits. They took two packs of cards. One was dealt round, the other laid on the table face downwards.

'Whoever holds this card,' said old Shelestov solemnly, lifting the top card of the second pack, 'his forfeit is to go straight to the nursery and kiss Nanny.'

The good fortune of kissing Nanny devolved upon Shebaldin. They all flocked round him, they took him to the nursery and they made him kiss the nanny in an uproar of laughing, clapping and shouting.

'Less passion, I insist!' shouted Shelestov, tears rolling down his cheeks.

Nikitin's forfeit was to take confession. He sat on a chair in the middle of the drawing-room, a shawl was brought and put over his head. Varya came to confess first.

'I know your sins, madam.' Nikitin gazed at her stern profile in the gloom. 'How, pray, do you account for going out with Polyansky every day? Oho, there's more to this than meets the eye!'

'Feeble,' said Varya. And went.

Then Nikitin saw big, lustrous, unwavering eyes under his shawl, a lovely profile emerged from the gloom, and he caught a familiar, precious fragrance redolent of Masha's room.

'Marie Godefroi, what are your sins?' he said, and did not know his own voice—so tender, so soft was it.

Masha screwed up her eyes, put out the tip of her tongue, laughed and went away. A minute later she was standing in the middle of the room clapping her hands.

'Supper, supper, supper,' she shouted, and all trooped into the dining-room.

At supper Varya had another argument, with her father this time. Polyansky stolidly ate his food, drank his claret, and told Nikitin about a winter's night which he had once spent knee-deep in a bog when on active service. The enemy had been so near that they were forbidden to speak or smoke, it had been cold and dark, there had been a piercing wind. Nikitin listened, watching Masha out of the corner of his eye while she gazed at him without wavering or blinking, as if deep in thought and oblivious of her surroundings. This pleased and tormented him.

'Why does she look at me like that?' he agonizingly wondered. 'It's embarrassing, someone may notice. Oh, how young, how innocent she is.'

The party broke up at midnight. When Nikitin had gone through the gate a first-floor window banged open, Masha showed herself, and called his name.

'What is it?'

'It's just that—.' Masha was obviously wondering what to say. 'Er, Polyansky's promised to bring his camera in a day or two and photograph us all. We must have a get-together.'

'Fine.'

Masha disappeared, the window slammed, and someone in the house at once started playing the piano.

'Oh, what a house,' thought Nikitin, crossing the street. 'A house where the only moaning comes from the turtle-doves, and that simply because they have no other way to express their joy.'

Fun was not confined to the Shelestovs', though, for Nikitin had not taken two hundred steps before piano music was heard from another house. He walked on a bit and saw a peasant playing a balalaika near a gate. The band in the park struck up a pot-pourri of Russian folk-songs.

Nikitin lived a quarter of a mile from the Shelestovs in an eight-roomed flat, rented at three hundred roubles a year, which he shared with his colleague Hippolytus, the geography and history master. This Hippolytus—a snub-nosed, reddish-bearded, middle-aged man with a rather coarse but good-natured expression more like a workman's than an intellectual's—was sitting at his desk correcting pupils' maps when Nikitin returned. According to Hippolytus, drawing your maps was the most crucial and essential aspect of geography, while with history it was knowing your dates—he would sit up night after night with his blue pencil correcting the maps of boys and girls he taught, or compiling lists of dates.

'Wonderful weather today,' said Nikitin, going into Hippolytus's room. 'I don't know how you can stay indoors.'

No great talker, Hippolytus would either say nothing at all or utter the merest platitudes. He now vouchsafed the following reply.

'It is indeed excellent weather. It is May now, and it will soon be full summer. Summer differs from winter. Stoves must be lit in winter, whereas in summer you can keep warm without them. Open your windows on a summer night and you'll still be warm, whereas in winter you are cold even with the double frames.'

After sitting near the desk for less than a minute, Nikitin felt bored and stood up, yawning.

'Good night,' he said. 'I wanted to tell you something romantic affecting myself, but you have geography on the brain. One talks to you of love, and you ask for the date of the Battle of Kalka. To hell with your battles and your Siberian capes.'

'But why are you so cross?'

'I'm just fed up.'

Annoyed at not having proposed to Masha and having no one to tell about his love, he went and lay on his study sofa. The room was dark and quiet. Lying and gazing into the darkness, Nikitin imagined that some errand would take him to St. Petersburg in a couple of years, and that the weeping Masha would see him off at the station. In St. Petersburg he would receive a long letter from her in which she would entreat him to hurry back home. He would write her a reply beginning 'Darling little rat——'

'Just so, "Darling little rat",' he laughed.

He was lying uncomfortably, so he put his hands behind his head and canted his left leg on to the sofa back. That was better. Meanwhile dawn was breaking beyond the window, sleepy cocks crowed outside. Nikitin went on thinking—how he would come back from St. Petersburg, how Masha would meet him at the station and throw her arms round his neck shrieking with joy. Better still, he would play a trick. He would come back secretly late at night, the cook would let him in, and he would tip-toe to the bedroom, undress noiselessly and dive into bed. She would wake up—ah, bliss!

It was quite light now, but instead of his study and its window he saw Masha, who sat talking on the steps of the brewery they had ridden past that afternoon. She took Nikitin's arm and they went to the country park where he saw those oaks and crows' nests like fur caps. One nest swayed and out peeped Shebaldin with a vociferous 'Who hasn't read his Lessing?'

Shuddering all over, Nikitin opened his eyes. There by the sofa stood Hippolytus, head thrown back as he tied his cravat.

'Get up, it's time for school,' he said. 'Now, you shouldn't sleep in your clothes, it spoils them. One sleeps in one's bed after first removing one's attire.'

And he embarked on his usual long, emphatic string of platitudes.

Nikitin's first period was Russian grammar with the second form. Going into the classroom at nine o'clock precisely, he saw two capital letters chalked on the blackboard: M. S. They stood for Masha Shelestov no doubt.

'So the little devils have found out,' thought Nikitin. 'How do they always know everything?'

His second period was Russian literature with the fifth form. Here too he saw an M. S. on the board, and as he left the classroom at the end of the lesson a cry rang out behind him like a catcall from a theatre gallery. 'Good old Masha!'

He felt muzzy after sleeping in his clothes, his body drooped from fatigue. His pupils, daily looking forward to the break before their examinations, were idle and depressed, and they misbehaved out of boredom. Also depressed, Nikitin ignored their little tricks and kept going to the window. He saw the street bathed in sunlight, the limpid blue sky above the houses, the birds—while far, far away beyond green gardens and houses stretched an infinitely remote expanse with dark blue coppices and a puff of steam from a moving train.

Two white-tunicked officers flicked their whips as they walked down the street in the shade of the acacias. A party of grey-bearded Jews in peaked caps drove past in a brake, the governess was taking the headmistress's grand-daughter for a walk, Fishface dashed past with two mongrels. And there went Varya in her plain grey dress and red stockings, carrying a *European Herald*—she must have been to the municipal library.

It was a long time before school would end at three o'clock. Nor could Nikitin go home or visit the Shelestovs after school, for he had to give a lesson at Wolf's. This Wolf was a rich Jewish protestant convert who did not send his children to school, but got schoolmasters to coach them privately at five roubles a lesson.

Nikitin was bored, bored, bored.

At three o'clock he went to Wolf's and spent what seemed like all eternity there. He left at five o'clock, and was due back at school by seven for a teachers' meeting to fix the oral examination timetable for the fourth and sixth forms.

That night, on his way from school to the Shelestovs', he felt his heart pounding and his face burning. A week ago, a month ago—every time he had been about to propose he had had an entire harangue ready complete with introduction and peroration, but now he didn't have one word prepared, his head was awhirl. All he knew was that he was going to declare himself this evening for sure and that there was no more putting it off.

He would ask her into the garden, he reflected. 'I'll stroll about a bit and I'll propose.'

There was no one in the hall. He went into the drawing-room and parlour, but there was no one there either. He heard Varya arguing with someone upstairs and the dressmaker clicking her scissors in the nursery.

There was a lobby with three names: the 'small', the 'corridor', the 'dark' room. It contained a big old cupboard full of medicines, gunpowder and hunting gear, and a narrow wooden staircase, with cats always asleep on it, leading to the first floor. The lobby had two doors—one to the nursery, one to the drawing-room. When Nikitin went in on his way upstairs the nursery door suddenly opened and slammed so hard that staircase and cupboard rattled. Out rushed Masha in a dark dress, carrying a piece of blue material, and darted to the stairs without seeing him.

'Hey,' Nikitin said to stop her. 'Hallo, Godefroi. May I, er——'

He gasped, he didn't know what to say, clutching her hand with one hand and the blue material with the other. Half frightened, half surprised, she gazed at him wide-eyed.

'Look here—,' Nikitin went on, afraid she would go away. 'I have something to say, only it's, er, awkward here. I can't do it, it's beyond me, Godefroi, it's more than I can manage and that's all there, er, is to it.'

The blue material slipped to the floor and Nikitin took Masha's other hand. She turned pale, moved her lips and backed away from him, ending up in the corner between wall and cupboard.

'I swear, I assure you,' he said softly. 'I take my oath, Masha, er——'

She threw back her head and he kissed her lips, holding her cheek with his fingers to make the kiss last longer. Then he somehow found himself in the corner between cupboard and wall, while she had twined her arms round his neck and was pressing her head against his chin.

Then they both ran into the garden.

The Shelestovs had a large, ten-acre garden with a score of old maples and limes. There was a fir, a sweet chestnut, a silvery olive, and all the rest were fruit-trees—cherries, apples, pears. There were masses of flowers too.

Nikitin and Masha ran down the paths, now silent, now laughing, now asking disconnected questions which went unanswered, while a half moon shone over the garden. On the ground—dark grass, dimly lit by the moon's crescent—drowsy tulips and irises stretched up as if they too longed to hear words of love.

When Nikitin and Masha came back to the house the officers and young ladies were already assembled, dancing a mazurka. Again Polyansky led a grand chain through the house, again they played forfeits after dancing. But when the guests went into the dining-room before supper, Masha was left alone with Nikitin.

She pressed close to him. 'You must talk to papa and Varya, I'm too embarrassed.'

After supper he spoke to the old man, who heard him out. 'I'm most grateful,' said he, after some thought, 'for the honour which you are conferring on myself and my daughter, but permit me to speak as a friend—not as a father, but as between gentlemen. Now, why oh why the great rush to marry so early? Only farm labourers marry so young, but then we all know they're a lot of bounders, sir. But you—what's got into you? A ball and chain at your tender age—where's the fun in that?'

Nikitin took umbrage. 'I'm *not* young, I'm nearly twenty-seven.'

'Father, the farrier's here,' shouted Varya from another room. And that ended the conversation.

Varya, Masha and Polyansky saw Nikitin home.

'Why does your mysterious Mr. Hippolytus never emerge?' Varya asked when they reached his gate. 'He might come and see us.'

The mysterious Mr. Hippolytus was sitting on his bed taking off his trousers when Nikitin went into his room.

'Don't go to bed yet, old man,' Nikitin gasped. 'Just give me a moment, please.'

Hippolytus quickly put his trousers on again and asked anxiously what the matter was.

'I'm getting married.'

Nikitin sat down beside his colleague with the amazed look of one who has succeeded in surprising himself. 'Just fancy, I'm getting married. To Masha Shelestov, I proposed this evening.'

'Well, she seems a nice girl. She is very young, though.'

'Yes, young she is,' sighed Nikitin with a worried shrug. 'Very young indeed.'

'She was a pupil of mine once. I remember her, she wasn't bad at geography but she was no good at history. And she was inattentive in class.'

Nikitin suddenly felt rather sorry for his colleague and wanted to say something kind and consoling. 'Why don't *you* get married, old man?' he asked. 'My dear Hippolytus, why don't you marry Varya, say? She's a splendid girl, quite first-rate. Oh, she is very argumentative, I know, but she's so very, very good-hearted. She was asking about you just now. So you marry her, old chap, how about it?'

That Varya wouldn't have this boring, snub-nosed character Nikitin knew perfectly well, yet he still tried to persuade him to marry her. Why?

Hippolytus pondered. 'Marriage is a serious step,' he said. 'One must look at all the angles, weigh every issue, one mustn't be too casual. Caution never comes amiss—especially in wedlock when a man, ceasing to be a bachelor, begins a new life.'

He began uttering his platitudes, but Nikitin stopped listening to him, said goodnight and went to his room. Hastily undressing, he quickly lay down in a great hurry to brood on his happiness, his Masha, his future. Then he smiled, suddenly remembering that he still hadn't read Lessing.

'I must read him,' he thought. 'But then again, why should I? To hell with him.'

Exhausted by bliss, he fell asleep at once and smiled through till morning. He dreamt of the clatter of horses' hooves on the wooden floor. He dreamt of black Count Nulin and the grey, Giant, with his sister Mayka, being brought out of the stable.

II

It was very crowded and noisy in church. At one point someone in the congregation actually shouted aloud, and the priest who was marrying me and Masha peered over his spectacles.

'Don't wander about the church,' he said sternly. 'Just keep still and worship. This is God's house, remember.'

I had two of my colleagues in attendance, while Masha was attended by Captain Polyansky and Lieutenant Gernet. The bishop's choir sang superbly. The sputtering candles, the glitter, the fine clothes, the officers, the mass of joyful, contented faces, Masha's special ethereal look, the entire ambience, the words of the nuptial prayers—they moved me to tears, they filled me with exultation. How my life has blossomed out, I thought. How romantically, how poetically it has been shaping of late. Two years ago I was just a student living in cheap lodgings in Moscow's Neglinny Drive, with no money, no relatives and—I then fancied—no future. But now I teach at the high school in one of the best county towns, I'm secure, I'm loved, I'm spoilt. For me this congregation is assembled, thought I. For me three chandeliers burn, for me the archdeacon booms, for me the choir puts forth its efforts. For me too this young creature, soon to be called my wife, is so youthful, so elegant, so happy. I remembered our first meetings, our country rides, my proposal and the weather which seemed to have gone out of its way to be wonderfully fine all summer. That happiness which, in my old Neglinny Drive days, only seemed possible in novels and stories—I was actually experiencing it now, apparently, I was taking it in my hands.

After the ceremony everyone crowded round Masha and me, they expressed their sincere pleasure, they congratulated us, they wished us happiness. A retired major-general in his late sixties congratulated Masha alone.

'I trust, my dear, that now you're married you'll still be the same dear little rosebud,' he told her in a squeaky, senile voice audible throughout the church.

The officers, the headmaster, the teachers—all gave the socially incumbent grin, and I could feel that ingratiating, artificial smile on my face too. Dear old Mr. Hippolytus—history master, geography master, mouther of platitudes—shook my hand firmly and spoke with feeling. 'Hitherto you've been a bachelor and have lived on your own. But now you're married and single no longer.'

From church we went to the two-storeyed house with unrendered walls which comes to me with the dowry. Besides the house Masha is bringing about twenty thousand roubles in cash and a place called Meliton's Heath complete with a shack where I'm told there are lots of hens and ducks running wild because no one looks after them.

When I got home from church I stretched and lounged on the ottoman in my new study, smoking. I felt more snug, more comfortable, more cosy than ever in my life. Meanwhile wedding guests cheered, a wretched band played flourishes and sundry trash in the hall. Masha's sister Varya ran into the study carrying a wineglass, her face oddly strained as if her mouth was full of water. Apparently she had meant to run on, but she suddenly burst out laughing and sobbing, while the glass rolled, ringing, across the floor. We took her by the arms and led her off.

'No one understands,' she muttered later as she lay on the old nurse's bed at the back of the house. 'No one, no one—God, no one understands.'

Everyone understood perfectly well, though, that she was four years older than her sister Masha, that she still wasn't married, and that she wasn't crying through envy but because she was sadly aware that her time was passing—or had perhaps already passed. By the time the quadrille began she was back in the drawing-room with a tearful, heavily powdered face, and I saw her spooning up a dish of ice-cream held for her by Captain Polyansky.

It is now past five in the morning. I have taken up my diary to describe my complete, my manifold happiness, intending to write half a dozen pages and read them to Masha later in the day, but oddly enough my mind is just a vague, dreamy jumble, and all I remember distinctly is this business of Varya. 'Poor Varya,' I want to write. Yes, I could go on sitting here and writing 'poor Varya'. And now the trees have started rustling, which means rain. Crows are cawing and my dear Masha, who has just fallen asleep, has a rather sad expression.

Nikitin did not touch his diary for a long time afterwards. He had various entrance and other school examinations at the beginning of August, and after the fifteenth of the month term started again. He usually left for school before nine, and an hour later was already missing Masha and his new home, and kept looking at his watch. In the lower forms he would get one of the boys to dictate and would sit in the window day-dreaming, eyes shut, while his pupils wrote. Picturing the future, recalling the past—he found everything equally splendid, like a fairy-tale. In the senior forms they read Gogol or Pushkin's prose aloud, which made him drowsy, conjuring up in his imagination people, trees, fields, horses.

'Superb,' he would sigh, as if bewitched by the author.

At the lunch break Masha would send him his meal in a snow-white napkin, and he would eat it slowly, with pauses to prolong his enjoyment, while Hippolytus—who usually lunched on a single roll—looked at him with respectful envy, uttering some such platitude as that 'man cannot live without food'.

From school Nikitin would go to his coaching, and when he at last reached home about half-past five he would feel as happy and excited as if he had been away a whole year. He would run panting upstairs, find Masha, take her in his arms, kiss her, swear he loved her and couldn't live without her, claiming to have missed her terribly, asking in panic whether she was well and why she looked so solemn. Then they would dine together. After dinner he would lie smoking on his study ottoman while she sat beside him, talking in a low voice.

His happiest days were Sundays and holidays, when he stayed at home from morning till evening. On these days he shared an unsophisticated but most agreeable life reminiscent of pastoral idylls. Constantly watching the sensible, practical Masha as she wove her nest, he too wanted to show that he was some use about the house, and would do something pointless like pushing the chaise out of the shed and inspecting it from all sides. Masha had set up a regular dairy and kept three cows. Her cellar and larder contained many jugs of milk and pots of sour cream, all of which she kept for butter. Nikitin would sometimes ask her for a glass of milk as a joke, and she would take fright at this breach of discipline, while he laughed and put his arms round her.

'There, there, it was only a joke, my treasure—just a little joke.'

Or he would laugh at how strict she was when she found an old stone-hard piece of salami, say, or cheese in the cupboard and solemnly said that 'they can eat that out in the kitchen'.

He would tell her that such a scrap was fit only for a mousetrap, while she hotly contended that men know nothing of housekeeping, and that you could send food out to those servants by the hundredweight and you still wouldn't get any reaction from them. He would agree and embrace her ecstatically. When she said something sensible he found it unique and astounding, and whatever contradicted his own sentiments was deliciously unsophisticated.

Sometimes, in philosophical vein, he would discourse on an abstract theme, while she listened and looked inquiringly into his face. 'I'm infinitely happy with you, darling,' he would say, playing with her fingers, or plaiting and unplaiting her hair. 'But I don't regard my happiness as a windfall or manna from heaven. My felicity is a wholly natural, consistent and impeccably logical phenomenon. I believe that man makes his own happiness, so I'm now enjoying something I myself created. Yes, I can say so without false modesty: I created this bliss, and I have every right to it. You know my past. Having no mother and father, being poor, an unhappy childhood, a miserable adolescence—all that was a struggle, a road to happiness built by myself.'

In October the school suffered a grievous loss when Hippolytus succumbed to erysipelas of the head and died. He was unconscious and delirious for two days before dying, but even when rambling he rambled only platitudes.

'The Volga flows into the Caspian Sea, horses eat oats and hay——'

There was no school on the day of his funeral. Colleagues and pupils carried coffin-lid and coffin, and the school choir sang the anthem 'Holy, holy, holy' all the way to the cemetery. The procession included three priests, two deacons, all the boys' high school and the bishop's choir in their best cassocks. Seeing so solemn a cortège, passers-by crossed themselves and prayed to God to 'grant us all such a death'.

Nikitin went home from the cemetery very moved, and took his diary from the desk.

> Today Mr. Hippolytus Ryzhitsky was consigned to his grave (he wrote). Rest in peace, thou humble toiler. Masha, Varya and the other ladies at the funeral all wept sincerely, perhaps because they knew that no woman ever loved so unattractive, so downtrodden a man. I wanted to say a word of appreciation at my colleague's grave, but was warned that the Head might take exception since he disliked the deceased. I think this has been the first day since the wedding that I've felt depressed.

There was no other event of note during the school year.

Winter was a half-hearted affair—sleety, without hard frosts. All Twelfth Night, for instance, the wind howled piteously as in autumn, the roofs dripped, and during the Consecration of the Waters in the morning the police stopped people walking on the frozen river because they said the ice had swollen up and looked dark. Despite the dismal weather Nikitin was just as happy as in summer, though, and had even acquired a new hobby—he had learnt to play bridge. There only seemed to be one fly in the ointment, only one thing that got on his nerves and riled him—the cats and dogs which he had acquired as part of the dowry. The house smelt like a zoo, especially in the mornings, and there was no getting rid of the stench. The cats often fought the dogs. That spiteful Bluebottle was fed a dozen times a day, but still wouldn't accept Nikitin, still treated him to her liquid, nasal-guttural growls.

One midnight in Lent Nikitin was on his way home from the club after cards. It was raining, dark and muddy. Things felt unsavoury, somehow. Was it the twelve roubles he had lost at the club? Or was it that when they were settling up one of the players had remarked that Nikitin had pots of money—a clear hint at that dowry? The twelve roubles didn't matter to him, and there had been nothing offensive in the man's words. Still, it was distasteful, and he didn't even feel like going home.

'Oh, how awful,' he said, halting by a street lamp.

The reason he didn't care about the twelve roubles was that he had got them for nothing, it struck him. Now, if he had been a labourer he would have valued every copeck, he would not have been so casual about winning or losing. But then, all his good fortune had come to him free and gratis, he reasoned—it was a luxury, really, like medicine to a healthy man. Had he been harassed like the great majority by worrying about his livelihood, had he been struggling for existence, had his back and chest ached from hard work, then his supper, his warm, snug quarters and his domestic bliss would be a necessity, a reward, an adornment of his life. As it was the significance of all that was oddly blurred, somehow.

'Oh, how awful,' he repeated, knowing full well that these very broodings were a bad sign.

Masha was in bed when he arrived home. Her breathing was even, and she smiled, obviously relishing her sleep. Next to her curled the white cat, purring. While Nikitin was lighting his candle and cigarette Masha woke up and thirstily drank a glass of water.

'I ate too much jam,' she laughed, and asked after a pause whether he had been visiting her family.

'No.'

Nikitin knew that Captain Polyansky, on whom Varya had been counting heavily of late, was being posted to the west country, and was now making his farewell visits in town for which reason there was an air of gloom at his father-in-law's.

Masha sat up. 'Varya called this evening. She didn't say anything, but you can see from her face how depressed she is, poor thing. I can't stand Polyansky. He's so fat, so frowsty, and his cheeks wobble when he walks or dances. He's not my type. Still, I did think he was a decent person.'

'Well, I still do think he is a decent person.'

'What, after he's treated Varya so badly?'

'Badly in what sense?' Nikitin was irked by the white cat stretching and arching its back. 'To the best of my knowledge he never proposed or made any promises.'

'Then why did he visit our house so often? He shouldn't have come if he didn't mean business.'

Nikitin put out the candle and lay down. But he did not feel like sleeping or lying there. His head seemed like some vast, empty barn with new, rather weird thoughts drifting about it like tall shadows. Away from the soft icon-lamp beaming on their quiet family happiness, away from this cosy little world in which he and that cat both lived in such delectable serenity, there was a very different world, he reflected. And for that other world he felt a sudden pang of anguished longing. He wanted to toil in some factory or big workshop, to lecture to audiences, to write, to publish, to make a splash, to exhaust himself, to suffer. He craved some obsession to make him oblivious of self and indifferent to personal happiness with its monotonous sensations. And then suddenly, in his mind's eye, the living image of clean-shaven Shebaldin arose and spoke in horror.

'Who hasn't even read Lessing? How backward you are—God, how you have gone to seed.'

Masha drank more water. He looked at her neck, plump shoulders and breasts, remembering what the retired major-general had called her in church that day—'a dear little rosebud'.

'Dear little rosebud,' he muttered. And laughed. Under the bed sleepy Bluebottle growled her guttural response.

Inside Nikitin a cold, heavy, spiteful urge seemed to hammer and twist. He wanted to be rude to Masha, or even jump up and hit her. His heart throbbed.

'So that's the way of it,' he stated, trying to restrain himself. 'By visiting your house I thereby undertook to marry you, I suppose?'

'Of course you did, you know that as well as I do.'

'Charming, I must say.'

A minute later he said it again. 'Charming.'

To stop himself adding something which he would regret, and to calm his emotions, Nikitin went to his study and lay on the ottoman without a pillow. Then he lay on the carpet on the floor.

He tried to reassure himself. 'This is all nonsense. You, a teacher, have a most admirable calling. What other world can you need? What utter rubbish!'

But then he at once answered himself with certainty that, far from being a teacher, he was a mediocre, featureless hack like the Greek master, a Czech. He had never had a vocation for teaching, he knew nothing of pedagogic theory, he had never been interested in it, he had no idea how to treat children. The significance of his teaching was lost on him, perhaps he was even teaching all the wrong things. The late Hippolytus had been frankly stupid, but all his colleagues and pupils had known who he was and what to expect of him—whereas he, Nikitin, was like the Czech who could conceal his dullness and adroitly deceive people by pretending that everything was, thank God, just as it should be. These new ideas alarmed Nikitin, he spurned them, he called them stupid, he put them down to nerves, he thought he would soon be laughing at himself.

Towards morning, indeed, he already was laughing at his nerves and calling himself an old woman. And yet he also realized that his peace of mind was lost, probably for ever, and that there was no happiness for him in this two-storeyed house with its unrendered walls. The illusion was gone, he sensed, and a new, uneasy, conscious life had begun—a life incompatible with peace of mind and personal happiness.

On the next day, a Sunday, he went to the school chapel where he met the headmaster and his colleagues. Their sole business in life seemed to consist of sedulously concealing their own ignorance and dissatisfaction, and he too smiled affably and indulged in small talk to avoid betraying his unease. Then he walked to the station. He watched the mail train come and go, pleased to be alone and not to have to talk to anyone.

At home he found his father-in-law and Varya who had come over for dinner. Varya's eyes were red from crying, and she complained of a headache, while Shelestov ate a lot and went on about young people being so unreliable and ungentlemanly nowadays.

'It's the act of a bounder,' he said. 'And so I shall tell him to his face—the act of a bounder, sir.'

Nikitin smiled amiably and helped Masha entertain their guests, but after dinner he went and locked himself in his study.

The March sun shone brightly, and warm rays fell on the desk through the double frames. It was only the twentieth of the month, but sledges had now given way to wheeled traffic and starlings were singing in the garden. He had the feeling that Masha was about to come in, put one arm around his neck, say that the horses or chaise had been brought round to the porch, and ask what she was to wear to keep warm. Spring had begun—a spring just as exquisite as the previous year's, promising just the same joys. But Nikitin thought he would like to take a holiday, go to Moscow and stay in his old lodgings in Neglinny Drive. In the next room they were drinking coffee and talking about Captain Polyansky while he tried not to listen.

Ye gods, where am I (he wrote in his diary)? I'm surrounded by smug, complacent mediocrities, dreary nonentities, pots of sour cream, jugs of milk, cockroaches, stupid women.

There is nothing more terrible, insulting and mortifying than the smug complacency of the second-rate. I must run away, I must escape this very day or I shall go out of my mind.

AT A COUNTRY HOUSE

[В усадьбе]

(1894)

AT A COUNTRY HOUSE

PAUL RASHEVICH paced up and down, stepping softly on the floor covered with Ukrainian rugs, throwing a long, narrow shadow on wall and ceiling. His guest Meyer, an acting coroner, sat on the ottoman, one leg tucked under him, smoking and listening. The clock said eleven, and they could hear someone laying the table in the room next to the study.

'From the standpoint of brotherhood, equality and all that, Mike the pigman may be as good as Goethe or Frederick the Great, I grant you that,' said Rashevich. But take the scientific view, have the courage to face the facts, and you'll see that breeding is no illusion or old wives' tale. Breeding, dear boy, has its biological validity, and to deny it is as odd, to my mind, as denying that a stag has horns. Just face up to things. As a lawyer you've confined your studies to the arts field—*you* can flatter yourself with illusions about equality, fraternity and all that. But I'm an incorrigible Darwinist. For me such terms as breeding, aristocracy, pedigree are more than empty sounds.'

Rashevich was excited, and spoke with emotion. His eyes gleamed, his pince-nez kept slipping down his nose, he nervously twitched his shoulders, he winked, and at the word 'Darwinist' he had cast a jaunty glance at the mirror, smoothing his grey beard with both hands. He wore a very short, shabby jacket and narrow trousers. His rapid movements, jauntiness, short jacket—they were not really his style, and it was as if his large, handsome head—complete with flowing locks and suggesting some bishop or venerable poet—had been stuck on the body of a tall, thin, affected youth. When he straddled his legs his long shadow was scissor-shaped.

Fond of a chat, he always felt he was saying something fresh and original, and in Meyer's presence he felt on top of his form—simply bursting with ideas. He liked the coroner. His youth, his health, his excellent manners, his reliability, and above all his affectionate attitude to Rashevich and his family—what a tonic they all were. Most of Rashevich's acquaintances disliked him, gave him a clear berth. As he was aware, they said he had talked his wife to death, and behind his back they called him Old Misery. Meyer alone, that go-ahead, open-minded man, was glad to be a frequent visitor, and had even remarked somewhere that Rashevich and his daughters were the only people in the county who made him feel really at home. Rashevich also liked him as a young man who might make a good husband for his elder daughter Zhenya.

Savouring his thoughts and the sound of his own voice, glancing with pleasure at the somewhat portly, elegantly barbered, respectable Meyer, Rashevich yearned to find his Zhenya such a husband, after which all the troubles with his estate would devolve on the son-in-law. And irksome troubles those were. His last two interest payments had not been made to the bank, and his various arrears and forfeitures came to over two thousand roubles.

Rashevich warmed to his theme. 'If some Richard Cœur de Lion, say, or Frederick Barbarossa, is brave and noble, these qualities are transmitted by heredity to his son along with his cranial convolutions and bumps, you take it from me. Now, if this courage and generous spirit are preserved in the son by education and cultivation, and if he marries a princess who is also noble and brave, then these qualities are transmitted to the grandson and so on, thus becoming a characteristic of the species and being, so to speak, organically transmuted into flesh and blood. Thanks to strict sexual selection, thanks to noble families instinctively shunning unions beneath their station, thanks to well-connected youngsters not marrying hell knows who, exalted mental characteristics have passed, all unalloyed, from generation to generation. They have been preserved, their cultivation has been perfected and refined in course of time. It is to nature—to nature, sir—that we owe mankind's assets, and that ordered, efficacious biological process which has over the centuries so sedulously set men of breeding apart from the common herd. Depend on it, dear boy—it wasn't your lower orders, your working-class lads, that gave us literature, learning, the arts, law, concepts of honour and duty.

'Humanity owes all that exclusively to its upper crust, in the light of which your most churlish backwoods squire belongs, biologically speaking—simply because he comes out of the top drawer—to a higher and more useful order of being than your finest businessman, one who has built fifteen museums. Say what you like, but if I refuse to shake hands with some common lout, if I don't invite him to my table, I am thereby conserving the finest fruits of the earth, and am implementing one of Mother Nature's loftiest designs for perfecting the species.'

Rashevich paused, stroking his beard with both hands, his scissor-shaped shadow projected on to the wall.

'Now, take good old Mother Russia,' he went on, thrusting his hands in his pockets and standing, now on his heels, now on his toes. 'Who are her élite? Take our first-class artists, writers, composers. Who are they? They all came straight out of the top drawer, dear boy. Pushkin, Gogol, Lermontov, Turgenev, Goncharov, Tolstoy—those were no sextons' sons.'

'The Goncharovs were in trade,' said Meyer.

'Aha! But exceptions only prove the rule. And Goncharov's talents are highly disputable anyway. But never mind the individuals. Back to the facts. Now, what of this fact, sir—one which speaks volumes? No sooner has your underdog invaded fields previously barred to him —high society, the academic world, literature, local government, the courts—than Nature herself has stepped forward to champion mankind's loftiest perquisites, she has been first to declare war on this rabble. No sooner, indeed, has your Mister Average Man quitted his proper station in life than he has begun to waste away, go off his head, wither on the bough, run to seed. Nowhere will you find so many neurotics, consumptives, mental cripples and miscellaneous ninnies as among these birds. They die like flies in autumn. But for this salutary degeneracy our civilization would have gone to rack and ruin long ago, your *hoi* bloody *polloi* would have gobbled it all up. Now, tell me, pray—what has this intrusion given us so far? What contribution have these scum made?'

Rashevich adopted an enigmatic, frightened air.

'Never have our literary and academic achievements sunk as low as they are now. People have no ideas or ideals nowadays, dear old boy. Whatever they're up to they have only one thing in mind—how to feather their own nests while beggaring their neighbours. Those who try to pass as progressive, "decent" men nowadays, they can all be bought for one rouble apiece, and the hallmark of your modern intellectual is just this—that you must keep hold of your pocket when talking to him, or you'll find yourself minus a wallet.'

Rashevich winked and roared with laughter. 'He'll have your wallet, believe you me,' he gleefully pronounced in a reedy little voice.

'Then there's morality. What price morality?' Rashevich looked round at the door. 'No one's surprised any more when a wife robs and deserts her husband—it's nothing, nothing. These days, old chap, a girl of twelve is already looking for a lover, and all these amateur theatricals and literary evenings have been invented solely to make it easier to hook some well-heeled bumpkin and become a kept woman.

'Mothers sell their daughters, and husbands are asked straight out how much they want for their wives. They'll even come down a bit if you bargain, dear boy.'

Meyer, who had sat still all this time saying nothing, suddenly rose from the sofa and looked at his watch. 'Excuse me, Mr. Rashevich, but it's time I went home.'

Rashevich had not finished, though. He put his arm round Meyer, sat him forcibly back on the sofa, swore he should not leave without supper. So Meyer once more sat listening, but was now giving Rashevich baffled and perturbed glances as if he was just beginning to take the man's measure. Red blotches appeared on his face. And when at last the maid entered and said that the young ladies would like them to come to supper, he gave a faint sigh and was first to leave the study.

At table in the next room sat Rashevich's daughters Zhenya and Iraida—twenty-four and twenty-two years old, both black-eyed, very pale, of the same height. Zhenya had her hair down, Iraida wore hers piled up. Before eating they both drank a glass of home-made spirits, looking as if they did so by accident, for the first time in their lives. Both were embarrassed and laughed.

'Now, don't you be such naughty children,' said Rashevich.

Zhenya and Iraida talked French to each other, but Russian to their father and his guest. Interrupting one another, mixing Russian with French, they rapidly explained how they had always gone off to their boarding school in the old days at exactly this time of year, August. What fun it had been! But now there was nowhere to go, and they had to live in the country all year round, summer and winter. And that was no fun at all.

'Now, don't you be such naughty children,' Rashevich repeated.

He wanted to do the talking. If others spoke in his presence he felt something akin to jealousy.

'Well, that's the way of it, dear boy.' He was off again, looking fondly at the coroner. 'In our kindness and simplicity, and because we fear to be thought retrograde, we fraternize with all sorts of scum, if you'll pardon the term. We preach brotherhood and equality with jumped up yokels and bartenders. But if we put our minds to it we'd see how criminal such kindness is. We've brought civilization to the edge of the abyss, dear boy. Our ancestors' age-old achievements will be desecrated and wrecked tomorrow by these latter-day vandals.'

After supper all went to the drawing-room. Zhenya and Iraida lit candles on the piano and prepared the music.

Rashevich was still at it, though, there was no knowing when he would be done. It was in agonized irritation that they looked at the selfish father for whom the pleasure of chattering and displaying his intellect was patently so much more precious and important than his daughters' happiness. Meyer, the only young man to visit their home, did so, they knew, for their charming feminine company. But the incorrigible old man had taken him over and gave him no inch of leeway.

'Just as the Western Knights flung back the Mongol invasion, so we too must unite before it's too late and strike a collective blow at our enemy,' Rashevich continued in prophetic tones, raising his right hand. 'Let me confront the common herd, not as Paul Rashevich, but as the dread and mighty Richard Cœur de Lion. And an end to the kid-glove treatment. Enough is enough. Let's all agree that as soon as one of these plebeians approaches us we'll at once fling our scorn right in his ugly mug. "Be off with you, sir! Know your place, insect!"'

'We'll let him have it straight between the eyes!' continued Rashevich gleefully, stabbing a bent finger in front of him. 'Plumb in the centre of his great fat face!'

Meyer turned away. 'I can't do that.'

'But why ever not?' Rashevich spoke forcefully, anticipating a long and interesting argument.

'Because I'm working class myself.'

With this Meyer blushed. His neck swelled, even, and actual tears appeared in his eyes.

'My father was a working man,' Meyer added in a harsh, abrupt voice. 'And I see nothing wrong in that.'

Rashevich was frightfully put out. He was shattered, as if caught committing a crime, and he stared at Meyer baffled, at a loss for words. Zhenya and Iraida blushed and bent over their music, ashamed of their tactless father. A minute had passed in silence and unbearable embarrassment when suddenly a voice—a neurotic, tense, jarring voice—rang in the air.

'Aye, I'm working class and proud of it.'

Then Meyer took his farewell, awkwardly bumping into furniture—and went quickly into the hall though his carriage had not yet been brought round.

'You'll find it a bit dark on the road tonight,' muttered Rashevich, following him. 'The moon doesn't rise till later.'

Both stood in the dark porch waiting for the carriage to be fetched. It was cool.

'There's a shooting star,' said Meyer, huddling in his overcoat.

'There are lots of those in August.'

When the carriage appeared Rashevich looked keenly at the sky.

'A phenomenon worthy of a Flammarion's pen,' he sighed.

Having seen his guest off he paced the garden, gesticulating in the dark, not wanting to believe that such an odd, such a silly misunderstanding had just occurred. He was ashamed, vexed with himself. First, it had been highly imprudent and tactless of him to raise this blasted question of breeding without finding out in advance who he was dealing with. Something similar had happened before. He had once started running down Germans in a railway compartment, whereupon his travelling companions had all turned out to be German. Secondly, he sensed that Meyer would never call again. They're so pathologically conceited, so stubborn, so rancorous, are these intelligent artisans.

'Bad, bad, very bad indeed,' muttered Rashevich, spitting. He felt put out and queasy, as if he had been eating soap.

From the garden he could see Zhenya through the drawing-room window—with her hair down, very pale and scared-looking, she was talking away at high speed by the piano.

Iraida faced the room, deep in thought. But then she too started speaking rapidly, looking highly indignant. Both were talking at once. Though no word was audible Rashevich guessed what they were saying. Zhenya was probably complaining that her father had driven all decent people from the house with his talk, talk, talk, and had today deprived them of their one friend—a prospective husband, perhaps—and now the poor young man had nowhere in the whole county where he could feel at home. Iraida, from the way she had raised her hands in despair, was probably saying how boring things were and how her young life had been ruined.

Rashevich went to his room, sat on his bed, slowly undressed. He felt dejected, still haunted by that sensation of having eaten soap. He was ashamed. After undressing he looked at his long, sinewy, old man's legs and remembered how he'd been nicknamed Old Misery in the county, and how every long conversation left him with this feeling of shame. Somehow or other, as if foredoomed, he would begin so gently, so kindly, with such good intentions, calling himself a former university man, an idealist, a tilter at windmills. But then, all unawares, he would gradually descend to abuse and slander. Oddest thing of all, he would criticize learning, the arts and morals in all sincerity, though he hadn't read a single book for twenty years, had never travelled farther than the local county town, and had no real idea of what went on in the world at large. If he sat down to write anything, be it a mere congratulatory letter, that too turned out full of abuse. And this was odd because he was a sensitive man, really, always on the verge of tears. Could there be some evil spirit inside him, spreading hate and slander against his will?

'A bad, bad business,' he sighed, lying under his quilt.

His daughters could not sleep either. There was loud laughter and a shout as if they were chasing someone—that was Zhenya having hysterics. A bit later Iraida too burst out sobbing. A barefoot maid ran up and down the corridor several times.

'Lord, what a business,' muttered Rashevich, sighing and tossing from side to side. 'Bad.'

He had a nightmare, dreaming that he, naked and tall as a giraffe, stood in the middle of a room talking and stabbing his finger in front of him.

'Fling it straight into their great fat faces!'

He awoke in terror, and the first thing he remembered was yesterday's misunderstanding—Meyer would never come back, of course. He remembered too that he must pay interest to the bank, marry off his daughters, eat, drink. Then there was old age, there were illnesses, there were other nuisances, and soon it would be winter and he had no firewood.

It was past nine a.m. Rashevich slowly dressed, drank his tea, and ate two large slices of bread and butter. His daughters did not come down to breakfast. They were avoiding him, and this offended him. He lay on his study sofa, then sat at his desk and started writing his daughters a letter. His hand quaked, his eyes itched. He wrote that he was old, unwanted and unloved, he asked his daughters to forget him and, when he died, to bury him in a simple pine coffin without ceremony, or to send the corpse to the medical research people at Kharkov. He felt that every line breathed malice and buffoonery, but he couldn't stop writing, writing, writing.

Then, from the next room, his elder daughter's voice—outraged, hissing—suddenly rang out. 'Old Misery, Old Misery!'

'Old Misery, Old Misery!' the younger echoed.

THE HEAD GARDENER'S STORY

[*Рассказ старшего садовника*]

(1894)

THE HEAD GARDENER'S STORY

THERE was a flower sale at Count and Countess N's greenhouse. But there were not many buyers, just myself, my landowning neighbour and a young timber merchant. While labourers carried our magnificent purchases out and packed them on carts, we sat by the greenhouse door discoursing of this and that. To sit in a garden on a warm April morning, to listen to the birds, and to see the flowers sunning themselves now that they had been brought outside—how very delightful.

The stowage of the plants was handled by the head gardener Michael Karlovich—a venerable, full-faced, clean-shaven old fellow in a fur waistcoat—he had taken off his frock-coat. He said nothing all this time, but listened to our conversation in case we might say anything new. He was an intelligent, easy-going, universally respected man. Somehow everyone thought he was German, though he was Swedish on his father's side and Russian on his mother's. He was an Orthodox church-goer, he knew Russian, Swedish and German, he read a lot in these languages, and you could give him no greater delight than lending him a new book or talking to him about Ibsen, for instance.

He had his foibles, but innocent ones. For instance, he called himself a 'head' gardener, though there were no under-gardeners. His expression was highly dignified and haughty. He did not permit contradictions, he liked to be listened to seriously and attentively.

'Now, that young spark over there—he's a frightful rogue, I can tell you.' My neighbour pointed to a workman with a florid gipsy's face riding past on a water-cart. 'He was had up in town for robbery last week and got off on grounds of insanity. But just look at the blackguard's face, he's as sane as can be. Russian courts are always acquitting scoundrels nowadays, explaining everything by ill health and temporary insanity, but these acquittals, this blatant leniency, this aiding and abetting—it bodes no good. It demoralizes the masses, blunting everyone's sense of justice because they're used to seeing vice going unpunished, so that one can boldly apply to our own day Shakespeare's lines.

> "For in the fatness of these pursy times
> Virtue itself of vice must pardon beg." '

'True, true,' agreed the merchant. 'These acquittals have caused a boom in murder and arson. Just ask the peasants.'

The gardener Michael Karlovich turned to us.

'For myself I'm always delighted with an acquittal, gentleman,' said he. 'A not guilty verdict doesn't make me fear for morality and justice. Far from it, it pleases me. Even when my conscience tells me that a jury has been wrong to acquit a criminal, even then I feel exultant. Judge for yourselves, gentlemen—if judges and juries believe more in *man* than in clues, circumstantial evidence and speeches, then is not this *faith in man* itself superior to all mundane considerations? Such faith is accessible only to those few who understand Christ and feel His presence.'

'A fine thought,' said I.

'But not a new one. I even remember once hearing a story on this theme long long ago, a most delightful story.' The gardener smiled. 'My old grandmother, now passed away—my father's mother, a wonderful old woman—used to tell me it. She told it in Swedish, but it doesn't sound as well in Russian, it's less classic.'

Still, we asked him to tell the story undeterred by the crudeness of the Russian language. Well pleased, he slowly lit his pipe, looked angrily at the labourers, and began.

In a certain small town there lived an elderly, ugly bachelor called Thomson or Wilson. The name doesn't matter, it's beside the point. He practised the noble calling of doctor, was always grim and unsociable, spoke only when his profession required it. He never made social visits, never carried acquaintanceship beyond a silent bow, lived as humbly as any hermit. He was a scholar, in fact, and in those days scholars were unlike ordinary people. They would spend their days and nights contemplating, reading books, healing sickness, rating all else mere frivolity and being too busy to speak without need. The townsfolk appreciated this, trying not to pester him with their visits and idle chat. They were overjoyed that God had sent them a healer at last, they were proud to have so remarkable a man living in their town.

They used to say that he 'knew everything'.

Nor was this all. We should also add his love for everyone. In the scholar's breast beat a wondrous, angelic heart. And in any case the townsfolk were strangers to him, they weren't his kith and kin after all, yet he loved them like his children, was ready to give his very life for them. He suffered from tuberculosis, he was always coughing, but when called to a patient he would forget his illness, not sparing himself, and would puff his way up mountains however high. He spurned heat and cold, despised hunger and thirst, never accepted money, and—odd, isn't it?—when one of his patients died he would follow the coffin with the relatives and weep.

He soon became so vital to the town that folk wondered how they had ever managed without him. Their gratitude knew no bounds. Adults and children, the good-natured and ill-natured, the honest men and rogues—everyone, in a word—respected him, valued him. No one in the little town and its environs would have done him an ill turn, or even thought of it. He never locked his doors and windows when leaving his quarters, being absolutely assured that no thief would venture to harm him. As a doctor he often had to walk highways, forests and mountains, the haunts of hungry vagabonds, but felt completely safe. One night on his way home from a patient he was waylaid in a wood by highwaymen who, when they saw who it was, respectfully doffed their hats and asked if he was hungry. When he said he was not, they gave him a warm cloak and escorted him all the way to town, happy that fortune had granted them this chance of conveying their thanks to one so noble-spirited. Then again, if you take my drift, my grandmother used to say that even horses, cows and dogs knew him and showed how glad they were to see him.

Yet this man whose saintliness seemed a bulwark against all evil, this man whom the very robbers and madmen wished well—he was found murdered one morning. Covered with blood, his skull smashed in, he lay in a gulley with a surprised look on his pale face. No, it was not horror but surprise which had frozen on his face when he saw his murderer before him. Now, imagine how heart-broken the townsfolk and locals were. All were in despair, not believing their eyes, wondering who could kill such a man. The court officers who conducted the investigation and examined the corpse pronounced as follows.

'Here is every evidence of murder. Since, however, no one on earth could bring himself to kill our doctor, it obviously cannot be murder and the accumulated clues must derive from pure coincidence. We must assume that the doctor stumbled into the gulley in the dark and died from the fall.'

With this opinion the whole town concurred. The doctor was buried, and there was no more talk of death by violence. The very existence of someone base and foul enough to murder him seemed improbable. After all, even vileness does have its limits, doesn't it?

But then suddenly, believe it or not, chance revealed the murderer. A certain scallywag, who had often stood trial and was known for his dissolute life, was seen in an inn with a snuff-box and watch, once the doctor's, which he was using to obtain drink. When questioned he showed embarrassment and told some blatant lie. His home was searched, and in his bed were found a shirt with blood-stained sleeves and the doctor's lancet in a golden case. What more clues were needed? They put the villain in prison, and the townsfolk were perturbed while claiming it as 'most unlikely' and 'impossible'.

'Look, there may have been a mistake. Clues can be misleading, after all.'

The murderer stubbornly denied his complicity in court. Everything was against him. His guilt was as plain as that this soil is black, but the magistrates had apparently taken leave of their senses. Ten times they weighed every clue, viewing the witnesses with suspicion, blushing, drinking water.

They began trying the case early in the morning, and did not finish until evening.

The presiding magistrate addressed the murderer. 'Prisoner in the dock, the court finds you guilty of the murder of Doctor Such-and-Such and sentences you——'

The chief magistrate was about to say 'to death', but dropped the paper on which the sentence had been written and wiped off cold sweat.

'No,' he shouted. 'May God punish me if this judgement is wrong, but I swear he is not guilty. That anyone would dare kill our friend the doctor I do not concede. Man cannot sink so low.'

'No indeed,' the other magistrates concurred.

'No,' echoed the crowd. 'Let him go.'

They let the murderer go scot free, and not a soul reproached the court with a miscarriage of justice. According to my grandmother God forgave all the townsfolk their sins because of their great faith in man. He rejoices when folk believe that man is His own image and likeness, and He is grieved if men forget their human dignity and judge their fellows to be worse than dogs. Even if the acquittal should harm the townsfolk, yet just consider how beneficent an influence their faith in man has had on them. That faith is no dead formula, now is it? It educates us in noble sentiments, always prompting us to love and respect everyone. Everyone—that's what's so important.

Michael Karlovich ended. My neighbour wanted to offer some objection, but the head gardener made a gesture signifying a dislike of all objections, and went over to the carts to continue supervising the loading with an expression of great dignity on his face.

THREE YEARS

[*Три года*]

(1895)

THREE YEARS

I

It was dark, but lights had already come on in some houses, and at the end of the street a pale moon was rising behind the barracks. Seated on a bench by a gate, Laptev waited for vespers to end at St. Peter and St. Paul's. He calculated that Julia Belavin would come past on her way back from church, that he would speak to her and perhaps spend the evening with her.

He had sat for an hour and a half visualizing his Moscow flat, his Moscow friends, his valet Peter, his desk. He gazed in bewilderment at the dark, unmoving trees, astonished that he was no longer living in his Sokolniki villa but in a provincial town, in a house past which a large herd of cattle was driven every morning and evening, raising terrible clouds of dust while the herdsman blew his horn. He remembered the long Moscow discussions in which he had so recently taken part, about life without love being possible, about passionate love being a psychosis, and finally about how there's no such thing as love but only sexual attraction—that sort of thing. Recalling it, he sadly reflected that if anyone now asked him what love was he would be at a loss for an answer.

The service ended, the congregation emerged, and Laptev stared intently at the dark figures. The bishop had driven past in his carriage, the bell-ringing was over, the red and green lights on the belfry had been extinguished one after the other—special illuminations, these, to celebrate the patronal festival—and people were making their way unhurriedly, talking and pausing beneath the windows. Then at last Laptev heard a familiar voice, his heart missed a beat, and he was seized with despair because Julia was not on her own, but with two other ladies.

'That's awful, truly awful,' he whispered, feeling jealous.

She stopped at the corner of a side-road to say good-bye to the ladies, and it was then that she looked at Laptev.

'I'm on my way to your place,' he said. 'I want to talk to your father. Is he in?'

'Probably. It's too early for him to be at his club.'

The side-road was rich in gardens. By the fences grew lime trees, now casting their broad shadows in the moonlight so that fences and gates on one side were blanketed in darkness from which proceeded the whisper of feminine voices, subdued laughter and the quiet strumming of a balalaika. It smelt of lime trees and hay. The unseen women's whispering and the smell aroused Laptev. He felt a sudden intense urge to embrace his companion, to cover her face, arms, shoulders with kisses, to burst into tears, to fall at her feet, to say how long he had been waiting for her. She brought with her a faint, elusive whiff of incense, reminding him of the time when he too had believed in God, had gone to evening service, had yearned for a pure, romantic love. But, since this girl did not love him, he now felt permanently deprived of the prospect of that happiness for which he had then longed.

She expressed concern about the health of his sister Nina, who had had an operation for cancer two months earlier. Now everyone was expecting a relapse.

'I saw her this morning,' said Julia. 'And it struck me that she had not just lost weight this last week, but all her vitality too.'

'Quite,' agreed Laptev. 'There has been no new crisis, but I see her growing feebler every day. She's sinking before my eyes, I can't think what's happening.'

'Goodness me, what a healthy, buxom, rosy-cheeked woman she was,' Julia said after a short pause. 'Everyone here called her "the girl from Moscow". How she did laugh. On holidays she would wear peasant dress, which suited her very well.'

Doctor Sergey Belavin was at home. A stout, red-faced man in a long frock-coat reaching below the knees, seeming short-legged, he was pacing his study, his hands thrust into his pockets, humming a sort of ruminating hum. His grey side-whiskers were dishevelled, his hair was as untidy as if he had only just got out of bed. And his study—with the cushions on the sofas, piles of old papers in the corners, and a large, dirty poodle under the table—had an air as unkempt and frowsty as its owner's.

'Mr. Laptev wishes to see you,' his daughter told him, going into the study.

He hummed his ruminative hum more loudly, came into the drawing-room, shook hands with Laptev, and asked 'what tidings?'

It was dark in the drawing-room. Laptev remained standing, kept his hat in his hands and apologized for the intrusion. He asked what could be done to help his sister sleep at night. And why was she so appallingly thin? He was embarrassed because he vaguely remembered asking the doctor these same questions already during this morning's visit. And he asked whether 'we shouldn't send for some specialist in internal diseases from Moscow'. What was the doctor's view?

The doctor sighed, shrugged, made a vague two-handed gesture.

He was offended, obviously. This was a very touchy, a very pernickety doctor, obsessed with being distrusted, not recognized, not sufficiently respected—a target, he felt, for general exploitation and his colleagues' malice. He was always mocking himself. 'Idiots like me exist only to be trampled on.'

Julia lit a lamp. The service had tired her, to judge from her pale, languid face and listless walk. Wishing to relax, she sat on the sofa, put her hands on her lap and was lost in thought, while Laptev—conscious that he was not handsome—now felt physically aware of his own ugliness. He was short, thin, with flushed cheeks, and with hair so sparse that his head felt cold. His expression wholly lacked that charm and simplicity which can make even a coarse, ugly face likeable. In women's company he was awkward, over-talkative, affected, and was almost despising himself for this at the moment. To avoid boring Julia he must say something. But what? Should he bring up his sister's illness again?

He began making trite remarks about medicine, he praised hygiene, he said that he had long wished to set up a poor people's hostel in Moscow, and already had a scheme afoot. A worker arriving in the evening was to receive for five or six copecks a portion of hot cabbage stew, bread, a warm, dry bed with a quilt, a place to dry his clothes and footwear.

Julia usually remained silent in his presence, while he—guided perhaps by the instincts of a man in love—had a strange faculty for guessing her thoughts and intentions. As she had not gone to her room to change and have tea after the service she must mean to go visiting this evening, he now calculated.

'But I'm in no hurry over the hostel,' he went on, annoyed and distressed. He was addressing the doctor, whose vague, lack-lustre and baffled gaze showed that he could not see why the man had to bring up medicine and hygiene.

'No, I don't suppose I shall carry out the project very soon,' Laptev went on. 'I fear it may fall into the clutches of Moscow's lady bountifuls and do-gooders, who ruin every initiative.'

Julia stood up, held out her hand to Laptev and asked him to excuse her. 'Time I was off. Give your sister my regards.'

The doctor hummed his ruminative hum.

Julia went out. Soon afterwards Laptev said good-bye to the doctor and set off home. What a vulgar atmosphere they do generate when one feels frustrated and unhappy—these lime trees, these shadows, these clouds, all these smug, unconcerned beauties of nature. The moon was high in the sky, clouds raced below it.

'Silly provincial moon,' Laptev thought. 'Pathetic, scraggy clouds.'

He was ashamed to have brought up medicine and that hostel just now. And he was aghast to think that he would not hold out tomorrow either, but would try to see and talk to her again, only to discover once more that he meant nothing to her. The day after tomorrow would be just the same. To what purpose? When and how would it all end?

When he arrived home he went to see his sister. Nina still looked strong, seeming a powerful, well-built woman, but her striking pallor made her corpse-like—especially when she lay on her back with her eyes closed, as now. By her sat her elder daughter, ten-year-old Sasha, who was reading to her from a school book.

'Alexis is here,' the sick woman said quietly to herself.

Between Sasha and her uncle a tacit agreement had long been reached, and they ran a shift system. So Sasha closed her reader and quietly left the room without a word. Laptev took a historical novel from the chest-of-drawers, found his place, sat down, began reading to her.

Nina had come from Moscow. Like her two brothers she had spent her childhood and youth at Pyatnitsky Road. The family was in business, and a long, boring childhood theirs had been. The father had been strict, even taking the birch to her several times, and her mother had been an invalid long before her death. The servants had been dirty, coarse, hypocritical. The house had been frequented by priests and monks no less rude and hypocritical. They drank, they ate, they crudely flattered her father, whom they disliked. The boys had had the good luck to go to a grammar school, but Nina had received no education at all, she had scrawled rather than written all her life, she had read nothing but historical novels. Seventeen years earlier, aged twenty-two, she had met her present husband Panaurov—member of a landowning family—at a Khimki villa. She had fallen in love and married him against her father's wish, in secret. Panaurov, a handsome and rather insolent person, a lighter of cigarettes from the icon lamp, a great whistler, had impressed her father as an utter nobody. Then

M. Rose

A long time ago
you asked for each
volume of chobbis's
short stories as
they were published.
Here is the latest.

JMG

Reserve   M. Rope

KING ALFREDS COLLEGE LIBRARY
WINCHESTER

AUTHOR *(CAPITALS)*   CHEKHOV

TITLE   Stories 1893-1895
(Oxford chekhov Vol. 7) ed. Hingley

EDITION AND DATE OF PUBLICATION   1978   PRICE

PUBLISHER   OUP

SOURCE OF ABOVE DETAILS   Aut. Bs

TUTOR   **DEPT.** Eng

	DATE ORDERED	OCT. 31. '78	DATE SUPPLIED	NO. OF COPIES 1
	ORDER NO.	09626		
LIBRARY USE ONLY	BOOKSELLER	H	BNB NO.	
	BOOKSELLER'S			

when the son-in-law's letters had begun insisting on a dowry, the old man had written to his daughter that he would send her some fur coats at her country home, some silver and oddments left by her mother, together with thirty thousand roubles in cash, but without his blessing. He sent another twenty thousand later. This money and the whole dowry had been squandered, the estate had been sold, Panaurov and his family had moved to town, and he had taken a local government job. He had started another family in town, which caused endless discussion every day since no secret was made of this illegitimate family.

Nina adored her husband. Listening to the historical novel, she reflected how much she had experienced and suffered all this time, how poignant any account of her life would be. Since hers was a tumour of the breast she was sure that her disease had been caused by love and family life, and that jealousy and tears had laid her low.

Alexis closed the book. 'That's the end, praise be. We'll start another tomorrow.'

Nina laughed. She had always been inclined to laugh, but it had begun to strike Laptev that her mind was sometimes enfeebled by sickness, so that she laughed at mere trifles and for no reason at all.

'Julia called before dinner while you were out,' she said. 'I can see she doesn't much trust that father of hers. "Let my father treat you," says she. "But you write to the Reverend So-and-So on the quiet, get him to say a prayer for you." This is some local sage of theirs. Julia left her umbrella here—send it her tomorrow,' she went on after a short pause. 'Anyway, if this is the end, neither your doctors nor your Reverend So-and-Sos will help.'

'Why can't you sleep at night, Nina?' Laptev wanted to change the subject.

'Oh, I don't know. I can't, and that's that. I just lie thinking.'

'What about, dear?'

'The children, you, my own life. I've been through so much, haven't I, Alexis? When you start remembering, when you—heavens!' She laughed. 'It's no joke having five children and burying three of them. Sometimes I'd be on the point of having the baby, but Gregory would be with another woman and there would be no one to send for the midwife or anything. You'd go into the hall or kitchen for the servants, and you'd find Jews, tradesmen, money-lenders—all waiting for him to come home. It used to make me quite dizzy. He didn't love me, though he never said so. But now I've come to terms with it,

I'm not heart-broken any longer. It did hurt me so much when I was younger, though. I did suffer, dear. Once, when we were still living in the country, I found him in the garden with another woman, and I just left—left without caring where I went, and somehow found myself in the church porch. I fell on my knees. "Mother of God", I prayed. It was dark outside, a moonlit night.'

Exhausted, she breathed heavily. Then, after resting a while, she took her brother by the arm. 'You're so kind, Alexis,' she went on in a feeble whisper. 'You're so intelligent. What a fine man you have become.'

At midnight Laptev wished her good night, and took with him as he left the umbrella left behind by Julia. Late though the hour was servants, male and female, were drinking tea in the dining-room. What chaos. The children were still up, and they were in the dining-room too. All were talking in low voices, not noticing that the lamp was fading and would soon go out. Everyone, large and small, was troubled by an accumulation of unfavourable auguries, and they felt depressed. The hall mirror was broken, the samovar whined every day —it was at it now, confound it. And as Mrs. Panaurov had been dressing a mouse had jumped out of her shoe, or so they said. The sinister portent of these omens was already known to the children. The elder, Sasha, a thin, dark-haired little girl, sat still at the table, looking scared and downcast, while the younger, Leda—seven years old, plump, fair-haired—stood near her sister, squinting at the light.

Laptev went down to his ground-floor rooms with their stuffy atmosphere, low ceilings and permanent smell of geraniums. In his drawing-room sat Nina's husband Panaurov reading a newspaper. Laptev nodded and sat opposite him. Neither spoke. They would some-times spend whole evenings like this, unembarrassed by their silence.

The little girls came down to say good-night. Silently, unhurriedly, Panaurov made the sign of the cross over both several times, gave them his hand to kiss. They curtsied and went up to Laptev, who also had to make the sign of the cross over them and let them kiss his hand. This kissing and curtsying occurred every evening.

When the girls had gone Panaurov put his paper on one side. 'This blessed town is such a bore.' Then he added with a sigh that he was 'frankly delighted that you've found some amusement at last, dear boy'.

'Meaning what?' Laptev asked.

'I saw you leaving Dr. Belavin's house just now. It was not on dear Daddy's account, I trust—your visit.'

'Of course it was.' Laptev blushed.

'But of course. Incidentally, what a wet blanket dear Daddy is, he must be unique. What dirty habits, what a dim, clumsy brute it is—you've no idea. Now, you Muscovites are only interested in the provinces from a romantic angle, so to speak—in the scenery, in picturesquely miserable bumpkins. But there's nothing romantic here, old man, believe you me. There's just barbarity, meanness, squalor—nothing else. Take our local lights of learning, our "professional men". Do you know we have twenty-eight doctors in this town? They've all made their fortunes, they've all bought their own houses, while the rest of the people are still in the same wretched plight as ever. For instance, Nina had to have an operation—a trivial one, actually, yet we had to have a man from Moscow because none of the local surgeons would do it. You've no idea what it's like—they know nothing, understand nothing, are interested in nothing. Ask them what cancer is, for instance—what it is, where it comes from?'

Panaurov went on to explain what cancer was. He was a specialist in all branches of learning, having a scientific explanation for everything under the sun. But he always had his own line on things. He had his own theory of the circulation of the blood, his own chemistry, his own astronomy. He spoke slowly, softly, convincingly, bringing out the words 'you haven't the remotest inkling' as if begging a favour. He screwed up his eyes, he sighed languidly, he smiled benevolently like royalty, patently self-satisfied and wholly unconcerned with being fifty years old.

'I'm a bit peckish,' said Laptev. 'I feel like something savoury.'

'But of course. That can be laid on at once.'

Soon afterwards Laptev and his brother-in-law were upstairs having supper in the dining-room. Laptev drank a glass of vodka and moved on to wine, but Panaurov drank nothing. He neither drank nor played cards, despite which he had contrived to run through his own and his wife's property, and to pile up a mass of debts. To squander so much money so quickly you need more than mere carnal appetites—you need something extra, a special flair. Panaurov liked tasty food, first-rate table appointments, music with his dinner, speeches, the bows of the waiters to whom he nonchalantly tossed tips of ten or even twenty-five roubles. He subscribed to everything, went in for all the lotteries, sent ladies of his acquaintance flowers on their name-days, bought cups, glass-holders, studs, ties, canes, scents, cigarette-holders, pipes, dogs, parrots, Japanese wares and antiques. His night-shirts were of silk, his bed was of ebony and mother-of-pearl, he had a real Bokhara dressing-gown and so on—all of which daily consumed what he called 'a mint of money'.

Over supper he kept sighing and shaking his head.

'Yes, everything in the world comes to an end,' he said quietly, screwing up his dark eyes. 'You'll fall in love and suffer. You'll fall out of love. You'll be deceived because there's no such thing as a faithful woman. You will suffer, you will despair, you too will be unfaithful. But in time all this will be only a memory, and you'll coolly reckon it as all utterly insignificant.'

Tired, slightly drunk, Laptev looked at the other's handsome head, at the clipped black beard, and felt he understood why women so loved this spoilt, confident, physically attractive man.

After supper Panaurov did not remain at home, but left for his other flat. Laptev accompanied him. Panaurov was the only man in the whole town who wore a top hat, and against the grey fences, the wretched three-windowed cottages, the clumps of nettles, his elegant, fashionable figure, top hat and orange gloves always evoked an air both strange and sad.

Laptev said good-night and returned to his quarters unhurriedly. The moon shone so brightly that every wisp of straw on the ground was visible, and Laptev felt as if the moonlight was caressing his uncovered head, which was like having his hair stroked with a feather.

'I'm in love,' he said aloud, and he suddenly felt like running after Panaurov to embrace him, forgive him, present him with a lot of money and then rush off into the fields or a wood somewhere, and run, run, run without looking back.

At home, on a chair, he saw the umbrella left behind by Julia, picked it up, kissed it passionately. It was of silk, no longer new, girded with an old piece of elastic. It had an ordinary cheap bone handle. Laptev opened it above him and felt enveloped in the very scent of happiness.

He sat down more comfortably and began writing to one of his Moscow friends while still holding the umbrella.

'My dearest Kostya,

'Here's news for you—I'm in love again. I say "again" because six years ago I was in love with a Moscow actress whom I never even managed to meet, and for the last eighteen months I've been living with the "personage" you know of, a woman neither young nor beautiful. I've always been so unlucky in love, old friend. I never had success with women, and if I say "again" it's only because it's so sad, so painful to realize that my youth has gone by without any love at all, and that I'm now well and truly in love for the first time at the age of thirty-four. So let me say I'm in love "again".

'If you only knew what she's like. You can't call her beautiful—her face is too broad, she's very thin, but what a wonderfully kind expression! And how she smiles! When she speaks her voice sings, it's so resonant. She's never the first to speak to me, and I don't really know her, but when I'm near her I sense in her a rare, exceptional creature imbued with intelligence and high ideals. She's religious, and you can't imagine how this moves me and raises her in my estimation. On this point I'm prepared to argue with you for ever. All right, have it your own way, but I still love her church-going. She's a provincial but she went to school in Moscow, she loves our city, she dresses like a Muscovite and for that I love her, love her, love her.

'I see you frown and stand up to read me a long lecture about what love is, and whom one may and may not love, and so on and so forth. But I too knew just what love was—before I fell in love, my dear Kostya.

'My sister thanks you for your regards, and often remembers how she once took Kostya Kochevoy to join the preparatory class. She still calls you "poor Kostya" because she still remembers you as the little orphan boy. So I'm in love, poor orphan. It's a secret for now, so don't say anything *there* to the "personage" known to you. That business will settle itself, I think. Or as the servant says in Tolstoy, "it will sort itself out." '

The letter finished, Laptev went to bed. He was so tired that his eyes closed of themselves. But sleep he somehow could not, apparently because of the noise in the street. The herd of cattle was driven past, the horn sounded, and soon after that the bells rang for morning service. Now a cart would creak past, now a woman's voice was heard on her way to market. And the sparrows never stopped twittering.

II

The morning was bright and cheerful. At about ten o'clock Nina, wearing a brown dress, hair tidied, was led into the drawing-room where she paced about, then stood by the open window, smiling a broad, innocent smile. Looking at her, one remembered the local artist, a drunkard, who had called her face a 'countenance' and had wanted to use her as a model in a picture of a Russian Shrovetide. Everyone—children, servants, even Nina herself and her brother—was suddenly convinced that her recovery was certain. Shrieking with laughter, the little girls ran after their uncle trying to catch him, and the house was full of noise.

Visitors came to ask about her health, bringing communion bread and saying that special prayers had been offered for her today in almost all the churches. She had done much good in the town, and was much loved. Charitable deeds came as naturally to her as to her brother, who gave money very readily without bothering whether he should or not. Nina paid poor boys' school fees, took old ladies tea, sugar and jam, equipped impecunious brides with dresses, and if she chanced on a newspaper she would first look for appeals or accounts of anyone being in desperate straits.

At the moment she held a bundle of chits with which sundry indigent beneficiaries had obtained goods at the grocer's. The man had sent them along yesterday with his request to pay eighty-two roubles.

'Dear me, they've been helping themselves quite shamelessly.' She could hardly make out her own ungainly hand-writing on the notes. 'Eighty-two roubles, that's no joke, I've a good mind not to pay.'

'I'll pay it today,' said Laptev.

'But why should you?' Nina was perturbed. 'It's enough that I get two hundred and fifty roubles a month from you and our brother, God bless you,' she added quietly, so that the servants should not hear.

'Well, I spend two thousand five hundred a month,' he said. 'I tell you again, dear, you've as much right to spend money as Theodore and I. Get that into your head once and for all. Our father has three children, and one in every three copecks is yours.'

But Nina, not understanding, looked as if she had been trying to do a very complicated sum in her head. This lack of money sense always worried and embarrassed Laptev. Besides, he suspected her of having some private debts which she was ashamed to confide in him and which pained her.

They heard steps and heavy breathing. The doctor was coming upstairs, dishevelled and unkempt as ever, humming his usual ruminating hum.

To avoid meeting him Laptev stepped into the dining-room, then

went down to his own quarters. To get on closer terms with the
doctor, to call on him casually—that was out of the question, Laptev
clearly realized. Even to meet this 'wet blanket', as Panaurov called
him, was unpleasant. That was why he saw so little of Julia. If he took
back her umbrella now that her father was out he would probably
find her at home on her own, and his heart leapt with joy. He must
hurry.

He picked up the umbrella and flew off in great excitement, on the
wings of love. It was hot in the street. In the doctor's house, in the
huge yard overgrown with tall weeds and nettles, a score of urchins
were playing ball. These were children of tenants—workpeople who
lived in the three unprepossessing old outbuildings which the doctor
was going to have repaired every year, but always postponed. Healthy
voices resounded. Far to one side near her porch stood Julia, arms
behind her back, watching the game.

Laptev hailed her and she turned round. She usually looked coolly
indifferent when he saw her, or tired, as she had been yesterday. But
now she looked as vivacious and playful as the boys with their ball.

'See, they never have such fun in Moscow.' She came towards him.
'Anyway, they don't have these huge yards there, do they? There's
nowhere to run about. Father has just left for your place,' she added,
looking round at the children.

'I know, but it's you I've come to see, not him.'

She looked so young—that was what Laptev admired, having
somehow never noticed it before today. He gazed, as if for the first
time, at her slim white neck with its little gold chain. 'It's you I've
come to see,' he repeated. 'My sister sent this umbrella that you left
behind yesterday.'

She held her hand out to take it, but he pressed it to his breast and
spoke ardently, uncontrollably, yielding once more to the delicious
pleasure experienced on the previous night under the umbrella.

'I beg you, give it to me, I'll keep it in memory of you—of our
friendship. It's so marvellous.'

'All right.' She blushed. 'But there's nothing marvellous about it.'

He looked at her entranced, silently, not knowing what to say.

'But why do I keep you out in the heat?' she asked after a pause, and
laughed. 'Let's go inside.'

'If I won't be interrupting you.'

They went into the hall. Julia ran upstairs with a rustle of her dress,
which was white with blue flowers.

'It's not possible to interrupt me.' She stopped on the staircase. 'You see, I never do anything—every day's a holiday from morning to night.'

'That's hard for me to understand.' He approached her. 'I grew up in surroundings where people work every day, all without exception, men and women.'

'But what if there's nothing to do?'

'So organize your life that work is inescapable. You can't live a decent, happy life if you don't work.'

Again he pressed the umbrella to his chest and, to his surprise, found himself speaking in a calm voice not his own. 'If you would consent to be my wife, I would give anything—anything at all. There's no price, no sacrifice I would not accept.'

She started, looking at him in surprise and fear.

'Don't, don't say such things.' She blenched. 'It's not possible, I assure you. I'm sorry.'

Then she rushed upstairs, her dress still rustling, and vanished through a door.

Laptev knew what this meant. Immediately and abruptly his mood changed, as if the light had suddenly gone out of his life. Shamed and humiliated, rejected as an unattractive, obnoxious, perhaps downright odious man shunned by one and all, he left the house.

'I would give anything.' On his way home in the heat, remembering the details of his declaration, he mocked himself. ' "Give anything"— what tradesman's talk. A lot of use your *anything* is!'

All he had just said seemed revoltingly stupid. Why had he told that lie about growing up in a family where everyone worked 'without exception'? Why had he spoken in that hectoring tone about a 'decent, happy life'? It wasn't clever or interesting, it was just eyewash, typical Moscow affectation. But then he gradually sank into the apathy of the criminal who has received a harsh sentence. Thank God it was all over and there was no more of that appalling uncertainty, he thought. No longer need he spend day after day waiting, suffering, obsessed with the one thing. Now all was clear. He must jettison every hope of personal happiness and live without desires, hopes, longings, expectations. To dispel the misery and boredom which he could no longer be bothered with, he might concern himself with other people's doings and happiness. Old age would arrive unnoticed. Life would end. That would be that. He didn't care, he wanted nothing, he could reason coolly, but his face felt somehow heavy, especially under the eyes. His forehead was taut like stretched elastic, tears seemed ready to spurt. Feeling weak all over, he went to bed. Five minutes later he was fast asleep.

III

Laptev's so unexpected proposal had plunged Julia into despair.

She didn't know him well, they had met accidentally. He was rich, he was a partner in the well-known Moscow firm Theodore Laptev and Sons, he was always very serious, he was obviously intelligent, and he was concerned about his sister's illness. He had seemed not to notice her at all, and she had been quite indifferent to him. But then there had been that declaration on the staircase, this pathetic, ecstatic face.

His proposal had upset her because it was so sudden, because the word *wife* was used, because she had had to refuse him. What she had said to Laptev she no longer remembered, but she still felt vestiges of the impulsive, disagreeable emotion with which she had turned him down. She didn't like him. He looked like a shop assistant, he was unattractive, she could only say no. Yet she still felt awkward, as if she had behaved badly.

'My God, without even going into the flat, right there on the staircase,' she said in despair, facing the icon above her bed-head. 'And he never showed any interest in me before. It's all so odd, so strange——'

In her loneliness she grew hourly more disquieted, unable to endure this oppressive sensation on her own. Someone must listen to her, tell her she had done the right thing. But there was no one to talk to. She had long ago lost her mother, she thought her father a crank and couldn't talk to him seriously. He embarrassed her with his caprices, his extraordinary touchiness, his vague gestures. Start a conversation with him and he at once began talking about himself. Even in her prayers she was not completely frank because she was unsure just what she should ask God for.

The samovar was brought in. Very pale, tired, looking helpless, Julia came into the dining-room, made tea—her responsibility—and poured her father a glass. The doctor wore that long frock-coat which reached below his knees. Red-faced, unkempt, hands in pockets, he paced the dining-room, not going from one corner to another but in random fashion like a caged beast. He would stop by the table, drink from his glass with relish, then stalk about again deep in thought.

'Laptev proposed to me this morning.' Julia blushed.

The doctor looked at her and seemed not to understand. 'What Laptev? Nina Panaurov's brother?'

He loved his daughter. She would probably marry sooner or later and leave him, but he tried not to think about that. He was terrified of loneliness. Should he be left alone in this large house he would have a stroke—so he vaguely felt without liking to say so outright.

'Then I'm delighted.' He shrugged. 'My heartiest congratulations. What a perfect chance to abandon me, how very nice for you. Oh yes, I see your point of view. To live with an aged, sick, unhinged father— what an ordeal for a girl your age. I understand you very well indeed. If only I could conk out soon, if only the foul fiend would whisk me off, how pleased everyone would be. My heartiest congratulations.'

'I refused him.'

The doctor was relieved, but had lost all self-control. 'I'm amazed. I've long wondered why I've never been put in a mad-house. Why do I wear this frock-coat and not a strait-jacket? I still believe in justice, in goodness, I'm wildly idealistic—surely that's insanity in our age! And what response do I get for being fair, for taking the decent line? I'm practically stoned in the street, I'm a general dogsbody. Even my nearest and dearest walk all over me, damn me, I'm just an old imbecile——'

'It's impossible to talk to you,' Julia said.

She abruptly stood up from the table and went to her room— furious, remembering how often her father was unfair to her. But she soon felt sorry for him, and when he left for his club she went downstairs with him and closed the door after him. The weather was disquietingly foul, the door shuddered from the wind's pressure, and in the hall there were draughts from all sides so that her candle nearly went out. Julia went all round her upstairs flat, making the sign of the cross over all windows and doors. The wind howled, someone seemed to be marching about on the roof. She had never known such depression, never felt so lonely.

She wondered whether she had been right to refuse a man solely because she did not like his looks. True, she did not love him, and marrying him would put paid to her dreams, her ideas of happiness in marriage. But would she ever meet and love the man of her dreams? She was already twenty-one. There were no eligible young men in town. She thought of all the men she knew—civil servants, school-teachers, officers. Some were married already, and their family life was palpably empty and dreary. Others were unattractive, colourless, stupid, immoral. Now, say what you like about Laptev, he *was* a Muscovite. He had been to college, he spoke French. He lived in Moscow, where there were so many intelligent, decent, distinguished people, where things were pretty lively, what with all the splendid theatres, the musical evenings, the excellent dressmakers, the cafés.

The Bible says that a wife must love her husband, and novels attach great importance to love. But couldn't that be a bit overstated? Is family life really impossible without love? They do say that love soon passes, don't they? That it just becomes a habit, that the goal of family life isn't love and happiness, but duty—bringing up children, housekeeping and so on. Anyway, perhaps the Bible views loving a husband as 'loving one's neighbour'—being respectful and considerate, that is.

That night Julia said her evening prayers attentively. Then she knelt down, clasped her hands to her breast, looked at the burning icon-lamp and prayed fervently that the Lord and Our Lady should 'lighten my darkness'.

She had met old maids in her time, wretched nobodies haunted by bitter regrets at having once turned down their suitors. Might that happen to her? Shouldn't she enter a convent, become a nurse?

She undressed and went to bed, crossing herself and making the sign of the cross in the air around her. Suddenly a bell rang sharply and poignantly in the corridor.

'Dear God!' The sound exasperated, utterly sickened her. She lay and thought about provincial life—so uneventful and monotonous, yet so disquieting. Every now and then it made you shudder, it made you apprehensive, angry, guilt-ridden, and in the end your nerves were so frayed that you were scared to peep out from under your quilt.

Half an hour later the bell rang again no less harshly. The servants must have been asleep and not heard it. Julia lit a candle and began dressing—shivering, annoyed with them. When she had dressed and gone into the corridor the maid was closing the downstairs door.

'I thought it was the master, but it was someone about a patient,' she said.

Julia returned to her room. She took a pack of cards from her chest-of-drawers, deciding to shuffle them thoroughly and cut them. If a red card showed up that would mean *yes*—she must accept Laptev's proposal. But if it was black she should say *no*. It was the ten of spades.

That calmed her and she went to sleep. But in the morning she was back with neither yes nor no. She could change her life now if she wanted to, she reflected. Her thoughts wearied her, she felt strained and ill. But soon after eleven o'clock she dressed and went to visit Nina. She wanted to see Laptev—perhaps he might look less unattractive now, perhaps she had been on the wrong tack.

Walking into the wind was difficult, and she could hardly make headway, holding her hat in both hands and seeing nothing for dust.

IV

Entering his sister's room and unexpectedly seeing Julia, Laptev again felt the humiliation of the suitor rebuffed. If, after yesterday, she could so casually visit his sister and meet him, she must find him beneath notice, a mere nonentity, he concluded. But when he greeted her and she—pallid, with dust beneath her eyes—looked at him sadly and guiltily, he saw that she too suffered.

She was feeling out of sorts, and stayed only a brief ten minutes before taking her departure.

'Please see me home, Mr. Laptev,' she asked as she was leaving.

They went down the road without speaking, holding their hats, while he walked behind and tried to shield her from the wind. In the side-road it was calmer and they walked together.

'Please forgive me if I was unkind yesterday.' Her voice quavered as if she was about to cry. 'I was so upset I didn't sleep all night.'

'Well, I slept very well all night.' Laptev did not look at her. 'But that doesn't mean I feel all right. My life's in ruins. I'm deeply unhappy and since you refused me yesterday I've felt as if I'd taken poison. The hardest thing was said yesterday. This morning I feel at ease with you, I can talk to you directly. I love you more than my sister, more than my dead mother. Without my sister and my mother I could and did live, but life without you—it has no meaning. I can't bear——'

As usual, he had divined her intentions. He saw that she wanted to continue yesterday's conversation, that this had been her sole purpose in asking him to escort her and in taking him to her house. But what could she add to her refusal? What new thought had occurred to her? Her glances, her smile, even the way she held her head and shoulders as she walked at his side—it all said that she still did not love him, that he was alien to her. So what was there for her to add?

The doctor was at home.

'Welcome, and delighted I am to see you, my dear Theodore,' said he, getting Laptev's name wrong. 'Delighted, delighted.'

He had never been so cordial before, and Laptev concluded that he knew of the proposal—a disagreeable thought, that. He was now seated in the drawing-room, where the miserable, vulgar appointments and dreadful pictures created an odd impression. There were armchairs and a huge lamp with a shade, but it still looked like a room not lived in, being more of a capacious barn. Only someone like the doctor could feel at home in this room, that was obvious. Another room almost twice as large was called 'the ballroom', and contained nothing but chairs, as if for a dancing class. Seated in the drawing-room, talking to the doctor about his sister, Laptev was nagged by a certain suspicion. Could Julia have called on Nina and then brought him here in order to announce her acceptance of his proposal? What an awful thought, but most awful of all was to have a mind open to such suspicions. He pictured father and daughter conferring at length during the previous evening and night. They might have had a long argument and concluded that Julia had behaved foolishly in refusing a rich man. His ears even rang with such words as parents speak on these occasions. 'It's true you don't love him, but think how much good you'll be able to do.'

The doctor prepared to go on his rounds. Laptev wanted to leave with him, but Julia asked if he would please stay behind.

Having suffered agonies of depression, she was now trying to convince herself that to refuse a decent, kindly man who loved her, solely because she found him unattractive, especially when this marriage offered her the chance to change her life, the unhappy, monotonous, idle life of one whose youth was passing and who could see no bright prospects for the future—to refuse him under these circumstances was insane, it was wanton self-indulgence, and God might even punish her for it.

Her father went out. When his steps had died away she suddenly stopped in front of Laptev and spoke decisively, turning terribly pale.

'I thought things over yesterday, Mr. Laptev, and I accept your proposal.'

He bent down and kissed her hand while she awkwardly kissed his head with cold lips. This amorous declaration lacked, he felt, something vital—her love—while containing much which was anything but vital. He felt like shouting aloud, running away, leaving for Moscow then and there. But she stood near him, seeming so lovely that passion suddenly seized him. Seeing that it was too late for further discussion, he embraced her ardently, clasped her to his chest and, muttering some words or other, spoke to her intimately, kissed her neck, cheek, head.

She retreated to the window, fearing these caresses, and both regretted their declarations, asking themselves in embarrassment why this had happened.

'I'm so unhappy, did you but know.' She wrung her hands.

'What's the matter?' He went towards her, also wringing his hands. 'For God's sake tell me, my dear. But only tell me the truth, I implore you, only the truth.'

'Pay no attention.' She forced herself to smile. 'I promise to be a faithful, devoted wife. Come and see me this evening.'

Sitting with his sister and reading the historical novel afterwards, he remembered all this, and was insulted that his splendid, pure, broad sentiments had evoked a response so trivial. He was unloved, but his proposal had been accepted—probably only because he was rich, so that preference had been given to that aspect of himself which he valued least of all. Julia, being pure and believing in God, had never thought of money—that could be conceded. Still, she didn't love him, did she? That she did not, and there had obviously been an element of calculation—confused and not fully deliberate, perhaps, but calculation for all that. The doctor's house repelled him with its vulgar appoint-ments, the doctor himself was like some miserable fat miser, a comic figure from an operetta, and the very name Julia now sounded plebeian. He imagined Julia and himself at the wedding ceremony—strangers to each other, essentially, and without a scrap of feeling on her side, as though this had been an arranged marriage. His only consolation now—one as banal as the marriage itself—was that he was neither the first nor the last, but that thousands of men and women had entered such marriages, and that Julia might come to love him in the end when she knew him better.

'Romeo and Julia.' He shut the book and laughed. 'I'm Romeo. You may congratulate me, Nina. I proposed to Julia Belavin today.'

After thinking that he was joking, Nina believed him and burst into tears. The news did not please her.

'All right, I congratulate you,' she said. 'But why does it have to be so sudden?'

'It isn't, it's been going on since March, only you never notice anything. I fell in love back in March when I met her here in your room.'

'And I thought you'd marry one of our Moscow friends,' said Nina after a pause. 'The girls from our own set are easier to get on with. But the great thing is for you to be happy, Alexis, that's what counts. Gregory never loved me, and you see how we live, there's no hiding it. Of course any woman might love you for your kindness and intelligence, but Julia went to an exclusive boarding school, didn't she? She's a lady, and intelligence and kind-heartedness won't get you far with her. She's young, Alexis, whereas you're neither young nor good-looking.'

To soften the last words, she stroked his cheek. 'You aren't good-looking, but you're a splendid fellow.'

She was so overcome that a slight flush appeared on her cheeks, and she enthusiastically discussed whether it would be proper for her to bless Alexis with an icon. She was his elder sister, after all, which made her a mother to him. And she kept trying to convince her gloomy brother that the wedding must be celebrated properly—solemnly and cheerfully so that no one should take it amiss.

As Julia's future husband he began visiting the Belavins three or four times a day, and was no longer free to take Sasha's place reading the historical novel. Julia would receive him away from the drawing-room and her father's study in her own two rooms which he liked very much. There were dark walls, there was an icon-case with its icons in a corner. There was a smell of good scent and lamp oil. She lived in the remotest part of the house, her bed and dressing-table were screened off, her bookcase doors were curtained inside in green, and she had carpets to walk on so that her steps were noiseless. All this persuaded him that she had a secretive character and liked a quiet, calm, enclosed life. Her status in the house was that of a child, she had no money of her own, and she was sometimes embarrassed during their walks because she had not a copeck on her. Her father would hand out a little cash for clothes and books, no more than a hundred roubles a year. The doctor himself hardly had any money anyway, despite his thriving practice, since he played cards at the club every evening and always lost. Besides, he was buying houses on mortgage through a mutual credit society, and renting them out. His tenants were irregular in paying their rent, but he called these housing operations highly profitable. He had mortgaged his own home, where he lived with his daughter. Having bought some derelict land with the money, he was already building a large two-storey house there so that he could mortgage that too.

Laptev was now living in a sort of haze, as though he wasn't himself but his own double, and he was doing much that he would not have ventured on before. He visited the club a couple of times with the doctor, had supper with him and offered him, unprompted, some money for his building. He even visited Panaurov in his second flat. One day Panaurov invited him to dinner, and Laptev accepted without thinking. He was welcomed by a lady of about thirty-five, tall and thin with some grey in her hair and black brows—obviously not Russian. There were white powder blotches on her face, she smiled a sickly smile, she pressed his hand impulsively, making the bracelets jingle on her white arm. Laptev felt that she used this smile to hide her unhappiness from others and from herself. He also saw two little girls, three and five years old, who resembled Sasha. The meal consisted of cream soup and cold veal with carrots, followed by chocolate. It was sickly-sweet and vaguely unpleasant, but there were gleaming gold forks on the table, pots of soy sauce and Cayenne pepper. There was a highly baroque gravy-boat and a golden pepper pot.

Only after the soup did Laptev realize how improper it was for him to dine here. The lady was embarrassed, smiling and showing her teeth all the time. Panaurov was expounding in scientific terms the meaning and origins of falling in love.

'We are confronted with a phenomenon in the electrical field.' He spoke in French, addressing the lady. 'Everyone's skin contains microscopic glands charged with current. Meet a person with currents parallel to your own and there you are—that's love.'

When Laptev was back home and his sister asked him where he had been he was embarrassed and made no reply.

Throughout the period before his marriage he felt in a false position. He loved Julia more and more each day. She seemed mysteriously sublime. Yet his love was unreturned and the plain fact was that he was buying her and she was selling herself. Sometimes, after much cogitation, he felt quite desperate and wondered whether to abandon it all. He was lying awake night after night and for ever imagining himself meeting the woman whom, in letters to his friend, he called 'a personage'—meeting her in Moscow after the wedding. And how would his father and brother, those awkward customers, react to his marriage and to Julia? He was afraid of his father saying something rude to her when they first met. And there was something odd about his brother Theodore of late. He wrote long letters about the importance of health, about the influence of illness on the psyche, about the nature of religion, but not a word about Moscow and busines

These letters irritated Laptev. His brother's character was deteriorating he thought.

The wedding was in September, and the ceremony took place after morning service at St. Peter and St. Paul's. Bride and groom left for Moscow that same day. When Laptev and his wife, in her black dress and train—no longer a girl in appearance, but a mature woman—said good-bye to Nina Panaurov the sick woman's whole face twisted, yet no tear flowed from her dry eyes.

'If I die, which God forbid, look after my little girls.'

'Yes, I promise,' Julia answered, her lips and eyelids also twitching nervously.

'I'll visit you in October.' Laptev was greatly moved. 'Get better, darling.'

They had the railway compartment to themselves. Both were sad and embarrassed. She sat in a corner without taking her hat off and pretended to be dozing, while he lay on the bunk opposite, perturbed by sundry thoughts—about his father, about the 'personage'. Would Julia like his Moscow flat? Looking at the wife who did not love him, he despondently wondered why it had all come about.

V

In Moscow the Laptevs had a wholesale haberdashery business dealing in fringes, ribbons, braid, knitting material, buttons and so on. The turnover was two million a year. As for the net profit, no one knew that except the old man. The sons and clerks reckoned it a cool three hundred thousand, saying that it would be a hundred thousand more if the old man hadn't 'dissipated his efforts' by allowing indiscriminate credit. In the last ten years they had collected nearly a million in worthless promissory notes, and when this topic cropped up the chief clerk would give a sly wink and use language which many found obscure.

'It's the psychological aftermath of our age.'

Their main business was done in the city's commercial district, in the building called the warehouse. It was approached from a yard sunk in gloom, smelling of matting. Dray-horse hooves battered the asphalt. The modest-looking door was iron-bound and led from the yard into a room where the walls, brown with damp, were bescribbled in charcoal. This was lit by a narrow iron-grilled window. Then there was another room on the left—larger, cleaner, with a cast-iron stove and two tables, but also with its prison-style window. This was the office, and from it a narrow stone stairway led to the first floor, the main centre of activity. It was a fairly large room, but being in permanent twilight, low-ceilinged and cluttered with crates, bales and scurrying people, it struck those new to it as no more prepossessing than the two lower ones. Up here, as also on the office shelves, were goods in stacks, bundles and cardboard boxes. There was no order or beauty in the arrangements, and had it not been for purple threads, tassles and bits of fringe peeping out of the paper-wrapped bundles here and there, no one could have divined at a glance what goods they dealt in. Looking at these rumpled paper-wrapped bundles and boxes, one could not believe that such trifles brought in millions, and that fifty persons, not counting buyers, were active in this warehouse every day.

When Laptev arrived at the warehouse at noon on the day after reaching Moscow, workmen were packing up goods and banging crates so loudly that no one in the first room or office heard him enter. A postman known to him came downstairs with a bundle of letters, frowning in the din, and he didn't notice Laptev either. First to greet him upstairs was his brother Theodore, who so closely resembled him that they were believed to be twins. This similarity regularly reminded Laptev of his own appearance. He now saw before him a short, red-cheeked man, thin on top, with narrow haunches of the lowest pedigree—so unprepossessing, so unprofessional-looking.

'Do I really look like that?' he wondered.

'And glad I am to see you.' Theodore exchanged kisses with his brother and firmly shook his hand. 'I've been so much looking forward every day to seeing you, my dear fellow. When you wrote that you were getting married I suffered agonies of curiosity. I have missed you, old man, as you can imagine—we haven't met for six months. Well, how are things, eh? How is Nina? Very bad?'

'Yes.'

'It's God's will,' sighed Theodore. 'And then your wife? I'll bet she's beautiful. I love her already—she's my dear little sister, isn't she? We'll both spoil her.'

Laptev glimpsed the long familiar, broad, bent back of his father, also a Theodore. The old man was sitting on a stool near the counter talking to a buyer.

'God has sent us great joy, Father,' shouted the younger Theodore. 'Alexis is here.'

Laptev Senior was tall and very powerfully built, so that he still looked a strong, healthy man for all his wrinkles and his eighty years. He spoke in a ponderous, deep, rumbling voice which came booming out of his broad chest as from a barrel. He shaved his chin, wore a clipped military moustache, smoked cigars. Never feeling the cold, he wore a roomy canvas jacket in the warehouse and at home, whatever the season. Having recently undergone a cataract operation, he had poor sight and no longer handled business, but just talked and drank tea with jam.

Laptev bent forward to kiss his father's hand and then his lips.

'It's a mighty long time since we met, sir,' said the old man. 'Aye, that it is. Now, you'll expect congratulations on your marriage, eh? Very well, then. Congratulations.'

He disposed his lips for a kiss, and Laptev bent forward to kiss him.

'And have you brought the young lady with you?' asked the old man. Then, without waiting for an answer, he addressed the buyer. '"I hereby inform you, Dad old man, that I'm marrying a Miss Such-and-Such." Aye. But as for asking our dear old Dad's blessing and advice, that's not our way. Oh, we do things our own way nowadays. Now, when I married I was over forty and I threw myself at my father's feet and asked his advice. There's none of that now.'

Glad to see his son, the old man thought it unseemly to show him affection or display pleasure. His voice, his style of speaking and that 'young lady' business put Laptev into the bad mood that the warehouse always did evoke. Every detail reminded him of the old days when he had been whipped and given bread and water to eat. That boys were still whipped and punched on the nose till they bled, that when these same boys grew up they would punch others in turn—of these things he was aware. And he had only to spend five minutes in the warehouse to expect to be shouted at or punched on the nose.

Theodore clapped the buyer on the shoulder and spoke to his brother. 'Let me present Gregory Timofeyevich, the old firm's main support in Tambov. What an example to today's young men! He's in his sixth decade but he has children who are no more than babies.'

The clerks laughed and the customer, an emaciated, pale-faced middle-aged man, laughed too.

''Tis flying in the face of nature,' remarked the chief clerk, standing behind the same counter. 'Things come out the way they go in.'

The chief clerk, a tall, dark-bearded, bespectacled man of about fifty with a pencil behind his ear, usually expressed his thoughts obscurely, in distant hints, his sly smile indicating that he attached some special,

subtle meaning to his words. He liked to obfuscate his speech with
bookish expressions which he understood in his own way, and he often
gave ordinary words a sense different from their true meaning—for
example, the word 'otherwise'. When stating an idea dogmatically and
not wanting to be contradicted, he would hold out his right hand
before him and give tongue.

'Otherwise!'

Oddest thing of all, the other clerks and the buyers understood him
very well. His name was Ivan Pochatkin and he came from Kashira.
Congratulating Laptev, he expressed himself as follows.

'Highly meritorious and courageous of you, for bold and proud is
woman's heart.'

Another warehouse notability was the clerk Makeichev—a stout,
fair-haired worthy with receding hair and side-whiskers. He came up
and congratulated Laptev respectfully in a low voice.

'I have the honour, sir. The Lord has hearkened to the prayers of
your good father, sir. The Lord be praised, sir.'

Then other clerks came up to congratulate him on his marriage—all
fashionably turned out, all with the air of utterly decent, educated men.
From their speech they were northerners, and since their every other
word was 'sir', their swiftly delivered congratulations whistled through
the air like so many whiplashes. 'Sir, here's wishing you every blessing,
sir.'

Laptev was soon bored with it all, and felt like going home, but it
was awkward to leave, for propriety dictated that he spend at least two
hours at the warehouse. Stepping aside from the counter, he asked
Makeichev whether they had had a successful summer, and whether
there was any news, and the man answered respectfully without looking
Laptev in the eye. A boy with close-cropped hair, wearing a grey shirt,
gave Laptev a glass of tea without a saucer. A little later another boy
knocked into a crate as he was passing, nearly falling over, and the
sedate Makeichev suddenly adopted a fearful, vicious, ogre-like look.

'You watch your step!' he yelled.

The clerks were glad that the young master had married and was
back again at last. They gave him inquisitive, friendly glances, each
feeling obliged as he passed to make some agreeable and respectful
remark. But Laptev was sure it was all false, that they flattered him
from fear. He could not forget one mentally ill clerk. Fifteen years ago
the man had run into the street in his underclothes, bare-footed, shaking
his fist at the boss's windows and shouting that they had made his life

hell. Long after the poor fellow had been cured people had teased him, reminding him how he had called the bosses 'brutoclats' instead of 'plutocrats'. The Laptev employees had a bad time of it on the whole —such had long been the talk of the entire commercial district. The worst thing was that old Mr. Laptev handled them with oriental duplicity. Thus no one knew what salary his favourites Pochatkin and Makeichev received—it was no more than three thousand a year each with bonuses, actually, but he pretended to pay them seven. Bonuses were paid to all the clerks each year, but secretly, so that those who got little were compelled by pride to say they'd had a lot. None of the office boys knew when he would be promoted to clerk, no employee knew whether the boss was satisfied with him or not. Nothing was directly forbidden to the clerks, and so they had no idea what was permissible and what was not. Though not actually forbidden to marry, they did not do so, fearing to displease the boss and lose their jobs. They could have friends, they could pay visits, but at nine in the evening the gate was locked. Every morning the boss suspiciously scrutinized all his employees, testing them to see if they smelt of vodka. 'Hey, let me smell your breath.'

Every saint's day employees had to attend early service and stand in church where the boss could see them all. The fasts were strictly kept. On special days, on the boss's and his family's name-days, for instance, the clerks had to subscribe for a cake from Fley's or an album. They lived on the ground floor of the house in Pyatnitsky Road and in an outbuilding, three and four to a room. They ate their meals from a common bowl, though each had his own plate before him. If any of the boss's family came in at mealtimes they all stood up.

Only those ruined by the old man's schooling could seriously regard him as their benefactor, Laptev realized. To the rest he was an enemy and a 'brutoclat'. Now, after six months' absence, he saw no improvements, and one innovation even boded ill. His brother Theodore— previously quiet, thoughtful, very sensitive—now had a great air of bustle and efficiency. Pencil behind ear, he scuttled round the warehouse clapping buyers on the shoulder and hailing the clerks as his 'old pals'. He was playing some part, obviously, a part in which Alexis found him unrecognizable.

The old man's voice rumbled on and on. Having nothing to do, he was instructing a buyer in the art of living and managing his affairs, and constantly invoked himself as a model. This boasting, this crushingly authoritative tone—Laptev had heard it ten, fifteen, twenty years ago. The old man adored himself. From his words it always transpired that he had made his deceased wife and relatives happy, bestowed advantages on his children, lavished benefactions on his clerks and employees, put the entire street and his whole acquaintanceship eternally in his debt. Whatever he did was excellent, and if others' dealings went awry, that was only because they wouldn't take his advice, without which no enterprise could succeed. In church he always stood in front of the rest of the congregation and even reprimanded the priests when he considered their performance of the ritual incorrect. All this he thought pleasing to God, since God loved him.

By two o'clock everyone in the building was at work except the old man, who was still booming away. Not wanting to be idle, Laptev took some braid from a female employee, dismissed her, and then listened to a buyer—a Vologda trader—and told a clerk to deal with him.

Since the prices and serial numbers of goods were denoted by letters, cries of 'T–V–A' or 'R–I–T' could be heard.

On his way out Laptev said good-bye to Theodore alone. 'I'll bring my wife to Pyatnitsky Road tomorrow. But I warn you I shan't stay a minute if Father says one rude word to her.'

'You're just the same as ever,' sighed Theodore. 'Marriage hasn't changed you. You must be nice to the old man, lad. All right, be there by eleven tomorrow. We'll look forward to it, you can come straight from church.'

'I don't go to church.'

'Then never mind. Just don't be later than eleven so as to leave time to worship the Lord before lunch. My regards to my dear sister-in-law, kiss her hand for me. I'm sure I shall like her,' Theodore added with an air of complete sincerity.

'How I envy you, old man,' he shouted when Alexis was already on his way downstairs.

Oh, why did the man cringe so humbly, as if he felt naked? Walking down Nikolsky Road, Laptev puzzled over the change in Theodore. Then there was this new style of speaking—this 'old man', 'dear brother', 'God's mercy', 'worship the Lord' stuff. What sickening humbug!

VI

At eleven next day, a Sunday, Laptev was driving down Pyatnitsky Road with his wife in a one-horse trap. Fearing some outburst by his father, he felt ill at ease before he had even arrived. After two nights in her husband's house Julia thought her marriage a disastrous mistake. Had life with him taken her to any town but Moscow she did not think she could have endured such a horror. Moscow amused her, though. The streets, houses, churches delighted her. Could she have driven about Moscow in this splendid sledge pulled by expensive horses— driven all day from morning to evening, careering at full tilt and breathing the cool autumn air—then perhaps she would have felt less miserable.

Near a white, newly plastered two-storey house the coachman halted the horse and turned right. Here they were awaited. At the gate stood the doorkeeper in a new caftan, high boots and galoshes, and two police constables. The whole area, from the middle of the street to the gate and down the yard to the porch, had been strewn with fresh sand. The doorman doffed his cap, the constables saluted. At the porch brother Theodore greeted them with an earnest air.

'So pleased to meet you, sister.' He kissed Julia's hand. 'Welcome.'

He led her upstairs by the arm, and then down a corridor through a group of men and women. Then came a vestibule, also crowded and smelling of incense.

'I shall now present you to our Dad,' whispered Theodore amid the solemn, tomb-like silence. 'A venerable old gent, the pater.'

In a large hall, by a table prepared for divine service, stood in evident anticipation old Mr. Laptev, a priest in his high purple hat, and a deacon. The old man gave his hand to Julia without a word. No one spoke. Julia was embarrassed.

The priest and deacon put on their vestments. A censer, scattering sparks and smelling of incense and charcoal, was brought. Candles were lit. Clerks tiptoed into the hall and stood by the wall in two ranks. It was quiet, no one even coughed.

'Bless us, O Lord,' began the deacon.

They celebrated the service solemnly, omitting nothing and intoning the prayers 'Sweetest Jesus' and 'Holy Mother of God'. The choir sang only from sheet music, and took its time about it. Laptev had noted how embarrassed his wife had been just now. While the prayers were read and the choristers were delivering their diversely harmonized triple 'Lord Have Mercy', he agonizingly expected the old man to look round at any moment and utter some reprimand like 'don't you know how to make the sign of the cross?' He was annoyed. Why all these people? Why this ceremony, these clergymen, this choir? Here was your old-fashioned Russian merchant style with a vengeance. But when Julia and the old man together allowed the Gospel to be laid on their heads, and when she several times genuflected, he saw that she liked all this and was relieved.

At the end of the service, during the anthem 'Long Life', the priest gave the old man and Alexis the cross to kiss, but when Julia came up he covered the cross with his hand and looked as if he wanted to speak. They waved to the choir to be quiet.

'The prophet Samuel came to Bethlehem at the Lord's command,' said the priest. 'And elders of the town besought him, trembling. "Comest thou peaceably, O prophet?" And the prophet said, "Peaceably: I am come to make sacrifice unto the Lord: sanctify yourselves, and rejoice this day with me." Shall we too question thee, O servant of the Lord Julia, whether thou dost come in peace unto this house?'

Deeply moved, Julia blushed. When he had finished, the priest gave her the cross to kiss and spoke in quite a different voice.

'Now it's time young Mr. Theodore was married, high time.'

The choir sang again, the congregation stirred, there was noise and bustle. Greatly touched, eyes brimming with tears, the old man kissed Julia three times and made the sign of the cross in front of her face.

'My house is yours,' he said. 'I'm old, I need nothing.'

The clerks offered congratulations and said something, but the choir was singing so loudly that nothing could be heard. Then they had lunch and drank champagne. She sat by the old man while he told her that it was wrong to live asunder, and right to live together in one house. Divisions and disagreements led to ruin.

'I made money, my children only spend it,' he said. 'Now, you must live in the same house with me and make money. I'm old, it's time I had a rest.'

Julia kept catching sight of Theodore. He looked so like her husband, but was more restless in his movements, more diffident. He fussed about near her and kept kissing her hand.

'We're just ordinary folk, sister dear.' Red blotches appeared on his face. 'We lead ordinary Russian, Christian lives, dear sister.'

On the way home Laptev was delighted that all had gone well, and that nothing untoward had occurred as he had feared.

'You wonder that a hefty, broad-shouldered father should have such small, narrow-chested children as me and Theodore,' he told his wife. 'Well, that's no problem. My father married my mother when he was forty-five and she was only seventeen. She would go white and tremble in his presence. Nina was born first, when Mother was comparatively healthy, so she turned out stronger and better than us. But Theodore and I were begotten and born when my mother was already worn out by a reign of terror. I remember that Father began teaching or, to put it bluntly, beating me before I was five. He birched me, boxed my ears, clouted my head, and when I woke up each morning my main worry was whether I'd be beaten that day. Theodore and I were forbidden to play and lark about. We had to attend matins and morning service, kiss the hands of priests and monks, recite the prescribed prayers at home. You're religious, you like all this, but I fear religion, and when I pass a church I remember my childhood and feel scared. When I was eight they took me on at the warehouse. I was an ordinary office boy, which was hard for me because I was beaten almost daily. Then, after I'd started school, I'd do my homework before dinner, and from then until night I'd be cooped up in the same old warehouse. So it went on till I was twenty-two and met Yartsev at the university. He persuaded me to leave my father's house. Yartsev has done me a lot of good. I tell you what.' Laptev laughed gleefully. 'Let's go and see Yartsev. He's a very fine man, and he'll be so touched.'

VII

On a Saturday in November Anton Rubinstein was conducting at the Conservatoire. The place was packed, and it was hot. Laptev stood behind some columns while his wife and Kostya Kochevoy sat far away in front, in the third or fourth row. When the interval began the 'certain personage'—Polina Rassudin—unexpectedly came by. Since marrying, he had often been worried by the thought of a possible meeting with her. As she glanced at him, frankly and openly, he remembered that he hadn't even got around to offering her any explanation or writing her a couple of friendly lines. It was as if he was hiding from her. He felt ashamed, he blushed. She shook his hand firmly and impulsively, and asked whether he had seen Yartsev.

Not waiting for his reply, she swept on with long strides as if impelled from behind.

She was very thin, ugly, long-nosed, she always looked utterly exhausted, as if it cost her enormous effort to keep her eyes open and not fall over. She had lovely dark eyes and a clever, kind, unaffected expression, but her movements were jerky and harsh. She was hard to talk to because she could not listen or speak calmly. And loving her had been an ordeal. When staying with Laptev she would sometimes go off in long, loud peals of laughter, hiding her face in her hands and claiming that love was not the basis of her existence. She was as coy as a maid of seventeen, and one had to put out all the candles before kissing her. She was thirty and had married a schoolmaster, but had not lived with her husband for many years. She made her living by teaching music and playing in quartets.

During the Ninth Symphony she again passed by, as if by accident, but a packed group of men standing behind the columns held her up, and she paused. Laptev noticed that she wore the same velvet bodice in which she had attended last year's concerts and those of the year before. Her gloves were new. So was her fan, but cheap. She would have liked to dress well but, lacking the knack and grudging the expense, rigged herself out so tastelessly and sloppily that she could easily have been mistaken for a young monk when striding swiftly down the street on her way to a lesson.

The audience applauded, there were shouts of encore.

Polina went up to Laptev, looked him sternly over. 'You are to spend this evening with me. We're going to have tea together when this is over, do you hear? I insist on it. You owe me a lot, and you have no moral right to deny me this trifle.'

Laptev agreed. 'All right then.'

The symphony evoked endless encores. The audience stood up and left very slowly. Since Laptev could not go without a word to his wife he had to wait by the door.

'I'm dying for some tea,' Polina Rassudin complained. 'I'm all parched inside.'

'We can get some here,' said Laptev. 'Come to the bar.'

'No, I've no money to waste on barmen. *I'm* not a tradesman's wife.'

He offered her his arm but she refused, pronouncing a long wearisome sentence which he had often heard from her, to the effect that she did not classify herself as one of the 'weaker' or 'fair' sex, and did not require the services of any male persons, thank you very much.

While talking to him she kept glancing at the audience, often greeting friends. These were fellow-alumnae of Guerrier's courses and the Conservatoire, and also her pupils, male and female. She shook hands firmly and impulsively with a sort of jerkiness. But then she began twisting her shoulders and trembling like a fever victim. In the end she spoke quietly, looking at Laptev with horror.

'What kind of wife have you married? Where were your eyes, maniac? Whatever did you see in that silly, insignificant little bitch? I loved you for your mind, for what you really are, didn't I? Whereas that little china doll only wants your money.'

'Let's forget that, Polina,' he begged. 'Anything you could say about my marriage I've told myself umpteen times already. Don't hurt me more than necessary.'

Julia appeared wearing a black dress and the large diamond brooch which her father-in-law had sent her after that prayer service. She was followed by her suite—Kochevoy, two doctors of her acquaintance, an officer and one Kish—a stout young man in student uniform.

'You go with Kostya, I'll come on afterwards,' Laptev told his wife.

Julia nodded and went off. Trembling all over and cringing nervously, Polina pursued her with a look of revulsion, hatred and pain.

Laptev feared to go to her room, foreseeing some disagreeable confrontation, with harsh words and tears. He suggested tea in a restaurant. But 'No, no, no', she said. 'Come to my place. Don't you restaurant me.'

She disliked restaurants because their air seemed poisoned with tobacco and male breath. She was oddly biased against strange men. To her they were all debauchees capable of leaping upon her at any moment. Besides, tavern music irritated her, gave her headaches.

Leaving the Gentry Club, they took a cab to Ostozhenka Road and Savelovsky Street where Polina lived. On the way there Laptev thought about her. He really did owe her a great deal. Laptev had first met her at his friend Yartsev's when she had been teaching him musical theory. She had fallen very much in love with him, with no thought of personal advantage. After becoming his mistress, she had gone on giving her lessons and working until she collapsed. Thanks to her he had begun to understand and love music, which had barely interested him before.

'Half my kingdom for a glass of tea,' she said hollowly, covering her mouth with her muff to avoid catching cold. 'Five lessons I've just given, blast it. My pupils are such dolts and dunderheads, I nearly died of rage. When this hell will end I don't know. I'm dead beat. When I've saved three hundred roubles I shall give it all up, go to the Crimea, lie on the beach and gulp oxygen. How I love, love, love the sea.'

'You won't go anywhere,' said Laptev. 'First, you won't save anything. And secondly, you're too mean. I'm sorry, but I'll ask you again—is it really less humiliating to amass your three hundred roubles copeck by copeck from idlers who study music with you because they have nothing else to do, than to borrow it from your friends?'

'I have no friends.' She was annoyed. 'So I must ask you not to talk nonsense. The working class, to which I belong, has one privilege—the consciousness of being incorruptible, together with the right to despise shopkeepers and not to borrow from them. No sir, I am not for sale. I'm not one of your Julias!'

Laptev did not pay the cabman, knowing that this would unleash a spate of all-too-familiar words. She paid herself.

She rented a small furnished room with board in a single lady's flat. Her Becker grand piano was at Yartsev's house on Great Nikitsky Road for the time being, and she went there every day to play. Her room contained armchairs in covers, a bed with a white summer quilt, flowers provided by the landlady. There were oleographs on the walls, and there was nothing to remind one that the tenant was a woman and a graduate. There was no dressing-table, there were no books, there was not even a desk. It was obvious that she always went straight to bed on arriving home, and that she left the house at once after getting up in the morning.

The cook brought the samovar, and Polina made tea. Still trembling, for it was cold in her room, she began criticizing the choir which had sung in the Ninth Symphony. Closing her eyes through excess of emotion, she drank one glass of tea, then another, then a third.

'So you're married,' she said. 'But don't worry, I shan't mope. I shall contrive to wrench you out of my heart. I'm just annoyed and upset to find you as worthless as everyone else, not wanting a woman's intellect and brains, but her body, her beauty, her youth. Youth, youth!' She spoke through her nose, as if mimicking someone, and laughed. 'You need purity, *Reinheit*.' She laughed aloud, lolling against the back of her chair. '*Reinheit*, I ask you!'

When she had finished laughing her eyes were full of tears. 'Are you at last happy?'

'No.'

'Does she love you?'

'No.'

Agitated, feeling miserable, Laptev got up and paced the room.

'No,' he repeated. 'I'm very unhappy, Polina, since you must know. But what can I do? I've done something foolish, but it can't be mended now. I must be philosophical. She married me without love, stupidly perhaps. She did marry me for money, yes, but without really thinking what she was doing. Now she obviously realizes she was wrong. She suffers, I can see that. We sleep together at night, but she's afraid to be alone with me for five minutes in daytime. She seeks entertainment, a social life. She's ashamed to be with me. Scared too.'

'But she still takes your money, doesn't she?'

'Don't be silly, Polina,' shouted Laptev. 'She takes my money because she simply doesn't care whether she has money or not. She's a decent, honourable woman. She just married me because she wanted to leave her father, that's all.'

'But are you sure she'd have married you if you hadn't been rich?' Polina asked.

'I'm not sure of anything at all,' said the agonized Laptev. 'I can't make sense of anything. For God's sake, let's stop talking about it, Polina.'

'Do you love her?'

'Madly.'

Silence ensued. She drank a fourth glass while he paced about, and reflected that his wife was probably having supper at the Doctors' Club at this moment.

'But can one really love without knowing why?' Polina asked with a shrug. 'No, that's just the voice of animal passion. You're intoxicated— poisoned by that beautiful body, all that *Reinheit*. Leave me, you're dirty. Go to your woman.'

She dismissed him with a gesture, took his hat, threw it at him. He put on his fur coat silently and went out, but she ran into the hall, frantically clutched his upper arm and burst into sobs.

'Stop it, Polina, do.' He could not unclench her fingers. 'Please calm yourself.'

She closed her eyes, she grew pale, her long nose turned an un-pleasant, waxen, corpse-like colour, and Laptev still could not un-clench her fingers. She had fainted. He carefully lifted her, laid her on her bed, sat by her for ten minutes until she came round. Her hands were cold, her pulse was weak and irregular.

She opened her eyes. 'Do go home, please, or I'll start howling again. I must pull myself together.'

After leaving her he did not go to the Doctors' Club, where he was expected, but went home. All the way there he asked himself re-proachfully why he had set up house with someone else instead of this woman who so loved him, this true wife and friend. She was the only person who was attached to him. And in any case it would surely have been a rewarding, worthwhile undertaking—to provide this intelligent, proud, toil-worn creature with happiness, with a peaceful haven.

'Are they really my style?' he asked himself of these hankerings after beauty, youth and that unattainable bliss which, by keeping him so miserably depressed for three months, seemed to punish or mock him.

The honeymoon had long been over, but he was still absurdly ignorant of his wife's true nature. She sent her old school-friends and father long letters on five sides of paper, and so she must find things to write about. But what did she speak to *him* of? The weather, that it was lunch time or supper time. When she said her long prayers before going to bed, and then kissed her wretched crosses and icons, he looked at her with hatred.

'She prays,' he reflected, 'but what, what does she pray about?' He insulted both of them, as he went to bed with her and took her in his arms, by telling himself that this was what he was paying for, and a revolting thought it was. He wouldn't have minded if she had been a lusty, bold, bad sort of woman, but there was all this youth, religious feeling, tenderness. There were those pure, innocent eyes.

During their engagement her devotions had touched him, but now the very conventional and explicit nature of her views and convictions seemed a barrier between him and the real truth. Everything in his domestic life was torture to him now. When his wife sighed or laughed unaffectedly as they sat together in the theatre, he was hurt that she should enjoy herself on her own, without sharing her pleasure with him. And she had hit it off with all his friends, oddly enough. *They* all knew what she was like, while he had no idea. He just sulked, said nothing. He was jealous.

Reaching home, Laptev donned dressing-gown and slippers, sat in his study and read a novel. His wife was out, but within half an hour the bell in the hall rang, followed by the hollow thud of Peter's steps as he ran to answer it. It was Julia. She came into the study in her fur coat, cheeks red with cold.

'There's a large fire at Presnya,' she gasped. 'There's a huge glow. I'm going there with Kostya Kochevoy.'

'Then good luck to you.'

Seeing her health, her freshness, the childlike panic in her eyes, Laptev calmed down. He read for another half hour and went to bed.

On the next day Polina sent two books once borrowed from him to the warehouse together with all his letters, his photographs and a note consisting of the one word *basta*.

VIII

At the end of October Nina had an unmistakable relapse. She was losing weight rapidly, her face was changing. Despite the agonizing pain she thought that she was recovering, put on her clothes every morning as if she was well—and then lay in bed all day fully dressed. By the end she had become downright garrulous. She would lie on her back and talk quietly away, panting with the effort. Her death came suddenly and these were its circumstances.

It was a clear, moonlit night and there was sleighing on the newly fallen snow in the street, the noise being borne into the room from outside. Nina lay on her back. Sasha, the only person to sit with her now, sat dozing by her side.

'I don't remember his second name,' said Nina quietly. 'But they called him Ivan. The surname was Kochevoy. He was a poor clerk and the most awful drunkard, may he rest in peace. He visited us, and we'd give him a pound of sugar and a small packet of tea every month. And sometimes money, of course. Ah, well. Now, here's what happened next. Our Kochevoy embarked on the most almighty bender and snuffed it—went out like a light. He left a son, a little boy of seven, a poor little orphan. We took him in and hid him in the clerks' quarters, where he survived for twelve months after a fashion, without Father knowing. When Father did see him he just dismissed him with a gesture and said nothing. When the little orphan was eight I tried to get him into a high school—this was when I was engaged to be married. I took him here, I took him there, but they wouldn't have him anywhere. He kept crying. "Why cry, you silly boy?" I asked. Then I took him to the Second High School on Razgulyay Square, where they accepted him, God bless them. The little lad would walk from Pyatnitsky Road to the Square and back every day. Alexis paid the fees. The boy was good at his lessons, he had a feel for them and he's turned out all right, praise be. Now he's a lawyer in Moscow, he's Alexis's friend, and they're each as brainy as the other. There's someone we didn't despise, we took him in, and now he mentions us in his prayers, sure enough. Ah, well——'

Nina spoke more and more quietly, with long pauses. After one brief silence she suddenly raised herself and sat up.

'I, er, I don't feel so grand,' she said. 'Oh mercy, I can't breathe.'

Sasha knew that her mother must die soon, and seeing the sudden pinched look on her face, she guessed that the end had come and took fright.

'No, Mother, no,' she sobbed. 'You mustn't.'

'Run into the kitchen, tell them to send for your father. I really do feel awful.'

Sasha ran through the whole house calling, but no servants were in. There was only Leda asleep on a chest in the dining-room—fully dressed, with no pillow. Just as she was, without galoshes, Sasha ran into the yard and then into the street. On a bench outside the gate sat her nanny watching the sleigh-riding. From the river, where there was a skating rink, a brass band could be heard.

'Mother's dying, Nanny,' Sasha sobbed. 'We must fetch Father.'

Nanny went up to the bedroom, looked at the patient, placed a lighted wax candle in her hand. Sasha was appalled and dashed about imploring someone, anyone, to fetch her father. Then she put her coat and kerchief on, and ran into the street. She knew from the servants that her father had another wife and two little girls with whom he lived in Market Street. From the gate she ran to the left, weeping, afraid of the strange people, and was soon getting stuck in the snow and shivering.

A free cab approached her, but she did not take it—perhaps the man would drive her out of town, rob her and throw her into the grave-yard. (There had been such an incident, the servants had spoken of it at tea.) She walked and walked—out of breath, weary, weeping. Emerging in Market Street, she asked where Mr. Panaurov lived. Some unknown woman gave her a long explanation and then, seeing that she wasn't taking it in, led her by the hand to a one-storey house with a porch. The door was not locked. Running through the hall and down the corridor, Sasha at last found herself in a light, warm room where her father sat over a samovar, and with him a lady and two little girls. By now Sasha could not get out a single word, she only sobbed. Panaurov understood.

'Mother's unwell, isn't she?' he asked. 'Tell me, dear, is Mother unwell?'

He was alarmed and sent for a cab.

When they arrived home Nina sat supported by pillows, candle in hand. Her face looked dark, her eyes were shut. In the bedroom, bunched near the door, were Nanny, cook, the chambermaid, the peasant Prokofy and others of the servant class—strangers. Nanny was whispering orders which were not understood. Pale and sleepy, Leda stood at the far end of the room by the window sternly surveying her mother.

Panaurov took the candle from Nina's hands and tossed it behind the chest-of-drawers, frowning with disgust.

'This is terrible.' His shoulders trembled. 'You must lie down, Nina,' he said kindly. 'Do lie down, dear.'

She looked at him without recognizing him. They laid her down.

When the priest and Dr. Belavin arrived the servants were piously crossing themselves and praying for her.

'What a to-do.' The doctor pensively emerged into the drawing-room. 'And so young, you know—not yet forty.'

The little girls' loud sobs were heard. Pale, with wet eyes, Panaurov went up to the doctor.

'Do me a favour and send a telegram to Moscow,' he said in a feeble, suffering voice. 'I'm just not up to it, old son.'

The doctor obtained ink and wrote the following telegram to his daughter.

NINA DIED EIGHT PM TELL HUSBAND HOUSE ON DVOR-
YANSKY STREET IS FOR SALE WITH TRANSFERABLE MORTGAGE
NINE THOUSAND TO PAY AUCTION IS ON THE TWELFTH
ADVISE YOU NOT TO MISS CHANCE

IX

Laptev lived in a side-street off Little Dmitrovka Street, not far from Old St. Pimen's Church. Besides a large house facing the street he also rented a two-storey cottage on the premises for his friend Kochevoy, a junior barrister known to all the Laptevs by the familiar name 'Kostya' because they had watched him grow up. Opposite that cottage stood another, also two-storeyed, occupied by a French family —husband, wife, five daughters.

It was twenty degrees below, and the windows were frosted up. When he awoke in the morning, Kostya swallowed fifteen drops of medicine with a worried air, then took two dumb-bells from his bookcase and did his exercises. He was tall, very thin, with large, reddish whiskers. But his most remarkable features were his extra-ordinarily long legs.

Peter, a middle-aged odd-job man in a jacket, his cotton trousers tucked into jack-boots, brought in the samovar and made tea.

'It's mighty fine weather today, Mr. Kochevoy,' he said.

'Fine it is. But you and I aren't managing too brilliantly, old son.' Peter sighed from politeness.

'What are the children doing?' asked Kochevoy.

'The priest ain't here yet. Mr. Laptev's teaching 'em himself, like.'

Kostya found an ice-free part of the window and looked out through binoculars. He pointed them at the French family's windows, but said that he couldn't see anything.

Meanwhile Laptev was giving Sasha and Leda a scripture lesson downstairs. They had now been living in Moscow for six weeks with their governess, on the ground floor of the cottage. A priest and a municipal schoolmaster came and taught them three times a week. Sasha was on the New Testament, Leda had just started the Old. Last time Leda had been told to revise everything up to Abraham.

'So Adam and Eve had two sons,' said Laptev. 'Very good, but what were their names? Try and remember.'

Leda, stern as ever, said nothing, staring at the table and just moving her lips while her elder sister Sasha looked at her face and suffered agonies.

'You know it all right—just don't be nervous,' said Laptev. 'Now then, who were Adam and Eve's sons?'

'Able and Cable,' whispered Leda.

'Cain and Abel,' corrected Laptev.

A large tear crawled down Leda's cheek and fell on the book. Sasha lowered her eyes and blushed, also ready to weep. Laptev felt so sorry for them that he was speechless. Tearfully gulping, he got up from the table and lit a cigarette. Then Kochevoy came down carrying a newspaper. The children stood up and curtsied without looking at him.

'For God's sake, Kostya, you teach them,' said Laptev. 'I'm afraid I'll cry as well, and I must pop over to the warehouse before lunch.'

'All right.'

Laptev went out. Frowning and looking most serious, Kostya sat at the table and drew the Bible towards him.

'Well, what are you on?'

'She knows the flood,' said Sasha.

'The flood? Fine, we'll cook something up on that. The flood it is.' Kostya ran through the short description of the flood in the Bible.

'I must observe that no flood like this actually took place,' he then added. 'Nor was there any Noah. Several thousand years before

Christ the earth experienced a remarkable inundation which is mentioned not only in the Hebrew Bible but also in the books of other ancient peoples, to wit the Greeks, the Chaldees and the Hindus. Whatever form this inundation took it can't have flooded the whole earth. It did fill the valleys if you like, but you can bet the mountains were still there. By all means read the nice book if you want, but don't take it too seriously.'

Leda's tears welled up again. Turning away, she suddenly burst out sobbing so loudly that Kostya shuddered and stood up from his seat in utter dismay.

'I want to go home to Daddy and Nanny,' she said.

Sasha also burst out crying. Kostya went up to his room and telephoned Julia. 'The girls are crying again, dear. This is beyond me.'

Wearing a knitted kerchief, with nothing over her dress, Julia ran across from the big house. Nipped by the frost, she comforted the girls.

'You must, you must believe me,' she pleaded, clutching first one and then the other to her. 'Your Daddy *will* be here today, he's sent a telegram. You're grieving for your mother, and so am I, my heart's breaking in two. But it can't be helped. What God has willed we can't unwill, can we?'

When they had stopped crying she wrapped them up and took them for a drive. They drove down Little Dmitrovka Street, then past the Strastnoy Boulevard to the Tver Road. At the Iverian Chapel they stopped and each set up a candle and knelt in prayer. On their way back they called at Filippov's Café and bought lenten cracknels with poppy seed.

The Laptevs would lunch between two and three, the meal being served by Peter. By day this Peter ran errands to the post office, to the warehouse or to the District Court for Kostya, and generally made himself useful. In the evenings he packed cigarettes, at night he was on the run opening the door, and between four and five in the morning he did the stoves. When he slept no one knew. He adored opening bottles of soda water, which he did easily and silently, not spilling a drop.

'Cheers!' said Kostya, and drank a glass of vodka before his soup.

Julia had not liked Kostya at first. That deep voice, those slangy sayings—all that 'shove off', 'sock on the jaw', 'scum of the earth', 'activate the samovar' stuff—his habit of clinking glasses and waxing maudlin over his vodka, it all seemed so puerile. But when she knew him better she felt very much at ease with him. He was open with her, liked talking to her quietly in the evenings, and even lent her novels of his own composition, which had so far been kept even from such close friends as Laptev and Yartsev. She read them, she praised them so as not to offend him, and he was pleased because he hoped to become a famous writer one day. His novels were all about the countryside and manor houses, though he only saw the country very occasionally when visiting friends who had a holiday cottage. And he had only been in one manor house in his life, on a visit to Volokolamsk over a court case. He shunned the theme of love as if ashamed of it, and he went in for nature descriptions, favouring such expressions as 'the hills' fussy silhouettes', 'the clouds' grotesque forms', 'a chord of mysterious harmonies'.

That his novels were never published he put down to censorship.

He liked being a lawyer. But it was those novels, not the law, that he considered his main life's work. He thought himself a subtle artistic organism. Art held a permanent fascination for him. He neither sang nor played a musical instrument, he had no ear for music at all, but he attended all the symphonic and philharmonic concerts, he organized charity performances and cultivated singers.

There was conversation at lunch.

'It's quite amazing,' said Laptev. 'Brother Theodore has completely floored me yet again. We must find out, says he, when our firm's centenary will be so that we can apply to be registered as gentlefolk. And he's completely serious! What *is* up with him? Frankly, I'm worried.'

They talked about Theodore, and about how posturing was all the rage nowadays. For instance, Theodore was trying to ape an old-style merchant, though he wasn't a merchant at all any more. And when the teacher—from the school where old Laptev was patron—called for his salary, Theodore even spoke and walked in a different way, behaving like the man's superior officer.

As there was nothing to do after lunch they went into the study. They spoke of modernism in the arts and *The Maid of Orleans*. Kostya delivered an entire soliloquy—he fancied himself at taking off Mariya Yermolov. Then they played bridge. Instead of going back to their cottage, the little girls sat on, pale and sad, both on the same armchair, listening to the street noises and hoping to hear their father arrive. In the dark and candlelight of evening they felt miserable. The talk over bridge, Peter's steps, the crackling in the fireplace—it all irritated them and they didn't want to look at the fire. In the evenings they no longer even wanted to cry, but felt on edge and sick at heart. How could people talk and laugh when their mother was dead? That was beyond them.

'What did you see through your binoculars this morning?' Julia asked Kostya.

'Nothing, but yesterday the old Frenchman himself had a bath.'

At seven o'clock Julia and Kostya left for the Maly Theatre. Laptev stayed behind with the girls.

'It's time your father was here.' He looked at his watch. 'His train must be late.'

The girls sat in the armchair, silently clinging to each other like little animals who feel the cold, while he paced the rooms, looking impatiently at his watch. The house was quiet. Then, just before ten, there was a ring, and Peter answered the door.

Hearing the well-known voice, the children shrieked, burst out sobbing, rushed into the hall. Panaurov wore a sumptuous fur coat. His beard and whiskers were white with frost.

'Yes, yes—in a moment,' he muttered while Sasha and Leda, sobbing and laughing, kissed his cold hands, his cap, his fur coat. Handsome, languid, spoilt by love, he unhurriedly caressed the children and went into the study.

'I shan't stay long, friends.' He rubbed his hands. 'I'm off to St. Petersburg tomorrow, they've promised me a transfer to another city.'

He had put up at the Hotel Dresden.

X

A frequent visitor at the Laptevs' was Ivan Yartsev, a well-built, powerful, black-haired man with a clever, pleasant face. He was considered good-looking, but had put on weight lately, which spoilt his face and figure, as did his habit of wearing his hair cropped almost to the scalp. His powerful build and his strength had once earned him a nickname, 'the Bruiser', at the university.

He had done an arts course with the Laptev brothers, had then transferred to science, and now held a master's degree in chemistry. He was not banking on a professorial chair, he had never even been a laboratory assistant, but taught physics and biology at a boys' secondary school and two girls' high schools. Enchanted by his pupils, especially the girls, he would say that the rising generation was wonderful. Apart from his chemistry he also studied sociology and Russian history at

home, and sometimes published short articles in newspapers and
magazines, signing them 'Y'. When he talked about botany or zoology
he resembled a historian, but when he discussed a historical problem
he looked like a scientist.

Another member of the Laptev inner circle was Kish, the 'eternal
student'. He had read medicine for three years before going over to
mathematics, and spending two years on each year of that course.
His father, a provincial pharmacist, sent him forty roubles a month,
while his mother sent him ten without his father knowing. This
sufficed for his living expenses, and even for such luxuries as a cloak
trimmed with Polish beaver, gloves, scent and photography—he often
had his picture taken and would give copies to his friends. A neat,
balding fellow with golden whiskers round his ears, modest, he always
looked poised to be of service. He was for ever doing people's errands,
dashing round collecting subscriptions, or freezing at dawn outside
some theatrical box-office to buy a ticket for a lady of his acquaintance.
Or he would go and order a wreath or bouquet at someone's behest.
The word was always 'Kish will fetch it, Kish will do it, Kish will buy
it'. These errands were ill-managed on the whole, Kish being showered
with reproaches while people often forgot to pay for what he had
bought them. But he never said anything. In crises he only sighed. He
was never greatly pleased or greatly grieved, he was always telling
long, boring stories, and his jokes always made people laugh—but
only because they weren't funny. For instance, he once addressed the
following would-be witticism to Peter. 'You, Peter, are no sturgeon.'
Everyone roared with laughter, and Kish himself joined in for quite a
time, delighted to have launched a shaft so felicitous. At professors'
funerals Kish would walk in front with the torch-bearers.

Yartsev and Kish usually came over for afternoon tea, and if the
host and hostess were not going to the theatre or a concert that tea
would drag on till supper time. One February evening the following
conversation took place in the dining-room.

'A work of art is significant and useful only when its theme embraces
a serious social problem,' said Kostya with an angry look at Yartsev.
'If a work protests against serfdom, if the author tilts against the
smugness of high society, then that work is significant and useful. But
novels and stories full of moaning and groaning, all about her falling
in love with him and him falling out of love with her—such works are
insignificant, say I. To hell with them.'

Julia told him that she agreed. 'These lovers' meetings, these acts of infidelity, these separations followed by assignations—is there nothing else to say? There are plenty of ill, unhappy, desperately poor people, aren't there? It must disgust them to read all this.'

Laptev disliked his wife discussing love so earnestly and coolly—a young woman not yet twenty-two. But he could guess why she did it.

'If poetry doesn't solve the problems you think important, then refer to technical works,' said Yartsev. 'Look up your criminal and financial law, read scientific articles. Why should *Romeo and Juliet* discuss educational freedom, say, or prison hygiene instead of love, when you can find all that stuff in specialist articles and reference works?'

'That's a bit steep, old man,' interrupted Kostya. 'We aren't talking about giants like Shakespeare or Goethe, we're talking about a hundred odd gifted and not so gifted writers who'd do a sight more good if they left love alone and tackled the popularization of knowledge and humane ideals.'

In a slightly nasal voice, pronouncing his 'rs' like a Parisian, Kish began telling the plot of a story which he had recently read. He related the details without haste. Three minutes passed, then five, then ten, and he was still at it, though no one knew what he was on about. His expression grew more and more apathetic, his eyes had lost their lustre.

Julia could not contain herself. 'Do get it over with, Kish, this is sheer agony.'

'Give over, Kish,' shouted Kostya.

Everyone, Kish included, burst out laughing.

Then Theodore came in, with red blotches on his face, rapidly greeted them and took his brother into the study. He had been avoiding crowded gatherings of late, preferring to talk to one person at a time.

'Let the young folk laugh, you and I must have a proper talk.' He sat in a low armchair away from the lamp. 'It's ages since we met, old son. How long is it since you were at the warehouse? A week, I reckon.'

'Yes, there's nothing there for me to do, and I'm frankly fed up with the old man.'

'They can manage without us two there of course, but you must have some sort of job. "In the sweat of thy face shalt thou eat bread", as the saying goes. Labour is pleasing to God.'

Peter brought a glass of tea on a tray. Theodore drank it without sugar and asked for more. He was a great tea drinker, and could put away ten glasses in an evening.

'I tell you what, old man.' He stood up and approached his brother. 'Why don't you simply go ahead and put up for the City Council, then we'll gradually winkle you on to the Executive Committee, and you'll end up as Deputy Mayor. The further you go the bigger you'll get. You're an intelligent, educated man, you'll be noticed and invited to St. Petersburg. Local government people are all the rage there, old son, and—hey presto!—you'll be an under-secretary or something before you're fifty and wear a ribbon round your neck.'

Laptev did not answer. Realizing that all this, the under-secretaryship, the ribbon, were Theodore's own ambitions, he didn't know what to say.

The brothers sat in silence. Theodore opened his watch and stared at it for an unconscionable time as if wanting to check the movements of the hands. To Laptev his expression seemed strange.

They were called in for supper, and Laptev went into the diningroom while Theodore stayed in the study. The argument was over, and Yartsev was talking like a professor lecturing.

'Differences of climate, energy, taste and age render human equality a physical impossibility. But civilized man can neutralize this inequality just as he has tamed swamps and bears. A scientist has contrived to teach a cat, a mouse, a falcon and a sparrow to eat from the same bowl. Education will do the same for people, one hopes. Life marches on, culture is visibly striding ahead, and a time will obviously come when the current position of factory-hands, say, will seem as absurd as serfdom—when they swopped girls for dogs—seems to us.'

'That won't be soon, oh dear me no,' Kostya laughed. 'It will be quite a while before Rothschild finds his gold vaults absurd, and until that day the worker must bend his back, starve till his stomach swells. Take it from me, old chap—we mustn't stand idly by, we must fight. A cat eating from the same bowl as a mouse—is *that* due to social consciousness? Not on your life. It was forced to do it.'

'Theodore and I are rich, our father's a capitalist, a millionaire, so we're the ones you have to struggle against.' Laptev wiped his forehead with his palm. 'A struggle against me—my consciousness finds that a bit hard to swallow. I am rich, but what have I got out of it so far? What has this power bestowed on me? In what way am I happier than you? My childhood was sheer hell, and money never saved me from the birch. My money was no use to Nina when she fell ill and died. If I'm not loved I can't make anyone love me even if I spend a hundred million.'

'But think how much good you can do,' said Kish.

'Good? What do you mean? Yesterday you asked me to help some mathematician who's looking for a job. I can do no more for him than you can, believe me. I can give him money, but that's not what he wants, now, is it? I once asked a famous musician to find a post for an indigent violinist, and he told me that only a non-musician would have made such a request. I give you the same answer—the reason you ask my help so assuredly is that you've never been in a rich man's shoes yourself.'

'But why this parallel with the famous musician?' Julia blushed. 'Why drag the famous musician in? It beats me.'

Her face shook with hate, and though she lowered her eyes to conceal this emotion, her expression was understood not only by her husband but by everyone at the table.

'Why drag in the famous musician?' she repeated quietly. 'Nothing's easier than to help the poor.'

Silence ensued. Peter served grouse, but no one would eat it, they only took salad. Unable to remember, now, what he had said, Laptev realized that it had not been his words, it had been the fact that he had taken part in the conversation at all which had aroused her hatred.

After supper he went to his study. Tensely, with pounding heart, anticipating further humiliations, he listened to the proceedings in the drawing-room. They had started another argument. Then Yartsev sat at the piano and sang a sentimental ditty. He was very versatile—sang, played, even did conjuring tricks.

'I don't know about you, gentlemen, but I don't want to stay at home,' said Julia. 'Let's go out.'

They decided on a trip out of town and sent Kish to the Merchants' Club for a troika. Their reason for not inviting Laptev was that he didn't usually go on such excursions and that he had his brother with him. But he took it that he bored them, and was utterly out of place among such jolly young people. Such was his annoyance, his resentment, that he almost wept. He even took pleasure in being treated so unkindly, in being this despised, stupid, boring husband, this mere moneybags. And should his wife betray him that night with his best friend, should she confess as much with a look of hatred—then he would be still more pleased.

The students, actors and singers whom she knew, Yartsev, even her casual encounters—all made him jealous to the point where he now yearned for her to be unfaithful. He wanted to surprise her with

someone, then poison himself and be rid of the whole nightmare once
and for all. Theodore drank tea, swallowing noisily, but then he too
made to leave.

'Something must be up with the old man,' he said, putting on his
fur coat. 'His eyesight's very bad.'

Laptev also put on his coat and went out. He saw his brother as far
as the Strastnoy Boulevard, then took a cab to the Yar Restaurant.

'So that's your married bliss, is it?' he taunted himself. 'That's love
for you.'

His teeth chattered, whether from jealousy or something else he
couldn't tell. At the Yar he paced about near the tables and listened to
a cabaret singer in the big room. He hadn't one sentence prepared in
case his wife and friends should appear, realizing in advance that if she
did show up he would only give a pathetic, silly smile, and everyone
would sense what emotions had brought him here. The electric
lighting, the noisy band, the smell of powder, the staring women—it
all confused him. He stopped by the door, trying to eavesdrop and spy
on the private rooms, and feeling as if he, the singer, the women—all
were playing some base and despicable role. Then he went on to the
Strelna, but saw none of them there either, and only when he was
approaching the Yar again on his way back did a troika noisily over-
take him with shouts from the drunken coachman and roars of
laughter from Yartsev.

When Laptev reached home after three in the morning Julia was in
bed. Seeing that she was not asleep, he went up to her.

'I understand your revulsion, your hatred,' he snapped. 'But you
might spare me in front of strangers, you might conceal your feelings.'

She sat up in bed with her feet hanging down, her eyes huge and
black in the lamplight.

'Please forgive me,' she said.

Agitated, trembling all over, he could not get a word out, but stood
silent in front of her. She too was shaking, and sat there like a criminal
waiting for him to state the case against her.

'I've been hurt so much,' he said at last, clutching his head. 'It's
sheer hell, I feel I've gone mad.'

'Do you think I find it easy?' Her voice shook. 'God only knows
how I feel.'

'You've been my wife for six months, but you haven't a spark of
love for me in your heart. There's no hope, no gleam of it. Why ever
did you marry me?' Laptev went on desperately. 'Why? What devil

drove you to my arms? What were you hoping for, what did you want?'

She looked at him in horror, as if fearing that he would kill her.

'Did you like me, did you love me?' He choked for breath. 'No. Then what? What? Tell me, what?' he shouted. 'It was that damned money, blast it.'

'It wasn't that, I swear,' she exclaimed. She crossed herself, flinching at the insult, and for the first time he heard her weep.

'As God is my witness, no,' she went on. 'I wasn't thinking of money, I don't need that. I simply felt I'd be wrong to refuse you. I was afraid I might ruin both your life and mine. And now I'm suffering for my mistake, suffering unbearably.'

She sobbed bitterly. Seeing how hurt she was, he sank on the carpet before her at a loss for words.

'Do stop, please,' he muttered. 'I insulted you because I love you so madly.' He suddenly kissed her foot and embraced her passionately. 'Just a tiny spark of love,' he muttered. 'Come on then, lie to me. Don't say it was a mistake.'

But she went on crying, and he felt that she only tolerated his caresses as the inevitable consequence of her mistake. As for the foot which he had kissed, that she had tucked beneath her like a bird. He felt sorry for her.

She lay down, covered herself up. He undressed and lay down too. In the morning both felt awkward, not knowing what to talk about, and he even sensed that she trod unsteadily on that kissed foot.

Before lunch Panaurov came to say good-bye, and Julia felt an irresistible urge to go back to her home town. How good to leave, she thought, to recover from married life, from this embarrassment and constant awareness of having behaved badly. It was decided at lunch that she would go with Panaurov and stay at her father's for two or three weeks until she was bored.

XI

She and Panaurov travelled in a private railway compartment, he wearing an odd-looking lambskin cap.

'Well, Petersburg was a disappointment,' he sighed, articulating deliberately. 'They promise you everything, but nothing specific. Yes, my dear, I've been a Justice of the Peace and a Permanent Secretary, I've chaired the local appeal court, and finally I've been a consultant to the County Council. I've served my country, I think, and I do have some claim to attention. But, do you know, I just can't get a transfer to another town.'

He shut his eyes, shook his head.

'I'm not recognized,' he went on sleepily. 'I'm no ace administrator of course, but I am a decent, honest man, and nowadays even that's a rarity. I confess I've deceived women a bit, but in my relations with the Russian government I've always been the perfect gentleman. Still, enough of that.' He opened his eyes. 'Let's discuss you. Why this sudden urge to visit your dear papa?'

'Oh, I'm not getting on too well with my husband.' Julia looked at his cap.

'Yes. Funny chap, isn't he? All the Laptevs are odd. Your husband's not that bad, he can pass at a pinch, but brother Theodore's a real nit-wit.'

Panaurov sighed. 'And do you have a lover?' he asked in all seriousness.

Julia looked at him in amazement, laughed. 'Heavens, what a question!'

At about half-past ten both got out at a large station and had supper. When the train moved off Panaurov took his overcoat and cap off, and sat by Julia's side.

'You're very lovely, I must say,' he began. 'You remind me of a freshly salted gherkin, if you'll excuse the snack-bar simile. It still has the whiff of the forcing bed, so to speak, but it has already absorbed a little salt and smells of dill. You're gradually shaping into a magnificent woman—a splendid, elegant creature. If this trip had taken place five years ago'—he sighed—'I'd have thought it my agreeable duty to place myself on the register of your admirers. But now, alas, I'm in retirement.'

Smiling a sad, yet compassionate smile, he put his arm round her waist.

'You must be mad.' She blushed, so scared that her hands and feet went cold. 'Stop it, Gregory.'

'What's so frightening, my dear?' he asked softly. 'What's so terrible? You're not used to it, that's all.'

To him a woman's protests only meant that he had impressed and attracted her. Holding Julia's waist, he firmly kissed her cheek, then her lips, in absolute certainty that he was affording her great pleasure. Recovering from her terror and embarrassment, she began laughing. He kissed her again.

'That's all you get from the old warrior.' He was putting on that comic hat. 'A certain Turkish pasha, a nice old boy, was once presented with—or, more probably, inherited—an entire harem. When his beautiful young wives paraded before him he inspected them, telling each one as he kissed her that this was "all I'm able to bestow on you now". Those are my sentiments too.'

She found it all foolish and unusual, it amused her. Feeling a little skittish, she stood on the seat, humming, and took a box of chocolates from the rack.

'Catch!' she shouted. And threw him one.

He caught it. She threw him another, loudly laughing, and then a third. He caught them all and put them in his mouth, looking at her with eyes full of yearning. There was much about his face, features and expression that was feminine and childlike, she felt. When she sat down out of breath, still looking at him and laughing, he touched her cheek with two fingers and pretended to be annoyed.

'Bad, bad girl!'

'Take it.' She gave him the whole box. 'I don't like sweets.'

He ate every single one and shut the empty box in his trunk, liking boxes with pictures on them.

'Enough of the horseplay,' said he. 'It's the land of Nod for the old warrior now.'

He took out his Bokhara dressing-gown and a cushion from a hold-all, lay down and covered himself with the gown.

'Good night, dearest lady,' he said, quietly sighing as if his whole body ached.

Soon his snores were heard. Feeling no constraint, she too lay down and was soon asleep.

As she drove home from the station next morning in her native town the streets seemed abandoned and deserted, the snow grey, the houses small and squashed. She encountered a funeral procession. The body was borne in an open coffin with banners.

'They say a funeral means good luck,' she thought.

In the house where Nina had once lived the windows were now pasted with white notices.

With sinking heart she drove into the yard, rang the door-bell. It was opened by a maid—a buxom, sleepy stranger in a warm quilted blouse. On her way upstairs Julia remembered Laptev declaring his love for her there. But the stairs were unwashed now, with footmarks everywhere. In the cold first-floor corridor waited fur-coated patients, and for some reason her heart thumped—she was almost too agitated to walk.

Stouter than ever, brick-red, hair dishevelled, the doctor was drinking tea, and even shed a tear in his delight at seeing his daughter. She was the old man's only joy, she reflected. Greatly touched, she embraced him heartily, and said that she would stay a long time, till Easter. After changing in her room, she went to the dining-room to drink tea with him, while he stalked about, hands in pockets, humming that ruminating hum which meant that he was vaguely annoyed.

'You have lots of fun in Moscow,' said he. 'I'm overjoyed for your sake, but I don't need anything myself, being old. I'll soon conk out and free you all. Why is my hide so tough, why am I still alive? Amazing, isn't it? Astonishing.'

He said he was a sturdy old donkey, not to say dogsbody. He had been saddled with treating Nina, with caring for her children, with her funeral, while this popinjay Panaurov would have nothing to do with it all, and had even borrowed a hundred roubles from him which still hadn't been returned.

'Take me to Moscow, put me in the mad-house,' the doctor said. 'I must be certifiable, seeing I'm naïve and infantile enough to go on believing in truth and justice.'

Then he reproached her husband with lack of foresight in not buying houses when they were on advantageous offer. No longer could Julia feel that she was the old man's only joy. While he received patients and did his rounds she stalked the house, not knowing what to do or think. She had grown away from her town and her home. She had no urge to go out in the street or visit people she knew, and when she remembered her former girl friends and her own life as a girl she neither felt sad nor hankered for the past.

That evening she dressed up and went to church. But the congregation consisted of no one in particular, and so her magnificent fur coat and hat went unappreciated. She felt as if the church and she herself had both undergone some change. At one time she had enjoyed hearing the canon recited at vespers, and listening to the choir sing anthems like 'I shall open my lips'. She had once enjoyed slowly drifting with the congregation towards the priest who stood in the centre of the church, she had liked the feel of holy oil on her forehead. But now she was just waiting for the service to end. Leaving church, she feared being accosted by beggars. It would be tedious to stop and search her pockets. She had no small change, anyway, only roubles.

She went to bed early, but fell asleep late and kept dreaming of certain portraits and that morning's funeral procession. They bore the open coffin with the body into a yard, stopped by a door, tossed the corpse on sheets for a time. Then they banged it full tilt into the door. Julia woke, leapt up in terror. There actually was a banging on the door downstairs. The bell-wire rustled on the wall, but she heard no ring.

The doctor coughed. Then the maid was heard going down and coming back.

'Madam!' It was the maid knocking at Julia's door.

'What?'

'A telegram.'

Julia went out carrying a candle. Behind the maid stood the doctor wearing his overcoat over his underclothes, also with a candle.

'The bell's broken.' He yawned, half asleep. 'It should have been mended ages ago.'

Julia opened the telegram and read it.

> WE DRINK YOUR HEALTH
>
> YARTSEV   KOCHEVOY

'Oh, how silly of them.' She laughed aloud, feeling relaxed and cheerful.

Returning to her room, she quietly washed and dressed, then spent some time packing until it was light. At noon she left for Moscow.

XII

In Easter week the Laptevs went to the School of Art to see a picture exhibition. They went as a family, Moscow fashion, taking both little girls, their governess and Kostya.

Laptev knew all the famous artists by name, and never missed an exhibition. He sometimes painted landscapes himself, at his country cottage in summer, thinking that he had excellent taste and might have made a fine artist had he studied. When abroad he would visit antique shops, inspect the wares with a knowing air, express an opinion, make some purchase. The dealer would charge whatever price he liked, and the object would then be stuffed in a box and lie around the coach-house before vanishing who knows where. Or he would go into a print-shop, scrutinize the pictures and bronzes carefully at length, make various observations—then suddenly buy some rough frame or box of worthless paper. The pictures in his home were of generous dimensions but poor quality, with some good ones which were badly hung. He had often paid a lot for what had turned out to be crude forgeries. Now, why should one so timid about life in general be so very bold and brash at picture exhibitions? Odd.

Julia looked at the pictures as her husband did—making a peep-hole of her fingers or through opera glasses—and was surprised that the people in them seemed alive and that the trees looked real. But they made no sense to her. She felt that many pictures at the exhibition were more or less the same, and that the whole aim of art came down to making the persons and objects depicted look real when observed through your fingers.

'This wood is a Shishkin,' her husband explained. 'He paints the same things over and over again. Now, you'll observe that real snow is never as mauve as this. And this boy has a left arm shorter than the right.'

When all were tired and Laptev had gone in search of Kostya so that they could return home, Julia stopped by a small landscape and idly looked at it. The foreground was a stream crossed by a wooden bridge with a path merging into dark grass on the far side. On the right was part of a wood with a bonfire near it—there must be grazing horses and watchmen hereabouts. Far away the sunset's last fires smouldered.

Julia imagined going over the bridge, and then further and further down the path. It was quiet there, sleepy landrails cried. A light winked far away. Suddenly she vaguely felt that she had often seen them long ago—those clouds spanning the red of the sky, that wood, these fields. She felt lonely, she wanted to walk on, on, on down the path. There, at the sunset's end, lay reflected an eternal, unearthly Something.

'How well painted.' She was surprised at her sudden understanding of the picture. 'Look, Alexis—see how quiet it is.'

She tried to explain why the landscape had so taken her fancy, but neither her husband nor Kostya understood. Sadly smiling, she continued to gaze at the scene, disturbed to find that the others saw nothing special in it. Then she began going round the gallery again, looking at the pictures, wanting to understand them, and no longer did the exhibition seem to contain so many identical works. Returning home, and noticing for the first time in her life the large picture above the grand piano in the hall, she felt animosity towards it.

'Who wants that sort of picture?'

After this the golden cornices, the Venetian mirrors with their flowers, the pictures like that above the grand piano, her husband's and

Kostya's debates on art—all depressed and irritated her, even arousing her occasional hatred.

Life went on as usual from day to day, promising nothing in particular. The theatre season was over, the warm weather had begun and was set fair. One morning the Laptevs were to go to the District Court and hear Kostya as defence counsel appointed by the court. After being held up at home they arrived when the cross-examination of witnesses had begun. A private of the reserve was charged with breaking and entering. Among the witnesses numerous laundresses testified that the accused often visited their employer, the laundry manageress. On the thirteenth of September—the day before the Exaltation of the Cross—he had turned up late in the evening with a hangover, demanding money for a drink, but no one had given him any. Then he had gone away, but had come back an hour later with beer and peppermint cakes for the girls. They had drunk and sung almost till dawn, but on looking round in the morning had found the lock on the loft entrance broken and some laundry missing—three men's nightshirts, a skirt, two sheets. Kostya ironically asked each witness whether she had drunk any of the beer brought by the accused that night. Obviously he was trying to make it look as if they had robbed their own laundry. He delivered his speech without the least emotion, looking angrily at the jury.

He explained what breaking and entering was, and what petty larceny was. He spoke circumstantially, convincingly, revealing a remarkable gift for solemnly retailing a long string of earnest platitudes. Just what was he driving at, though? From his oration a juror could only conclude either that there had been breaking and entering without larceny—in that the proceeds of the linen had been consumed by the laundresses—or else that there had been larceny without breaking and entering. Yet he was saying just the right things, evidently, since his speech greatly affected the jury and the public, being highly popular. Julia nodded to Kostya when the acquittal was brought in, and later gave him a hearty hand-shake.

In May the Laptevs moved to a cottage at Sokolniki, Julia now being pregnant.

XIII

More than a year passed. At Sokolniki, not far from the Moscow–Yaroslavl railway line, Julia and Yartsev sat on the grass. A little to one side lay Kochevoy, his hands under his head, looking at the sky. All three had walked far enough, and were waiting for the six o'clock excursion train to pass so that they could go home for tea.

'All mothers think their children are unusual, that's nature's way,' said Julia. 'A mother stands by the cot for hours observing her baby's little ears, eyes, nose, and delighting in them. If a stranger kisses baby the poor woman thinks this affords him the utmost pleasure. And a mother can talk only of her baby. I know this maternal weakness and guard against it. But my Olga *is* special, honestly. The look she gives when she's feeding! And her laugh! She's only eight months old, but I've honestly never seen such intelligent eyes, even in a child of three.'

'Which do you love more, by the way,' Yartsev asked. 'Your husband or your baby?'

Julia shrugged. 'I don't know. I never did love my husband much, and Olga's really my first love. I didn't marry Alexis for love, as you know. I used to be so silly, suffering agonies and obsessed with having ruined both our lives. But now I see that one doesn't need love, that's all nonsense.'

'Then what feeling does attach you to your husband, if not love? Why do you stay with him?'

'I don't know—well, habit, I suppose. I respect him, I miss him when he's away for a while. But that's not love. He's an intelligent, decent man, and that's enough to make me happy. He's very kind and unaffected.'

'Alexis is intelligent, Alexis is kind.' Kostya lazily raised his head. 'This intelligence, this kindness, this charm of his—until one's known him for donkeys' years one doesn't even notice them, my dear. And what use are his kindness and intelligence? He'll shell out all the cash you want, that *is* within his range. But when it comes to force of character, and standing up to some boor or bounder, then he jibs and loses heart. People like dear kind Alexis are all very well, but they're utterly unfit for struggle. They're no use for anything, actually.'

At last the train appeared. Steam, bright pink, surged from the funnel and soared above the wood. Two windows in the last carriage suddenly flashed blindingly in the sun.

'Tea time.' Julia stood up.

She had put on weight recently, and now walked in leisurely, matronly style.

'Still, it's a poor look-out without love.' Yartsev followed her. 'We keep talking and reading about love, but we do precious little loving. A poor look-out, say I.'

'None of that matters, Ivan,' said Julia. 'That's not where happiness lies.'

They had tea in the garden where mignonette, stocks and tobacco flowers were blooming, with the early gladioli opening out. Julia was going through a blissful phase of spiritual calm and equilibrium, as Yartsev and Kochevoy could tell from her expression. She needed nothing beyond what she had, and they too began to feel gloriously at peace with themselves. Things were panning out so nicely—just right, there was no denying that. The pines were wonderful, there was a uniquely splendid aroma of resin, the cream was delicious, Sasha was a clever, good little girl.

After tea Yartsev sang ditties to his own piano accompaniment while Julia and Kochevoy sat listening silently, except that Julia stood up now and then, and quietly went out to look at her baby and at Leda, who had had a temperature for two days and had eaten nothing.

'My love, my gentle love,' sang Yartsev. He shook his head. 'Well, friends, I don't know what you have against love, cross my heart I don't. If I wasn't busy fifteen hours a day I'd fall in love myself. Definitely.'

Supper was laid on the terrace. It was warm and quiet, but Julia huddled in her shawl and complained of the damp. When it grew dark she felt vaguely uneasy, couldn't stop shivering, and asked her guests to stay on. She plied them with wine, and had cognac brought in after supper to stop them leaving. She didn't want to be left alone with the children and servants.

'We—the ladies staying in the resort, that is—are putting on a show for the children,' she said. 'We already have everything—the theatre, the actors. All we lack is a play. We've been sent a score of odd plays, but none of them's any good.' She turned to Yartsev. 'Now, you like the theatre, you know your history. So write us a historical play.'

'Very well.'

The guests drank up the cognac and made to leave. It was past ten o'clock, late by holiday standards.

Julia saw them through the gate. 'It's so dark, pitch black. How you'll find your way I can't think, friends. It is cold, I must say.'

She wrapped herself up tighter and returned to the porch. 'Alexis must be playing cards somewhere,' she shouted. 'Good night.'

Coming out of the brightly-lit house, Yartsev and Kostya could see nothing, but blindly groped their way to the railway line and crossed it.

'Can't see a bloody thing.' Kostya spoke in a deep voice, pausing to look at the sky. 'And the stars, look at them. Just like new fifteen-copeck pieces, they are, Hey, Yartsev!'

'What?' replied Yartsev's voice.

'I can't see, I say. Where are you?'

Yartsev went up to him whistling, took his arm.

'Hey, everyone round here!' Kostya suddenly shouted at the top of his voice. 'We've caught a socialist.'

In his cups he was always rather rowdy—shouting, picking quarrels with policemen and cabbies, singing, laughing crazily.

'To hell with Mother Nature!' he shouted.

Yartsev tried to calm him. 'Now, that's enough of that. Please.'

The friends soon grew used to the dark, and began to make out the silhouettes of the tall pines and telegraph poles. From Moscow's stations occasional whistles were heard, wires whined piteously. But the wood itself gave off no sound—the silence had a proud, powerful, mysterious air. The tips of the pines almost seemed to brush the night sky. The friends found the right cutting in the forest, and walked down it. It was pitch dark. Only the long strip of sky festooned with stars, and the trodden earth beneath their feet, showed that they were on a path. They walked silently side by side, both fancying that people were approaching from the other direction. Then their intoxicated mood subsided. Yartsev had the idea that the wood might be haunted by the ghosts of Muscovy's Tsars, boyars and patriarchs. He wanted to tell Kostya so, but refrained.

When they came to the city gate the sky was faintly paling. Still silent, Yartsev and Kochevoy marched down a paved road past cheap holiday cottages, taverns, timber-yards. Under the bridge of a branch line they felt a sudden dampness—pleasant, with a smell of lime trees. Then a long, broad street opened up without a soul or a light on it.

Dawn was breaking when they reached Krasny Prud.

'Moscow town has many agonies in store.' Yartsev gazed at St. Alexis's Convent.

'What put that into your head?'

'I don't know, I love Moscow.'

Yartsev and Kostya were both Moscow-born. They adored it, being vaguely hostile to other towns. That Moscow is a wonderful city and Russia a wonderful country they were convinced. In the Crimea, in the Caucasus, in foreign parts they felt bored, out-of-place, frustrated. Dear old Moscow's drab weather was the nicest and healthiest kind they found. The days when cold rain raps the windows, when twilight comes on early, when the walls of houses and churches take on a sombre brown hue, when you don't know what to wear when you go out—those days were an agreeable stimulus to them. They found a cab near the station in the end.

'It really would be nice to write a historical play,' said Yartsev. 'But without all the—you know—the Lyapunovs and Godunovs. I'd take Yaroslav's and Monomakh's times. I hate all Russian historical plays, Pimen's soliloquy excepted. When you handle a historical source, when you read a Russian history text-book, even, everything Russian strikes you as phenomenally accomplished, proficient and fascinating. But when I see a historical play at the theatre, Russian life seems so drab, morbid, tame.'

At Dmitrovka Street the friends parted and Yartsev went on to his lodgings in Nikitsky Road. He was dozing and swaying, he kept thinking about the play. Suddenly he imagined an appalling racket, a clanging, shouts in an incomprehensible language like Kalmuck. Then there was some village engulfed in flames, while near-by woods, decked with hoar frost and delicately pink in the fire's glow, were so clearly visible far and wide that every fir tree stood out. Savages, mounted and on foot, careered through the village, both they and their horses as crimson as the sunset.

'Those are Polovtsians,' thought Yartsev.

One of them—old, terrifying, bloody-faced, charred all over—was tying a young girl with a white, typically Russian face to his saddle. The old man was shouting furiously and the girl had a sad, intelligent look.

Yartsev shook his head and woke up.

'My love, my gentle love,' he sang.

Paying the cabby and then going upstairs to his room, he could not shake off his hallucination, but saw the flames move into the trees. The wood crackled and started smoking. Crazed with fear, a huge wild boar hurtled through the village.

The girl tied to the saddle kept watching.

When Yartsev entered his room it was light. On the grand piano near open music books two candles were burning low. On the sofa lay Polina in a dark dress with a sash, holding a newspaper, fast asleep. She must have been playing for a long time waiting for him, and had fallen asleep before he arrived.

How utterly worn out she looked, he thought.

Carefully removing the paper from her grasp, he covered her with a rug, put out the candles, went into his bedroom. As he lay down he thought about the historical play and he couldn't get the tune 'My love, my gentle love' out of his head.

Two days later Laptev looked in for a moment to say that Leda had diphtheria, and that Julia and the baby had caught it from her. Then, five days later, came news that Leda and Julia were recovering, but the baby had died and the Laptevs had fled from their Sokolniki villa to the city.

XIV

Laptev disliked spending much time at home these days. His wife often went over to the cottage in their yard, saying that she must help the girls with their studies, but he knew that she didn't go there for that but to cry at Kostya's place. Came the ninth day, the twentieth, the fortieth and he kept having to go to the St. Alexis Cemetery to attend the requiems, and then suffer agonies for twenty-four hours, thinking only of this unhappy baby and uttering sundry common-places to console his wife. He rarely visited the warehouse nowadays, charitable activity being his sole occupation. He invented odd chores and troubles for himself, and he was glad when he had to spend a whole day driving about on some trivial errand.

He had recently been intending to go abroad and study the organization of hostels for the poor, and this idea now diverted him.

It was autumn. Julia had just gone over to the cottage to weep, while Laptev lay on his study sofa trying to think of somewhere to go. Then Peter announced Polina Rassudin. Laptev delightedly jumped up to greet the unexpected guest—his former, now almost forgotten, friend. She had not changed at all since the evening when he had last seen her.

'It's been ages, Polina.' He held out both hands. 'I'm so glad to see you, you've no idea. Do come in.'

She greeted him with a snatch of the hand, entered the study, sat down without removing hat or coat.

'I only dropped in for a moment, I've no time for small talk. Pray sit down and listen. Whether you are or are not glad to see me I don't in the least care, not giving a rap for the condescending attentions of personages of the male tribe. If I am here now it is because I've been in five places already today and been turned down in all of them, and the matter is urgent. Now, then.' She looked him in the eye. 'Five students of my acquaintance, persons of limited intelligence but indubitable poverty, have failed to pay their fees and are being sent down. Your wealth imposes the obligation to go to the university this instant and pay up.'

'I'll be glad to, my dear.'

'Here are the names.' She gave Laptev a note. 'Off with you this instant, you can bask in domestic bliss later.'

A vague rustle came from the door into the drawing-room—the dog scratching itself, most likely. Polina flushed and jumped up.

'Little Miss Whatnot's listening at the key-hole,' she said. 'How revolting!'

Laptev was offended on Julia's behalf.

'She's not here, she's over at the cottage,' he said. 'And don't talk about her like that. Our baby died and she's dreadfully unhappy.'

'Then you can set her mind at rest.' Polina laughed and sat down again. 'She'll have a dozen more.

"A person well may stupid be,
Yet still engender progeny." '

Laptev remembered often hearing this or something like it in days gone by, and caught the evocative scent of time past, of his free bachelor existence—when he had felt young and capable of anything, when love for his wife and memories of his child still lay ahead of him.

He stretched himself. 'Let's go together.'

When they reached the university Polina waited by the gates while Laptev went to the registry. Returning soon afterwards, he handed her five receipts.

'Now where are you off to?' he asked.

'Yartsev's.'

'Well, I'm going with you.'

'You'll interrupt his work, you know.'

'No, I assure you.' He gave a pleading look.

She was wearing a black mourning hat with crêpe trimmings and a very short, threadbare overcoat with bulging pockets. Her nose seemed longer than ever, there was no colour in her face despite the cold. Laptev enjoyed following her, obeying her, listening to her complaints. What inner resources the woman must have, he reflected on the way—ugly, angular, restless, lacking all dress sense, with hair always dishevelled, always vaguely ungainly, she was yet enchanting.

They reached Yartsev's room by the servants' entrance through the kitchen, where they were greeted by the cook, a trim old girl with grey curls. Much embarrassed, she gave a sweet smile which made her tiny face look like a pie.

'Come in, do.'

Yartsev was out. Polina sat at the piano and embarked on some boring, difficult exercises after telling Laptev not to interrupt. Not seeking to distract her with talk, he sat on one side leafing through *The European Herald*. After playing for two hours, her daily stint, she ate something in the kitchen and went off to give her lessons. Laptev read an instalment of some novel, then just sat for a while, neither reading nor feeling bored, delighted that he would be late for dinner at home.

'Ha, ha, ha.' That was Yartsev's laugh, and he followed it in person—healthy, hearty, red-cheeked, in a new tail-coat with bright buttons.

The friends dined together. Then Laptev lay on the sofa while Yartsev sat by him and lit a cigar. Twilight fell.

'I must be getting old,' said Laptev. 'Ever since my sister died I keep thinking about death for some reason.'

They spoke of death and immortality. How nice it indeed would be to be resurrected and then fly off to Mars or somewhere, to be for ever idle and happy, and above all to think in some special non-terrestrial manner.

'But I don't want to die,' said Yartsev quietly. 'No philosophy can reconcile me to death, I look at it simply as annihilation. I want life.'

'Do you enjoy life, old friend?'

'Indeed I do.'

'Now, in that sense I just don't understand myself. My mood varies from dejected to apathetic. I'm timid, I lack self-confidence, my conscience makes me craven, I just can't adapt to life and master it. Some people talk nonsense or behave like scoundrels—and with what zest! Yet I sometimes consciously perform good works while feeling only anxiety or utter indifference. I put it all down to being a slave, old man—the grandson of a serf. A lot of us plebeians will come to grief before we find the right path.'

'That's all very well, my dear chap.' Yartsev sighed. 'It just shows once again how rich and varied Russian life is. Ah, rich indeed it is. You know, I'm more convinced every day that we're on the brink of some colossal achievement. I'd like to live to see it, have a part in it myself. Believe it or not, we have a wonderful new generation now, that's my view. Teaching children, especially girls, is sheer delight—those children are superb.'

Yartsev went to the piano and struck a chord.

'I am a chemist,' he went on. 'I think like a chemist, I shall die a chemist. But I'm greedy, I fear to die without glutting myself. Chemistry alone, that's not enough. I clutch at Russian history, at the history of art, at the theory of education, at music. This summer your wife told me to write a historical play, and now I'd like to write, write, write. I think I could sit in one place for three days and three nights, just writing. Images have drained me, they crowd my head—I feel my pulse pounding in my brain. It isn't that I want to make anything extraordinary out of myself or achieve greatness. Not a bit of it—I just want to live, think, hope, be everywhere at once. Life is short, my dear chap, and one must do one's best to live it.'

After this friendly conversation, which ended only at midnight, Laptev took to visiting Yartsev almost daily. He felt drawn there. He usually arrived in the late afternoon, lay down and waited patiently for Yartsev to arrive, not in the least bored. Yartsev would come back from his job, have his meal and sit down to work, but Laptev would ask a question, conversation would start up, work would lose its interest. The friends would part at midnight, delighted with each other.

It didn't last long, though. Reaching Yartsev's one day, Laptev found Polina there on her own. She was doing her piano exercises. She gave him a cold, almost hostile, look and did not shake hands.

'Tell me, pray, when will all this end?' she asked.

'All what?' Laptev did not understand.

'You come here every day, you stop Yartsev working. Now, he's not some damned tradesman, he's a scholar. Every moment of his life is precious. I should have thought you might see that and show at least *some* sensitivity.'

'If you think I'm interfering I shall discontinue my visits,' said Laptev shortly. He was embarrassed.

'A very good thing too. And leave now, or he'll come and find you here.'

Polina's tone, her look of indifference, completed his embarrassment. She felt nothing for him, she just wanted him to hurry up and go— what a change from their former love. He went out without shaking hands, expecting her to call him back. But the scales rang out again. Slowly making his way downstairs, he knew that they were strangers now.

Three days later Yartsev came over for the evening.

'I have news.' He laughed. 'Polina has moved in with me.' Somewhat embarrassed, he went on in a low voice. 'Well, we're not in love of course, but I, er, I don't think that matters. I'm glad to offer her a peaceful refuge and a chance to give up work if she falls ill. Now, *she* feels that by living with me she'll bring order into my life, that I'll become a great scholar under her influence. That's her view, so let her keep it. They have a proverb down south—"if wishes were horses, beggars would ride." Rather funny, that.'

Laptev said nothing. Yartsev paced the study—looking at the old, familiar pictures, sighing.

'Yes, my friend, I'm three years older than you. It's too late for me to think of real love now. A woman like Polina—that's a stroke of luck for me, in fact, and naturally I shall live happily with her until my old age. But I still have vague regrets, damn it, and vague yearnings. I keep seeing myself lying in a valley in the Caucasus, I dream I'm at a ball. Man's never satisfied with what he has, in other words.'

He went into the drawing-room and sang some songs as if he had no care in the world, while Laptev sat in his study with his eyes shut and tried to understand why Polina had taken up with Yartsev. How sad to think that all attachments lacked solidity and permanence. Polina's liaison with Yartsev annoyed him. He was annoyed with himself too because his feelings for his wife had completely changed.

XV

Laptev sat in an armchair reading and rocking himself. Julia was also in the study, reading. There seemed to be nothing to say, and both had been silent since morning. He cast her occasional glances over his book. You marry because you're passionately in love, he thought, or you marry without love at all. It makes no difference, does it? The jealous, emotional, suffering phase—how distant it seemed to him now. He had already fitted in a foreign trip which he was now recovering from, reckoning to return to England in the spring. He had liked England.

Having come to terms with her grief, Julia no longer went over to the cottage to cry. She did not visit shops or attend theatres and concerts that winter, but stayed at home. Disliking large rooms, she was always in her husband's study or in her own room where she kept her icon-cases—part of her dowry—and where the landscape she had so fancied at the exhibition hung on the wall. She spent hardly any money on herself, and her expenses were now as small as they had been back in her father's house.

The winter passed cheerlessly. People were playing cards all over Moscow, but when an alternative entertainment was conceived—singing, reciting or sketching, say—that turned out an even greater bore. The scarcity of accomplished persons in the city, the participation of the same old singers and lecturers at the same old functions—it gradually made the joys of artistic appreciation pall and become a tedious, monotonous obligation for many.

Besides, no day passed without tribulations for the Laptevs. Old Mr. Laptev's eyesight was very poor. He had stopped going to the warehouse, and the eye specialists said he would soon be blind. Theodore didn't go there any more either for some reason, but spent all his time at home writing. Panaurov had obtained his transfer to another town with promotion to a higher rank, and was now staying at the Dresden Hotel and visiting Laptev almost daily to borrow money. Finally, Kish had left the university and was hanging round the Laptevs' place for days on end telling long, boring stories and expecting them to find him a job. It was all irksome and tiring, and it took the zest out of life's daily round.

Peter came into the study and announced a lady visitor unknown to them and described on the card which he presented as a 'Joséphine Milan'.

Julia stood up lazily and went out, slightly limping from pins and needles in the leg. In the doorway appeared a woman—thin, very pale, dark-browed, dressed all in black. She clenched her hands on her breast.

'Monsieur Laptev, save my children,' she pleaded.

The jangle of bracelets and powder-blotched face were familiar to Laptev, and he recognized the woman at whose home he had once so maladroitly chanced to dine before his marriage. This was the second Mrs. Panaurov.

'Save my children!' she repeated. Her face quivered, and she suddenly looked old and pathetic. Her eyes reddened. 'Only you can save us. I've spent all I have on this visit to Moscow. My children will starve.'

She made to sink to her knees while Laptev, panic-stricken, clasped her arms above the elbows.

'Sit down, I beg you,' he muttered, offering her a chair.

'We have no money left for food,' she said. 'Gregory is going off

to his new job, but he doesn't want to take me and the children with
him. All the money you've sent in your generosity—he spends it on
himself. So what can we do, I ask you? My poor, unfortunate children.'

'Calm down, I beg you. I'll tell the office to send the money to you
personally.'

She burst into sobs. Then she calmed herself and he noticed the tear
furrows running down her powdered cheeks. And she had a moustache.

'You're infinitely generous, Monsieur Laptev. But do be our
guardian angel, our fairy godfather—do persuade Gregory not to
abandon me, to take me with him. I love him so much, I'm crazy
about him. He is my joy in life.'

Laptev gave her a hundred roubles and promised to talk to Panaurov.
He saw her to the hall, terrified of her bursting into sobs again, or
falling on her knees.

Kish arrived next. Then Kostya turned up with a camera. He had
recently taken up photography, and would snap everyone in the house
several times a day, an occupation which caused him much distress.
He had even lost weight.

Before tea Theodore arrived. Sitting in a corner of the study, he
opened a book and spent some time looking at one page, obviously
not reading it. Then he dawdled over his tea, his face red. He depressed
Alexis, whom even his brother's silence irked.

'You may congratulate Russia on acquiring a new pundit,' said
Theodore. 'Quite seriously, though, I have given birth to a certain
little article, old man, just to try out the old pen as it were, and I've
brought it to show you. Read it, my dear chap, and tell me what you
think. But do be frank.'

He took an exercise book from his pocket and gave it to his brother.
The article was called 'The Russian Soul'. It was written in the flat,
featureless style commonly cultivated by persons with no talent and
much secret conceit. The main idea was as follows. An intellectual has
the right not to believe in the supernatural, but has the duty to conceal
his scepticism so as not to create a stumbling-block and shake the faith
of others. Without faith there can be no idealism, and idealism is
destined to save Europe and show Man his true path.

'But you don't say what Europe is to be saved *from*,' Laptev remarked.
'It's obvious.'

'Not at all.' Laptev strode up and down excitedly. 'I can't see why
you wrote it. Still, that's your business.'

'I want to publish it as a pamphlet.'

'That's your business.'

They said nothing for a minute, and Theodore sighed. 'I profoundly, I infinitely regret that we don't see eye to eye. Oh, Alexis, my dear brother Alexis. We're Russians, you and I, we belong to the Orthodox Church, we have a certain breadth. All these wretched German and Jewish ideas, how ill they suit us. We aren't a couple of mountebanks, you and I, we represent an illustrious merchant house.'

'An illustrious house—fiddlesticks!' Laptev tried to contain his irritation. 'An illustrious house! Our grandfather was always being kicked around by the nobs, and the most wretched little jack-in-office used to slap his face. Grandfather beat Father, Father beat you and me. What did your "illustrious house" ever give either of us? What kind of nerves and blood have we inherited? For nearly three years you've been maundering on like some canting cleric, mouthing miscellaneous clap-trap. As for what you've just written—why, it's the ravings of a flunkey! And what of myself? Well, just look at me. I lack adaptability, audacity, strength of mind. I'm as scared of taking the smallest step as if I risked a flogging. I quail before nobodies, imbeciles and swine, my utter inferiors intellectually and morally. I fear hall porters, janitors, policemen of all kinds, I fear them all because I was born of a mother who was hounded to death, and because I have been beaten and terrorized from infancy. We'd do well not to have children, you and I. Oh, let's hope your illustrious merchant house ends with the two of us.'

Julia came into the study and sat by the desk.

'Were you arguing?' she asked. 'Am I interrupting?'

'No, sister dear,' answered Theodore. 'We're discussing matters of principle. Now, you'—he turned to his brother—'say our family is this that and the other. Yet this family created a business worth millions. That means quite a bit!'

'To hell with your business worth millions. A man with no special intelligence or ability accidentally becomes a trader, makes his pile. He does business day in day out without system, without purpose, without even any lust for money, operating like some machine, and the money flows towards him without his taking a step. He's at his business all his life, only liking it because he can boss his clerks and mock his customers. He's a church elder because he can bully the choir and make them dance to his tune. He's a school trustee because he likes to see the schoolmaster as an underling and can boss him around. It's not business, it's throwing his weight about your merchant likes, and that warehouse of yours is no commercial enterprise, it's a torture chamber. Oh yes, for your kind of business you need clerks devoid of personality, with no stake in anything, and that's how you breed them. From infancy you make them grovel for every bite of food, from infancy you condition them to believe you their benefactors. You'd never take a university man into the warehouse, that's for sure.'

'Graduates are no use in our business.'

'Untrue!' shouted Laptev. 'Lies!'

'I'm very sorry, but you seem to be spitting on your own doorstep.' Theodore stood up. 'You hate our business, but you benefit from our profits.'

'Ah, so we've reached the point at last, have we?' Laptev laughed and looked angrily at his brother. 'Certainly—if I didn't belong to your illustrious house, if I had a jot of will-power or courage I'd have jettisoned your "profits" years ago, I'd have gone and earned my own living. But you and your warehouse have sapped my individuality since infancy. I am your creature.'

Theodore looked at his watch and hurriedly said goodnight. He kissed Julia's hand and made to leave, but instead of going into the hall he went into the drawing-room and then into a bedroom.

'I'd forgotten which room was which.' He was most embarrassed. 'This is an odd house. Odd, eh?'

As he put on his furs he seemed struck by something and his face expressed pain. Laptev was no longer angry. He felt scared, and also sorry for Theodore. That good, deep love for his brother which seemed to have dimmed inside him during the last three years—it now awoke, and he felt a strong desire to express it.

'Come to lunch tomorrow, Theodore.' He stroked his brother's shoulder. 'How about it?'

'All right then, but give me some water.'

Laptev ran into the dining-room himself, and picked off the sideboard the first thing that came to hand, a tall beer jug, poured some water and took it to his brother. Theodore began drinking thirstily, but suddenly bit into the jug, and was then heard gnashing his teeth and sobbing. The water spilt on his fur coat and frock-coat, and Laptev —who had never seen a man cry before—stood there confused and scared, not knowing what to do. Gazing in perplexity at Julia and the maid who had removed Theodore's coat and taken him back into the house, he followed them, feeling guilty.

Julia helped Theodore to lie down and sank to her knees beside him.

'It's all right, it's just nerves,' she said soothingly.

'My dear, I feel so awful,' said he. 'I'm so, so unhappy, but I've been trying and trying to hide it.'

He put his arm round her neck. 'I dream of Nina every night,' he whispered in her ear. 'She comes and sits in the armchair by my bed.'

An hour later he was putting on his coat again in the hall, smiling and embarrassed in the maid's presence. Laptev drove with him to Pyatnitsky Road.

'Do come to lunch tomorrow,' he said on the way, holding his brother's arm. 'And at Easter we'll go abroad together. You need an airing, you've rather gone to seed.'

'Yes, yes, yes—certainly I'll come. And we'll take sister Julia along.'

Returning home, Laptev found his wife highly distraught. This business of Theodore had shocked her, and she just could not get over it. She was not weeping, but was very pale—tossing about in bed, tightly grasping her quilt, her pillow and her husband's hands in cold fingers. Her eyes were dilated with fear.

'For heaven's sake don't leave me,' she said to her husband. 'Tell me, Alexis, why don't I say my prayers any more? Where's my faith? Oh, why did you have to discuss religion in my presence? You've confused me, you and your friends. I don't say my prayers any more.'

He placed compresses on her forehead, warmed her hands, gave her tea, while she huddled up to him in terror.

By morning she was tired, and she fell asleep while Laptev sat holding her hand. So he had no sleep. All next day he felt crushed, deadened and vacuous, wandering listlessly through the house.

XVI

The doctors said that Theodore was mentally ill, but what was happening at Pyatnitsky Road Laptev had no idea. The gloomy warehouse, where neither the old man nor Theodore were to be seen any more—it seemed just like a morgue. Whenever his wife told him he must visit the warehouse and Pyatnitsky Road every day, he either gave no answer or spoke irritably about his childhood—about how he couldn't forgive his father for the past, about how he loathed Pyatnitsky Road and the warehouse. And so on.

One Sunday morning Julia went to Pyatnitsky Road herself. She found the old man in the same large room where that service had once been held to celebrate her arrival. In his canvas jacket, without a tie, in slippers, he sat unmoving in an armchair, blinking his blind eyes.

'It's me, your daughter-in-law.' She went up to him. 'I came to see how you are.'

He breathed heavily, overcome by emotion. Touched by his unhappiness and loneliness, she kissed his hand while he felt her face and head. Then, having so to speak assured himself that it was really she, he made the sign of the cross over her.

'Thank you indeed,' he said. 'My eyes have gone, I see nothing. I can just make out the window, and the light too, but I don't notice people and objects. Yes, I'm going blind, and Theodore's ill. Aye, 'tis a bad business with no boss's eye on them. With no one to keep them up to scratch the lads will get out of hand if things go wrong. And what's this illness of Theodore's, a chill or something? Now, I've never been ill myself, never gone to the doctor. Nay, I've had no truck with doctors.'

The old man had started bragging as usual. Meanwhile servants were swiftly laying the table in the same room, putting out the *hors d'œuvre* and bottles of wine. They brought a dozen bottles, one shaped like the Eiffel Tower. They served a dishful of hot pasties smelling of boiled rice and fish.

'Help yourself, dear,' said the old man.

She took his arm, led him to the table, poured him vodka.

'I'll come back tomorrow,' she said. 'I'll bring your grandchildren Sasha and Leda. They'll love you and be nice to you.'

'Don't you bring them here, they ain't legitimate.'

'What do you mean? Their father and mother were married, weren't they?'

'Not with my permission. I never blessed them and I want nothing to do with them, confound them.'

'That's a strange way to speak, Father.' Julia sighed.

'Children should respect and fear their parents, the Gospels say.'

'Not at all. The Gospels say we should forgive even our enemies.'

'You can't forgive people in our business. Start forgiving everyone and you'll go bust in three years.'

'But to forgive, to say a kind, friendly word, even to someone who's done wrong—that's more important than business and making money.'

Julia wanted to mollify the old man, to instil compassion and evoke contrition, but he only heard her out with the condescension of an adult listening to a child.

'You're an old man, Father.' Julia spoke decisively. 'Soon God will call you to Himself. He won't ask you what your business was, or whether your affairs prospered, but whether you showed mercy to others. Were you harsh with those weaker than yourself—your servants and clerks, for instance?'

'I've always been good to my workpeople, and they should always mention me in their prayers.' The old man spoke with assurance. But, touched by Julia's air of sincerity and wishing to please her, he added that it was all right—she could bring his little granddaughters tomorrow. 'I'll have some presents bought.'

The old man was untidily dressed, and had cigar ash on chest and lap. No one was keeping his boots or clothes clean, obviously. The rice in the pasties was under-cooked, the table-cloth smelt of soap, the servants no longer trod quietly. The old man, the whole house in Pyatnitsky Road—they looked neglected. Julia sensed this and felt ashamed on her own and her husband's behalf.

'I'll definitely be back tomorrow,' said she.

She marched round the house telling them to tidy up the old man's bedroom and light his icon lamp. Theodore was in his own room gazing at an open book, not reading. Julia spoke to him, told them to tidy his room as well and then went down to see the clerks. In the middle of the room where they had their meals stood an unpainted wooden post to shore up the ceiling. The ceilings were low, the wallpaper was cheap, there was a smell of stove fumes and cooking. As it was Sunday the clerks were all at home, and were sitting on their beds waiting for their meal. When Julia came in they jumped up and answered her questions diffidently, looking at her as sullenly as convicts.

'Heavens, you *are* badly housed.' She threw up her hands. 'Don't you feel cramped?'

'Aye, cramped we be, but we ain't no worse for that,' Makeichev said. 'We are most grateful to you, and we lift up our prayers to merciful God.'

'In proportion commensurate to the dimensions of the personality,' said Pochatkin.

Seeing that Julia had not understood Pochatkin, Makeichev hastened to explain. 'We're humble folk and must live as fits our station.'

She inspected the boys' quarters and kitchen, she met the house-keeper—and was most dissatisfied.

Returning home, she spoke to her husband. 'We must move to Pyatnitsky Road as soon as we can. And you'll visit the warehouse every day.'

Then both sat in the study side by side, not speaking. He felt depressed, not wanting to go to Pyatnitsky Road or the warehouse, but he had guessed what was in his wife's mind and lacked the strength to gainsay her.

He stroked her cheek. 'I feel as if our life was over,' he said. 'It's as if a dim half-life was beginning. I wept when I learnt that brother Theodore's illness was incurable. We spent our childhood and youth together, I loved him dearly once. But then came this catastrophe, and I feel as if losing him means a complete break with my past. And when you just said we must move to Pyatnitsky Road, that prison, I began to feel I'd have no future either.'

He stood up and went over to the window. 'Anyway, I can say good-bye to any hope of happiness.' He gazed at the street. 'There's no such thing. I've never had it, so it must be an impossibility. I was happy once in my life, though—the night I sat under your umbrella. Remember leaving your umbrella at Nina's?' He turned towards his wife. 'I was in love with you then, I remember sitting under that umbrella all night, experiencing a state of bliss.'

In the study near the bookcases was a mahogany chest-of-drawers with bronze fittings where Laptev kept various unneeded objects, including that umbrella. He took it out and gave it to his wife.

'There it is.'

Julia looked at the umbrella, recognized it and smiled sadly.

'I remember,' she said. 'You were holding it when you told me you loved me.'

'Please come back early if you can,' she added, noticing that he was just going out. 'I miss you.'

Then she went to her room and gazed at the umbrella for a while.

XVII

There was no accountant at the warehouse, despite the complexity of the business and huge turnover, nor could any sense be made of the book-keeper's records. Buyers' agents, German and English, visited the warehouse every day and discussed politics and religion with the clerks. There was a genteel alcoholic—a sick, pathetic creature—who came and translated the foreign correspondence in the office. The assistants called him the Midget, and put salt in his tea. By and large the entire operation was, to Laptev, just one vast exercise in eccentricity.

He visited the warehouse every day, trying to introduce new methods. He forbade them to whip boys and mock customers, he was furious when laughing clerks merrily consigned useless, shop-soiled goods to the provinces as if they were new and in fashion. He was now the boss, but he still did not know how large his property was, whether his business was flourishing, what salary his senior clerks received. And so on. Pochatkin and Makeichev thought him young and inexperienced, kept a great deal from him, exchanged mysterious whispers with the blind old man every evening.

One day in early June, Laptev and Pochatkin went to Bubnov's Inn for a business lunch. Pochatkin had worked at Laptev's for years—he had gone there at the age of eight. He was very much at home there, enjoying complete trust. When, on leaving the warehouse, he removed all the takings from the cash-box and filled his pockets with them, this aroused no suspicion. He was the senior person in the warehouse, in the house and also at church, where he functioned as elder in the old man's place. His cruelty to subordinates had earned him the nickname 'Old Nero' from the clerks and boys.

When they reached the tavern he nodded to the waiter. 'Bring us half a cynosure, my good man, and a couple of dozen indelicacies.'

A little later the waiter brought half a bottle of vodka on a tray and several dishes of *hors d'œuvre*.

'Now, my man,' said Pochatkin. 'Bring a portion of the main author of slander and calumny with mashed potatoes.'

Not understanding, the waiter became embarrassed and made to say something, but Pochatkin looked at him sternly and spoke.

'Otherwise!'

The waiter racked his brains and went to consult his colleagues, but guessed right in the end and brought a helping of tongue.

When each had drunk two vodkas and had a bite, Laptev spoke. 'Tell me, Pochatkin, is it true that our business has been declining in recent years?'

'Not at all.'

'Tell me frankly and openly—what are the profits, past and present? What's the extent of the property? One can't go round blindfold, after all. The warehouse was recently audited, but I don't believe that audit, I'm sorry. You think fit to hide things from me, the only person you tell the truth to is my father. You've been steeped in chicanery since infancy, and now you can't do without it. But what use is that? Now, please be frank, I beg you. What is our business position?'

'That depends on credit fluctuation,' Pochatkin answered after some thought.

'And credit fluctuation means what?'

Pochatkin began explaining, but Laptev understood nothing and sent for Makeichev. He reported at once, said grace, ate some *hors d'œuvre*, and held forth in his portentous, fruity baritone—largely about the clerks' duty to pray for their benefactors night and day.

'All right then, but permit me not to consider myself one of your benefactors,' Laptev said.

'Every man must remember what he is, must be conscious of his station. You are our father and benefactor by God's grace, and we are your slaves.'

'Once and for all I'm sick of all this.' Laptev was angry. 'Will *you* please be *my* benefactor now, and explain our business situation to me. Pray cease treating me as a child, or I shall close down the warehouse tomorrow. My father's blind, my brother's in the mad-house, my nieces are still young. I hate the business, and I'd like to get out of it, but there's no one to take my place, you know that. So leave out the jiggery-pokery, for God's sake.'

They went to the warehouse to do the accounts, and they were still at it in the house that evening, helped by the old man. As he initiated his son into his business secrets, his tone suggested that he had not been practising commerce, but the black art. It transpired that the profits were increasing ten per cent per annum, and that the Laptevs' fortune, in cash and securities alone, totalled six million roubles.

When Laptev went out for some fresh air after doing the accounts it was nearly one o'clock in the morning, and he felt mesmerized by the figures. The night was quiet, moonlit, fragrant. The white walls of the houses in south-bank Moscow, the sight of the heavy locked gate, the quiet, the silent, black shadows—they produced the general impression of a fortress. All it needed was an armed sentry. Laptev went into the garden and sat on a bench near the fence—there was a garden next door too. The bird-cherry was in bloom. Laptev remembered this cherry being just as gnarled and just as big when he had been a boy—it hadn't changed since then. Every corner of the garden and yard reminded him of the distant past. As a boy he had been able, just as now, to see through the sparse trees the whole premises bathed in moonlight with shadows as enigmatic and stern as ever. A black dog lay in the middle of the yard, just as before, and the clerks' windows were wide open. But none of these were cheerful recollections.

Beyond the fence light footsteps were heard in the next-door yard.

'My darling, my dear one,' a man's voice whispered, so close to the fence that Laptev could even hear breathing.

A kiss followed. These millions of roubles, that so uncongenial business—they would ruin Laptev's life and enslave him in the end, of that he was certain. He imagined himself gradually adjusting to his situation, gradually assuming the role of head of a commercial house. He would grow dim and old, he would finally die, as dullards generally do die—in a dirty, sloppy fashion inducing melancholia in their associates. But what was there to stop him giving up these millions and that business, abandoning this garden and yard which he had loathed since boyhood?

The whispering and kissing behind the fence disturbed him. He went into the middle of the yard, unbuttoned his shirt, gazed at the moon. He felt like asking for the garden gate to be unlocked, going out and never coming back. The thought of freedom was a delicious pang in his heart. He laughed happily, imagining what a wonderful and romantic—perhaps, even, saintly—life that might be.

But he still stayed where he was, wondering what on earth kept him there. He was annoyed, both with himself and with the black dog which lay sprawled on the cobbles without escaping into the woods and fields where it would be independent and happy. He and the dog, both were prevented from leaving the yard by the same thing, obviously—the habit of bondage and slavery.

At noon next day he went to see his wife, asking Yartsev along as an insurance against boredom. Julia was staying at a cottage at Butovo, and it was five days since he had visited her. Reaching the station, the friends got into a carriage, and Yartsev sang and rhapsodized about the wonderful weather as they drove along. The cottage was in a large park not far from the station, and Julia sat under a broad old poplar awaiting the guests just where the main avenue began, about twenty yards from the gate. She wore an elegant lace-trimmed dress, light cream in colour, and she was holding the same old umbrella. After greeting her, Yartsev went towards the cottage, whence Sasha's and Leda's voices were heard, while Laptev sat down beside her to talk business.

'Why have you been so long?' she asked, not releasing his hand. 'I've been waiting here and looking out for you for days on end. I do miss you so.'

She got up, passed a hand through his hair, gazed at his face, shoulders and hat with lively interest. 'I do love you, you know.' She blushed.

'You're very dear to me. Now you're here, now I can see you, I'm happier than I can say. Let's talk, then. Say something.'

While she declared her love he felt as if they had already been married ten years. He also wanted his lunch. She put her arms round his neck, tickling his cheek with the silk of her dress. He carefully removed her hand, stood up, went wordlessly towards the cottage. The children ran to meet him.

'How they've grown,' he thought. 'And what changes there have been during these three years. But then I may have another thirteen or thirty years to live. What else has the future in store? Time alone will tell.'

He embraced Sasha and Leda, who hung round his neck.

'Grandfather sends his regards,' he told them. 'Uncle Theodore will soon be dead, Uncle Kostya has written from America and sends his regards. He's bored with the Exhibition and will soon be home. And Uncle Alexis is hungry.'

Then he sat on the terrace and watched his wife sauntering down the path towards the cottage. She looked pensive, she had an expression of bewitching sadness, and tears shone in her eyes. She was no longer the slim, brittle, pale-faced girl, but a mature, beautiful, strong woman. Laptev noticed how ecstatically Yartsev gazed at her, and how her own new, beautiful expression was reflected on Yartsev's face—also sad and entranced. This was like looking at her for the first time in his life, Laptev felt. As they lunched on the terrace Yartsev smiled a vaguely happy, shy smile, and could not take his eyes off Julia and her beautiful neck. Laptev observed him involuntarily, thinking of the thirteen or thirty years which might lie ahead.

What experiences awaited him during that time? What has our future in store?

'Time alone will tell,' he thought.

APPENDIXES

APPENDIX I

THE TWO VOLODYAS

1. Composition
2. Text
3. Variants

1. COMPOSITION

All that is known of the story's composition is contained in two references in Chekhov's letters. On the day of the story's first publication he wrote mentioning certain cuts which had been officiously imposed, without consultation with the author, by the editor of the newspaper in which it appeared: *Russkiye vedomosti* [*The Russian Gazette*]. 'They cropped it so hard that they cut off the head with the hair. What utterly infantile prudishness and astonishing cowardice! I wouldn't have minded if they'd only thrown out a line or two, but they've gutted the middle and docked the tail, and so it has moulted to the point where I'm downright sick of it. All right, let's grant the story *is* cynical. Then it should never have been published at all. But wouldn't it have been fairer to say a word to the author? Or else to write to him? All the more so, surely, as it didn't get into the Christmas number, but was held up' (letter to V. A. Goltsev, 28 Dec. 1893).

Three months later Chekhov again referred to these cuts when writing to a French translator, Jules Legras. 'If you've finished translating *The Two Volodyas* already, don't be in any hurry to publish. The fact is that *The Russian Gazette*'s editors made a lot of cuts out of cowardice and prudishness. I shall send you a complete version without fail' (letter to J. Legras, 27 Mar. 1894). But Chekhov did not keep this promise. Nor did he restore the excised material in later editions (see Variants, below). It has been lost, one presumes irretrievably. We neither know how extensive the editors' cuts were, nor to what points in Chekhov's text we should assign them.

2. TEXT

The present translation is made from the text in *Works*, 1944–51, vol. viii, itself based on that of Chekhov's *Collected Works* (1901), vol. viii.

There are two previous recensions:
(*a*) that published in the newspaper *Russkiye vedomosti* [*The Russian Gazette*] on 28 December 1893;
(*b*) that published by I. Sytin in Chekhov's *Tales and Stories* (Moscow, 1894).

3. VARIANTS

When revising the *Russkiye vedomosti* text for Sytin's edition Chekhov made a few insignificant changes which are ignored here. He also slightly expanded the last paragraph. This originally read as follows:

Calling at the convent almost daily, she complained of her unbearable sufferings to Sister Olga, who told her that none of it mattered, it would all pass.

When further revising the story for his *Collected Works* (1901), Chekhov made two cuts.

'*I mustn't, mustn't think about that,*' *she whispered* (p. 21). And no sooner had thoughts of God, of death, of Olga occurred to her than Sophia was trying to push them out with other thoughts, inaudibly humming a march which she had recently heard in the arcade and beating time in her head.

... *lurking like a beast of prey* (p. 21).
'How dared you marry me?' she wondered, staring at him angrily. 'You knew perfectly well that you were old, older than my father. What gave you the right, then? Your money, eh? Was that it?'
She felt like doing something—something horrible—just to spite herself, her husband and the father who had allowed her to embark on so dishonourable a marriage. What had she to lose, anyway? She didn't believe in God, she was nowhere near to dying. And if God did exist she was doomed to eternal torment since her situation was as hopeless as if she was neck-deep in a bog. She would not take the veil because that would be boring. And if she was going to renounce life it would be better to commit suicide—destroy herself in a moment with knife, poison, rope—than to enter a convent.

APPENDIX II

THE BLACK MONK

1. Composition
2. Text
3. Variants

1. COMPOSITION

The Black Monk was completed by 28 July 1893 (letter to A. S. Suvorin of that date). Its theme had been suggested to Chekhov by a nightmare which he had recently experienced at Melikhovo; and also by a conversation about mirages with the peasants of that locality (M. P. Chekhov, *Anton Chekhov i yego syuzhety* [Moscow, 1923], p. 110).

Chekhov declined to send *The Black Monk* to the newspaper *Novoye vremya* [*New Time*], where he had placed no less than thirty-seven stories in the years 1886–92, but which he was now in process of abandoning. On 18 August 1893 he wrote to Suvorin, the paper's proprietor, as follows: 'I shan't be sending you my new story because I've decided not to send to newspapers any stories requiring serialization.' He elsewhere described *The Black Monk* as 'a medical story, the case history of a disease. The subject is megalomania' (letter to M. O. Menshikov, 15 Jan. 1894). On 25 January 1894 Chekhov wrote to Suvorin to deny the suggestion that *The Black Monk* was a description of the author's own mental condition. 'I believe myself to be sane. True, I'm not specially keen on living. Still, that doesn't yet rate as an illness in the true sense, but rather as a transitory and natural everyday condition. Anyway, if an author depicts a mentally ill person it doesn't follow that he must be ill himself. I wrote *The Black Monk* without any despondent thoughts, out of cold deliberation. I just felt like describing megalomania. As for the monk whizzing over the fields, that was a dream which I described to Misha [the author's brother Michael] on waking up in the morning.'

2. TEXT

The present translation is made from the text in *Works*, 1944–51, vol. viii, itself based on that of Chekhov's *Collected Works* (1901), vol. viii.

There is one previous recension: that published in the magazine *Artist* [*The Artist*], January 1894.

3. VARIANTS

When revising the *Artist* version for the recension of 1894 (identical with the final version), the author changed only a single adjective.

APPENDIX III

A WOMAN'S KINGDOM

1. Composition
2. Text
3. Variants

1. COMPOSITION

Nothing is known of the composition of *A Woman's Kingdom*, except that the story had been completed by November 1893, as is shown by a letter from Chekhov to A. S. Suvorin of the 25th of that month. On 18 December Chekhov again wrote to Suvorin, announcing the forthcoming appearance of the story in the magazine *Russkaya mysl* [*The Russian Idea*] of the following January, and referring to it as 'the description of a certain spinster'.

2. TEXT

The present translation is made from the text in *Works*, 1944–51, vol. viii, itself based on that of Chekhov's *Collected Works* (1901), vol. viii.

There is one previous recension: that published by I. Sytin in Chekhov's *Tales and Stories* (Moscow, 1894).

3. VARIANTS

When revising the text for the recension of 1894, and again for the final version of 1901, Chekhov made a few minor changes which are not recorded here.

APPENDIX IV

ROTHSCHILD'S FIDDLE

1. Composition
2. Text
3. Variants

1. COMPOSITION

All that is known of the composition of *Rothschild's Fiddle* is an entry, probably made in 1892, on pp. 12–13 of Chekhov's Notebook II:

A coffin-maker's wife dies. He makes coffin. She will die in three days, but he hurries the coffin because the next day and the days after that are holidays, e.g. Easter.

She didn't die on the third day after all. Someone comes to buy a coffin. He, in a quandary, sells it. She dies. He curses her while she is given the last sacraments. When she dies he enters 'coffin' under Debits. He measures his wife for it while she is still alive. She: 'Remember us having a fair-haired little baby thirty years ago? We sat by the river.' After her death he goes to the river. The willow has grown substantially in thirty years (*Works*, 1944–51, xii, 285–6).

2. TEXT

The present translation is made from the text in *Works*, 1944–51, vol. viii, itself based on that of Chekhov's *Collected Works* (1901), vol. viii.

There are two previous recensions:

(*a*) that published in the newspaper *Russkiye vedomosti* [*The Russian Gazette*] on 6 February 1894;

(*b*) that published by I. Sytin in Chekhov's *Tales and Stories* (Moscow, 1894).

3. VARIANTS

In the first stage of revision Chekhov made three minor changes, not recorded here. In the second stage of revision he made one minor change, also unrecorded here, and cut out the following sentence:

... *looking scared and troubled* (p. 97). He wouldn't have minded showing her a bit of affection or buying her something now, but it was too late, there was no turning back.

APPENDIX V

THE STUDENT

1. Composition
2. Text
3. Variants

1. COMPOSITION

Chekhov wrote *The Student*, originally entitled *In the Evening*, during a visit to the Crimean resort of Yalta in April 1894 (*Works*, 1944–51, xvi, 141, 462).

According to two separate witnesses, the writer Ivan Bunin and Chekhov's brother Ivan, the author held *The Student* in particularly high esteem and regarded it as evidence that he himself possessed an optimistic outlook. 'How can anyone call me a pessimist [Bunin reports Chekhov as asking]? Why, of all my works *The Student* is my favourite.' According to Ivan Chekhov, too, *The Student* was his brother's favourite work. 'He thought it the most polished' (I. Bunin and I. Chekhov, cited in *Works*, 1944–51, viii, 564).

2. TEXT

The present translation is made from the text in *Works*, 1944–51, vol. viii, itself based on that of Chekhov's *Collected Works* (1901), vol. viii and identical with that published by I. Sytin in Chekhov's *Tales and Stories* (Moscow, 1894).

There is one previous recension: that published by the newspaper *Russkiye vedomosti* [*The Russian Gazette*] on 16 April 1894 with a different title: *In the Evening*.

3. VARIANTS

Besides changing the original title, *In the Evening*, to *The Student*, Chekhov also made a small number of minor corrections (not recorded here) when revising his original text for the *Tales and Stories* version.

APPENDIX VI

THE RUSSIAN MASTER

1. Composition
2. Text
3. Variants

1. COMPOSITION

The Russian Master has a most unusual history in that the first of its two chapters had been published as a self-contained story under a different title in 1889, five years before the work appeared as a whole in 1894. The independently-published first chapter had been entitled *Obyvateli* [*Mediocrities*], and dedicated to a doctor, N. N. Obolonsky, whose patient Chekhov's elder brother Nicholas had been before his death from tuberculosis in June 1889. Chekhov had written *Mediocrities* in early November of the same year. 'Your contributor . . . Chekhov has begun to give birth. . . . The beginning isn't bad' (letter to A. S. Suvorin, 1 Nov. 1889). On 12 November Chekhov sent *Mediocrities* to Suvorin's newspaper *Novoye vremya* [*New Time*] with a comment which shows him acceding to the appeals of his family by refraining from implementing an expressed intention to disrupt the happy conclusion of the story as it then stood. He omitted, that is, in 1889 to supply the astringent dénouement (Chapter Two in the completed story) which he already had in mind and which was eventually, in 1894, to convert the happily ending one-tier *Mediocrities* into the very different, two-tier, *Russian Master* with its falling-cadence ending. 'I enclose a story [Chekhov wrote to Suvorin on 12 November]. . . . It's a facetious trifle from the lives of some provincial guinea-pigs. You must excuse the self-indulgence. Incidentally, the said story has an amusing history. I intended an ending which was to smash my heroes to smithereens, but some damn silly impulse made me read it to my family [including at this time his mother, father, sister and youngest brother]. All begged me "to have mercy and let them off". So I did let my heroes off, and that's why the thing turned out so sloppy.'

Of the history of the conversion of *Mediocrities* into *The Russian Master* by the addition of a second chapter we know nothing beyond the bare fact of its occurrence. The following entry in Chekhov's Notebook I, p. 101, is apparently related to an early stage in the planning of the work:

'Dog hates teacher, is forbidden to bark at him. Dog stares, doesn't bark but cries with rage.'

2. TEXT

The present translation is made from the text in *Works*, 1944–51, vol. viii, itself based on that of Chekhov's *Collected Works* (1901), vol. viii.

There are three previous recensions:

(*a*) that published as a self-contained story in the newspaper *Novoye vremya* of 28 November 1889 under the title *Mediocrities*, but consisting of the first chapter only;

(*b*) that published in the newspaper *Russkiye vedomosti* [*The Russian Gazette*] of 10 July 1894;

(*c*) that published by I. Sytin in Chekhov's *Tales and Stories* (Moscow, 1894).

3. VARIANTS

The only major variant (the addition of Chapter Two) has been discussed above.

For the *Tales and Stories* version a few minor stylistic changes were made, including the replacement of the former surname 'Shidlovsky' by 'Shelestov'. The following sentence was cut:

... *sure she was going to get married, in other words* (p. 114). She danced the mazurka with massive grace, like a Polish girl, sang ballads very nicely, played the piano tolerably, and her company would have been indispensable had it been in the least degree possible to talk to her.

For the *Collected Works* version some further minor changes of wording, not recorded here, were also made.

APPENDIX VII

AT A COUNTRY HOUSE

1. Composition
2. Text
3. Variants

1. COMPOSITION

Nothing is known of the composition of *At a Country House*.

2. TEXT

The present translation is made from the text in *Works,* 1944–51, vol. viii, itself based on that of Chekhov's *Collected Works* (1901), vol. viii.

There are two previous recensions:

(*a*) that published in the newspaper *Russkiye vedomosti* [*The Russian Gazette*] of 28 August 1894;

(*b*) that published by I. Sytin in Chekhov's *Tales and Stories* (Moscow, 1894).

3. VARIANTS

Both stages of revision included some minor changes in wording, not recorded here. For the *Tales and Stories* version Chekhov also made a sizeable cut, as follows:

. . . *her young life had been ruined* (p. 138). Both girls were beautiful and appealing. Rashevich wanted to knock at their door and explain that he hadn't had the remotest intention of insulting poor Meyer. How could he have foreseen that the conversation would take so unexpectedly foolish a turn? Why, he'd have been delighted for Zhenya to marry Meyer, for all his lower-class origins. His own wife hadn't exactly come out of the top drawer, and if he'd weighed in about 'breeding' just now it had only been because he thought his ideas fresh and original, and because he wanted to gratify and please this very same Meyer. Why, he'd be delighted to chase after the coroner at this very moment, and embark on a new harangue. This one would be about professional men of humble origins, what a fresh and rejuvenating force they represented and so on. As for your much-vaunted upper crust, they'd really have been hauled over the coals!

APPENDIX VIII

THE HEAD GARDENER'S STORY

1. Composition
2. Text
3. Variants

1. COMPOSITION

As had previously occurred with *The Two Volodyas*, the editors of the newspaper *Russkiye vedomosti* [*The Russian Gazette*], in which *The Head Gardener's Story* was first published, made a cut in the text out of apprehensions about possible censorship objections. In this case, however (by contrast with *The Two Volodyas*), we can trace the material excised, since Chekhov quotes the relevant passage in a letter of 31 December 1894 to I. I. Gorbunov-Posadov.

'*Russkiye vedomosti* . . . in craven fear cut from the beginning of the Gardener's speech the following passage: "It's not hard to believe in God. Even the Inquisitors believed in Him. So too did Biron and Arakcheyev [tyrants, notorious minions of the Empress Anne (ruled 1730–40) and the Emperor Alexander I (ruled 1801–25) respectively]. *You* believe in Man." ' In the same letter Chekhov accepted Gorbunov-Posadov's proposal to publish the story in an edition specially designed for the *narod* (peasants, the Russian 'underprivileged' in general). But he added, while giving his permission, that the story was not, in his own view, suitable for this particular readership, and in any case the project fell through.

Despite his indignation over the cut made by *Russkiye vedomosti*, Chekhov omitted to restore the passage concerned in later editions.

2. TEXT

The present translation is made from the text in *Works*, 1944–51, vol. viii, itself based on that of Chekhov's posthumous *Collected Works* (1906), vol. xi.

There are two previous recensions:

(*a*) that published in the newspaper *Russkiye vedomosti* [*The Russian Gazette*] of 25 December 1894;

(*b*) that published in the symposium *A Toiler's Journey: for the Thirty-Fifth Anniversary of D. Tikhomirov's Literary and Pedagogical Activity* (Moscow, 1901).

3. VARIANTS

Chekhov made a few minor alterations at both stages of revision. These included the excision for the *Collected Works* edition of two passages:

. . . *would puff his way up* (p. 145) to a high place, and before he could approach his patient was obliged to cough gobs of coagulated blood off his chest.

. . . *never accepted money* (p. 145). Being wise, he was naturally the first to appreciate that life on this earth is impossible without death.

APPENDIX IX

THREE YEARS

1. Composition
2. Text
3. Variants

1. COMPOSITION

Numerous entries in Chekhov's Notebooks, later exploited in the story—the most important are given in translation below—go back to March 1891, which suggests that the gestation period of *Three Years* was, roughly, three years (Gitovich, pp. 288, 300, 333-4).

Chekhov began writing *Three Years* in autumn 1894, and finished it in December of the same year. On 29 September 1894 he wrote to his sister as ollows: 'If you see Goltsev, tell him I'm writing a novel about Moscow life for *Russkaya mysl* [*The Russian Idea*, the magazine of which V. A. Goltsev was co-editor]. . . . But they shouldn't expect it before December since it's a long work, of six to eight signatures.' On 6 October Chekhov wrote to Goltsev directly, stating that the story was 'not small, but not particularly large either. I'm working meticulously, so I doubt if I'll finish before December.'

On 28 November Chekhov informed another correspondent, N. M. Yezhov, that he was writing a story for the January issue of *Russkaya mysl*, adding that 'I'm hurrying with it and it's turning out a bit dull and lifeless.' On 4 December, when Chekhov was finishing the story, he wrote to a correspondent that 'the conception was one thing but the realization is something quite different, rather lifeless—not silky, as I wanted, but like a piece of cambric. . . . I'm fed up with always writing the same old things, and want to describe devils, wizards and terrifying, volcanic women. But, alas, people want well-meaning tales from the lives of the Ivan Gavriloviches and their spouses.' When despatching the story to Goltsev, on 11 or 12 December, Chekhov wrote as follows: '*Three Years: Scenes from Family Life*. That's the title of the . . . story. If you don't like the "scenes", just leave the "from family life", or just sub-title it "a story".' In fact Goltsev chose the last-mentioned solution.

That the censor imposed certain cuts—unrestored by Chekhov and untraced by his posthumous editors—is evident from his letter to A. S. Suvorin of 19 January 1895. 'The censor banned the lines referring to religion—and, as you know, *Russkaya mysl* is subject to pre-publication censorship. This takes away all one's urge to write freely. It's like plying your pen with a bone stuck in your throat.'

In a letter to Suvorin of 21 January 1895 Chekhov protested against the suggestion that Laptev *père*, in *Three Years*, was to be equated with his own father. Here is a significant biographical point: disparaging though the author's attitude to the fictional Laptev Senior may seem, he rated his own father even lower. 'The old merchant . . . does not resemble my father since, at the end of his days, Father is still what he has been all his life: a small-calibred person of limited range.' Nor would Chekhov countenance the suggestion that Polina Rassudin, in *Three Years*, was based on his real-life friend Olga Kundasov, an eccentric mathematician and astronomer.

Despite Chekhov's refusal to equate Laptev Senior with his own father, the warehouse in *Three Years* was almost certainly inspired by Gavrilov's, the large Moscow wholesale haberdashery suppliers at which Chekhov's father had been employed as a clerk from 1877 onwards, and where his cousin Michael also served for many years.

Chekhov's Notebooks contain particularly numerous entries which relate to the planning of *Three Years*, and which (as stated above) go back to March 1891. They include the following items from Notebook I:

p. 5.
2. O.I.'s brother [Panaurov] drank only champagne. It was less tobacco than cigarette-holders and pipes which attracted him, and he adored cups, glass-holders, studs, ties, canes, scents.

p. 12.
7. He was not jealous of the students who took his wife to theatres and symphony concerts, but of the actors and singers who were bound to attract his young wife.
8. His sister's husband had children by a mistress, and loved them more than his legitimate children. Those were called Sasha and Zoya.
9. His brother played cards at the Doctors' Club of an evening.
10. His father is a school visitor. Talking to the teacher, his brother adopts an authoritarian tone. Businessmen usually do like to boss people around. The father is a church elder. The choir fears him.

p. 17.
1. His brother dreamt of being a mayor, then a vice-governor or departmental director, and then an assistant minister. His dream: 'I'll write a patriotic article, publish it in *The Moscow Gazette*, it will be read by the big shots, and I'll be invited to run a department.'

p. 18.
2. Kostya did not sing, having neither voice nor ear, but he loved arranging concerts, selling tickets, meeting singers.

p. 19.

8. The boys in the warehouse were whipped.

9. Tries to find out when the firm's centenary will be so that he can apply to be registered as a gentleman.

10. She dressed Moscow fashion, had been to school in Moscow, and this appealed to him.

12. The brother-in-law drank either little or nothing. It was not on drink, but on food, that he had wasted his substance.

p. 22.

7. He was pleased that his future wife was devout, that she held precise views and convictions. But when she became his wife this very precision upset him.

p. 23.

1. His brother-in-law makes advances to his young wife. Tells her she 'needs a lover'.

2. Looking at her new friends in Moscow, she thought: 'How ugly Moscow men are.'

3. Brother-in-law: 'Every woman is capable of being unfaithful, believe me. But that means nothing. It does no one any harm.'

4. In the compartment, brother-in-law to her: 'But what are you afraid of? What's so terrible about it? What would you lose by it?'

7. She: 'Why the comparison with the famous musician? That's what I can't see. What has the famous musician got to do with it (expression of hatred)?'

p. 24.

4. Kostya went to America for the Exhibition.

5. Kostya doing lesson with girls: 'The flood didn't actually happen.'

7. Conversation with chief clerk. 'Is our business really in a bad way?' 'Not in the least.'

9. The dealings are extensive, but there's no accountant.

10. A peasant, not particularly intelligent or capable, becomes a merchant and then a rich man by accident, conducts his business day in day out mechanically, quirkily, bossing his clerks and mocking his customers. The warehouse is visited by buyers' agents, Germans, Englishmen, as also by a drunken, penniless intellectual nicknamed 'Midget', who translates the foreign correspondence.

p. 25.

1. 'For your kind of business you need clerks devoid of personality, with no stake in anything . . . making them go to church and grovel to you. You'd never take a university man into the warehouse, that's for sure.'

'University men are no use in the business.'

'Untrue! Lies!'

2. Sister, as they say good-bye: 'If, which God forbid, I should die, give my little girls a home.'

Wife, touched: 'Oh, that I promise you.'

3. Father goes completely blind. Brother is ill. They go to the New Trinity Inn. Conversation.

'What's the state of our business, Pochatkin?'

'It all depends on the fluctuation in promissory notes.'

'And what do you mean by that?'

'When a customer owes money and doesn't want to pay it.'

4. On learning of his brother's illness he wept. As a boy and youth his brother had been a splendid person. Astonishing that this timid, gentle, intelligent man's illness should have begun with megalomania.

5. She fell in love with me for my money—i.e. that attribute of myself by which I set least store.

6. The old man is proud and boastful. Calls Sasha and Zoya 'illegitimate'.

8. The chief clerk Ivan Pochatkin comes from Kashira. Acts as church elder in the old man's place.

p. 26.

2. Brother-in-law in compartment after kisses tells story of old pasha presented with harem.

3. A woman won't last long without an attachment, which is why X. took up with Yartsev.

4. Zoya, the baby and she herself contracted diphtheria. Baby died. She went to Kostya's rooms to cry.

6. 'I loved you for your mind and spirit—whereas with her it was your money, wasn't it?'

9. To her the air in the restaurant seemed poisoned by tobacco and male breath. She thought all men dissolute and liable to leap upon her any moment.

10. Brother-in-law, laying newspaper aside: 'This blessed town is such a bore.'

p. 27.

4. The clerks are not forbidden to marry, but as things are none of them ever do marry because they are afraid of annoying the boss and losing their jobs. They don't marry, they lead clandestine, dissolute lives, they fall ill.

p. 28.

1. 'I'm so depressed, old boy. But I've been hiding it all the time. I am so unhappy.'

His brother had this breakdown in front of the maid, which is why he felt embarrassed later, when leaving.

7. I'd give anything to have you as my wife. 'Give anything'—what trades-man's talk. A lot of use your *anything* is.

9. After the baby's death he looked at her—so lifeless and silent—and he thought: 'Whether you do or do not marry for love, it comes to the same in the end.'

p. 29.

2. He writes on 'The Russian Soul'. That soul is characterized by the highest degree of idealism. As for your Russian admirer of western Europe—let him disbelieve in miracles and the supernatural if he likes, but let him not dare destroy the faith in the Russian's soul, since this is a form of idealism pre-destined to save Europe.

'But you don't say what Europe is to be saved *from*.'

'That's obvious.'

5. 'Where have you been, Uncle Kostya?'

'In court defending a burglar. Fellow broke into a loft and stole the washing from some laundry maids.'

p. 30.

1. There are no firm, permanent attachments. He is annoyed with X. for going to live with Y., and with himself because his feelings for his wife have begun to cool.

3. Kostya secretly writes novels, but no one publishes them because of their extreme tendentiousness and worthlessness.

5. They went to the picture exhibition as a family, merchant-fashion—he, she, Kostya, the governess, both little girls. He paid for them all. He did not understand and gazed intently, making a peep-hole of his fingers. Kostya was put off by the lack of content while the governess was making sure the children didn't misbehave, and tried to divert their attention when they approached a naked nymph. She was bored, but then suddenly overcome with emotion in front of one landscape. She suddenly understood painting, and they bought the landscape.

p. 31.

1. He and she went to the District Court to hear Kostya, who had invited them. It was a boring case, and Kostya—no whit perturbed, with angry eyes—pronounced lengthy platitudes in a deep voice, working up the spectators' emotions. When the burglar was acquitted he would not return home but went to tackle someone about some piece of impertinence.

5. He can't forgive the old man for the past. But she's sorry for the old boy. She goes to see him. He asks her: 'Why is Theodore ill? Has he got a chill or something? Now, I was never ill.'

And he starts bragging. Still, he does love his children.

6. 'But is it really impossible to avert the relapse?' Her doctor father sighed and shrugged his shoulders, as if to say that doctors aren't gods.

8. While walking at Sokolniki, she tells Yartsev how nice it is to have a baby.

He to her: 'Tell me, doesn't your love for your baby detract from your love for your husband?'

'I don't know. I didn't marry for love. At first I suffered agonies, but now I've calmed down and I think that there's no such thing as love and that one can manage without it.'

p. 32.

2. In the warehouse. They were northerners from their speech, and they said 'sir' so often that some of their sentences sounded like one long hiss.

p. 34.

7. When she reached her home town the houses seemed lower, and the people fewer. A dead body was carried past in an open coffin accompanied by banners.

9. By the old man's reckoning he had made his wife and her family happy, rewarded his children, lavished benefactions on his clerks and employees, given the whole street cause to mention him in their prayers.

10. His mother had married his father when she was seventeen and he was forty-two, and she had gone in fear and trembling of him.

11. Father shows no trace of repentance. Stern and unjust. God loves him and no one else. People's affairs fail to prosper because they won't take his advice. No deal ever succeeds without his advice. All he does is excellent.

p. 35.

9. Panaurov has put up at the Dresden Hotel in Moscow.

14. People like Laptev can't stand up to boors and bounders, which is why we find such ugly abuses in our society along with the evolution of high ideals.

15. He was only happy once in his life—under the umbrella.

16. A burglar broke into the laundry loft and stole washing worth 74 roubles. The laundry girls suspected a retired soldier who kept saying in court that he'd 'drunk a skinful'. The women wanted him put away at all costs. Kostya in his speech: 'One can't be robbed of one's honour, one can only lose it.'

p. 36.

6. While she was praying it occurred to him: 'There she is praying, but she has treated me like a whore.'

12. The old man thought himself a higher order of being, infallible.

13. Arriving in her home town, and passing the house where poor Nina had lived, she saw white notices on the windows.

14. She wanted to put the old man on the right path, thinking that he would soon die and must repent, but none of this could prevail against his adoration of himself.

p. 37.

4. On Pochatkin. Has worked at Laptev's since childhood, starting as office-boy. He was trusted completely. When, on leaving the warehouse of an evening, he stuffed his pockets with money taken from the cash-box, this aroused no suspicion. He was the senior man at the warehouse, at the lodgings, and also at church, where he acted as elder in the old man's place.

p. 38.

2. Pochatkin at Bubnov's inn: 'Bring me half a cynosure and a couple of dozen indelicacies.'

5. Panaurov was made a vice-governor.

6. Conversation at holiday villa: 'I'll write a historical play.' Yartsev and Kostya returned to town along a forest clearing.

7. Panaurov in compartment: 'I've been a justice of the peace, I've chaired the local justices' committee, and finally I've been consultant to the county council. I think I'm entitled to some consideration by the authorities, but I've just been putting out some feelers in St. Petersburg and received a vague sort of answer.'

11. Panaurov has received a transfer and promotion to a higher rank, but doesn't want to take his unofficial family along, on the grounds that an irregular life style would accord ill with his new appointment.

p. 39.

5. So far we've only got through three years. But there will be thirteen or thirty more to get through, surely. Grandfather's blind, Uncle Theodore will soon be dead, Uncle Kostya sends his regards by letter—he's in America at the Exhibition—and Uncle Alexis is tired out.

6. She: 'Parents think that their own children are the élite of creation, that strangers like kissing their children and so on. All the same, my little Olga really is special.'

7. We all do nothing but talk and read about love, yet we do precious little loving. The Daghestan valley.

p. 40.

2. She came back from the old man tired out: 'We must move to Pyatnitsky Street.'

He takes her arm: 'Now, I feel as if our life was over and we were embarking on a half-life, a time of boredom.' Was once happy, under umbrella.

4. Bring me a portion of the main author of Slander and Calumny with mashed potatoes.

Not understanding, the waiter became embarrassed to be so slow on the uptake, and was about to raise some objection. But Poch[atkin] looked at him sternly and spoke.

'Otherwise!'

Soon afterwards the waiter brought tongue and mashed potatoes. So he *had* understood.

Other entries relating to the planning of *Three Years* are to be found in Chekhov's 'Notes on Separate Sheets' (*Works*, 1944–51, xii, 304 ff.).

Sheet 12.

12. She had the impression that there were many identical pictures at the exhibition.

13. He had sometimes paid a lot for what had later turned out to be crude forgeries.

14. Before us filed a whole parade of laundresses.

15. Kostya's line was that they had burgled themselves.

16. Laptev put himself in a juror's shoes, and concluded that there had been breaking and entering . . . but no petty larceny, since the laundresses had spent the proceeds of stealing the laundry on drink, or, if there had been larceny, then it had been without breaking and entering.

24. Kostya began telling the plot of a story he had once read.

27. Today the old Frenchman himself had a bath.

31. She lied when she said that she liked his novels very much. He could get tickets at any time. He had a mania for describing the country and manor houses, though he hadn't been in such houses more than half a dozen times in his life.

40. His novels were never published, which he put down to censorship conditions.

'I'm no ace administrator of course, but I am a decent, honest man, and that means a lot these days. I confess I've deceived women, but in my relations with the Russian government I've always been the perfect gentleman.'

2. TEXT

The present translation is made from the text in *Works*, 1944–51, vol. viii, itself based on that of Chekhov's *Collected Works* (1901), vol. viii.

There is one previous recension: that published in the magazine *Russkaya mysl* of January and February 1895 with the sub-title *A Story*.

3. VARIANTS

When preparing the story for his *Collected Works* Chekhov made extensive cuts and alterations, of which the following are the most significant:

(a) *Material on Laptev*

... *his sister's illness again* (p. 153)?
'But is there really no way of averting a relapse?' he asked. 'Is medicine really so powerless?'
He began making trite remarks about medicine, saying that it only cures symptoms, and still hasn't reduced the mortality rate, for all its successes.
'Indeed, its successes are generally expressed in its progressive self-elimination,' he went on, addressing Julia. 'It is gradually consuming itself. People used to cure themselves with herbs, but then chemistry gradually expelled all these herbs from the dispensary, and we're now treated with alkaloids. Dispensaries once flourished on an artificially extensive scale, and may be expected to disappear entirely in the end. Hygiene will replace medicine.'
'This really isn't at all interesting to a girl,' Laptev thought irritably. 'People praise hygiene to the skies,' he went on, 'even claiming that it is sometimes effective in reducing the mortality rate through such hygienic measures as the establishment of soup kitchens and doss-houses. And, by the way, this problem greatly concerns me personally. I've been recommended to set up a hostel in Moscow, we even have a draft scheme afoot. Should our plans be realized, a *worker arriving in the evening* . . .'

At home (p. 158) he stalked round the downstairs rooms laughing at himself and calling himself a lunatic. His arms and legs trembled, his head still felt that feathery touch. He suddenly saw on a chair *the umbrella left behind by Julia* . . . *old piece of elastic.* The handle was white, not of bone but of some sort of composition. Laptev gazed at it enraptured for a while, then sat down and opened it above him. Now he felt fine, free and easy. Observing his own sensations from habit, he was amazed, and told himself that he had never known such ecstasy before. He *felt enveloped* . . .

'. . . *prepared to argue with you for ever* (p. 159). You can talk till you're blue in the face, but I'll always insist that those who believe in God, the triumph of justice, the Last Judgement, eternal bliss—they're far more solid, far nearer to the truth than we insubstantial idealists who believe in nothing definitely and who only try to convince ourselves that truth exists and can be attained. I also love her because *she went to school in Moscow.* . .'

. . . *he saw so little of Julia* (p. 161). Anyone else would have given up the doctor long ago, and found any number of means to meet his daughter away from home, but he was too nervous, he brooded a lot and didn't know what to do. Even now, knowing that she was alone in the house, he still dared not approach her straightforwardly, but was as flustered by apprehensive anticipations as a callow youth—would his visit be the proper thing, wouldn't it be better to send a servant with that umbrella?

'*Frankly, I'm worried* (p. 190).'
They spent a long time talking about Theodore and the Russian intellectual's cult of simulated mysticism, pig-headedness, arrogant bluster and mental feebleness. Many even change their voice and walk just to seem coarse and ponderous. *Theodore was trying* . . .

. . . *like the man's superior officer* (p. 190).
'Such simulated aberrations pave the way to genuine delusions,' said Laptev. 'If a man's brain is neurotically receptive to miscellaneous mumbo-jumbo, then he'll never break free of it, he's completely done for. Whatever is obscure, vague, blurred, imperfectly expressed—these gentry all lump it together in one weird mish-mash. If a member of this fraternity takes up spiritualism or magnetism then he just has to throw in homoeopathy, metaphysics and symbolism as well. He believes that three candles and the number thirteen are unlucky, he curses civilization in the name of Chinese culture of which, never having been to China, he has no notion, and he won't recognize the kind of scholarship that transcends the bounds of nationality. This frame of mind is unsatisfactory, of course, and the man feels vaguely inadequate. He is forever irked, riled, obsessively anti-suggestible. Out of pure conceit he's now prepared to claim that the Russian's highest aspirations are brute ignorance, poverty and the lash.'

. . . *took a cab to the Yar Restaurant* (p. 196)—why, he had no idea.
'So that's what's called family happiness,' he jeered at himself, deliberately unbuttoning his fur coat so as to catch cold. 'That's love for you.'
Ashamed of his jealousy, cursing it, he paced about at Yar's *near the tables* . . .

. . . *might have made a fine artist had he studied* (p. 201). But he had occasional bouts of a peculiar mood when he was certain that painting and sculpture had no meaning for him, that he understood them not at all. *When abroad* . . . *express an opinion.* The dealer would listen attentively and agree, obviously flattering his ignorance while privately despising him. Sensing this, Laptev would buy some rough frame or box of worthless paper out of sheer obstinacy, and betray his ignorance.

... *turned out to be crude forgeries* (p. 202). And there were many such instances. Meanwhile he couldn't recall any evidence at all of possessing mature sensitivity and developed taste. Now, why should one so timid—at meetings, at the theatre, in the warehouse—be so bold and brash at picture exhibitions? From knowing that he could buy up all these pictures he derived confidence, but then he would catch himself out thinking this very thought—and would lose his confidence. When he stood in front of a picture, and loudly expressed his opinion, something deep down inside him—his conscience, no doubt—whispered that merchant blood, a wayward fluid, swirled in his veins, and that he who so boldly criticized the artist was very like his brother Theodore rebuking some erring clerk or teacher.

'. . . *one doesn't even notice them, my dear* (p. 204). You can't tell what he's like until he lets himself go. A real stick-in-the-mud he is. *He'll shell out . . . unfit for struggle.* There are lots of his sort. And that, sir, is why our society's rapid progress, and the extensive deployment of its civilized ideals, go hand in hand with sheer barbarity and miscellaneous horrors.'

'. . . *fiddlesticks!* (p. 215). A line of dead-beats, more like!' shouted Laptev furiously, hurling a chair at the hearth. 'A line of louts and down-and-outs! Though our grandfather wasn't a serf, I know for certain that he was always being kicked around *by the nobs. . . . Father beat you and me.* A rotten, seedy sort of bloody breed!'

Laptev quickly went out, but came back at once and went on, banging his fist on the table. '*What did your* "*illustrious house*" . . . *just look at me*—I'm like some sort of shell-fish or cretin, *I lack adaptability . . . not to have children, you and I.* Our line must end with us, or else—and I'm quite certain of this—our progeny will all be cowards, criminals and lunatics.'

Theodore shuddered. 'That's crude, Alexis. Don't say such things.'

Julia came into the study . . .

(*b*) *Material on Julia*

'. . . *how much good you'll be able to do* (p. 167).'

Now he saw her sitting down, standing up, going out of the drawing room. To conceal the strength of her feelings she would hold her handkerchief to her mouth, and he sensed that she had made no definite decision, but was still struggling with herself.

The doctor said it was time for him *to go on his rounds . . .*

. . . *no one should take it amiss* (p. 169). She was horrified to think of poor Julia having to manage without a mother. Somebody, after all, must deal with the dowry and see to it being arranged properly. And 'that monstrosity'—her name for the doctor—didn't understand a thing, now, did he?

By evening the weather was calm and fine, and Laptev went to the town park with Julia. Taking her arm, he told her about his childhood, the university, Moscow life in general, while she listened most attentively. On a dark path he could not help embracing her passionately and kissing her on the lips, while she kissed him on the cheek. This peck on the cheek, her serious attention —he would have exchanged them for a single smile. He was embarrassed to think that she was already studying her 'faithful and devoted wife' role—that of a spouse rather than a wife. Even while embracing her and enjoying doing so, he could not forget that she did not love him.

. . . *which he liked very much* (p. 169). Her mother had once occupied them, as one could vaguely sense, especially in the twilight of evening before the lamp had been lit. Dark colours predominated, and there was a smell of very good scent or lamp oil. There were many icons with metallic trimmings.

. . . *could have endured such a horror* (p. 177). In Moscow she could constantly have fun, worship, read, not think about herself. She very much liked Moscow's streets, houses and churches, and she now felt that if she could *have driven about Moscow* . . .

'. . . *whether thou dost come in peace unto this house* (p. 178)?'
Calling the Laptev business and his house a 'vineyard', he went on to explain that all his relatives and employees had been tremulously awaiting the wife of the master's eldest son—tremulously because the welfare, the very fate, of many of them would be in her hands henceforth. Having power, she could do much good, but also much harm.

'*She prays*,' *he reflected*, '*but* (p. 184) she has behaved essentially like a whore in relations between the two of us.' Cynically, he even tried to console himself, calculating that he had had what he'd paid for, *and a revolting thought it was* . . .

. . . *without sharing her pleasure with him* (p. 184). When leaving the house only today to drive to a concert, she had angrily shouted at Kostya that he did not know 'how to take a lady's arm'. 'But why is she so insincere with me?' Laptev wondered.

. . . *Julia now being pregnant* (p. 203). She bore it lightly without illnesses and fuss, only smoking occasional cigarettes, and was angry with the name Julia, saying that it only suited pretty parlour-maids. Kochevoy and Yartsev laughed and called her Constance.

(c) Material on Nina

The family was in business (p. 154). She was older than her brothers, so the servants and boys had once called her 'nanny'. Her childhood had been long and boring. *The father had been strict . . . before her death.* Then her little brother Theodore had been unable to sleep at night, he kept shouting that he was dreaming about his mother. The servants had been dirty, coarse, hypocritical. The house had been frequented by priests and monks who had addressed lengthy homilies at the children while helping themselves to the food. The governess who had been hired for the little girl, an emaciated, large-toothed personage resembling a fish, had taught them nothing and had only stopped them misbehaving. The boys had been sent *to a grammar school, but Nina . . .*

'*This is some local sage of theirs* (p. 155).'

Nina feared death and prayed daily to be cured, but had been rather against holy men, monks and pilgrims since childhood. She retained a dim memory of grey-haired people in long robes flattering her rich father and being rude to her ill, frightened mother, as also to the children and servants. She disliked talking about them.

. . . without bothering whether he should or not (p. 160). All one heard at Nina's home, usually, was how could she get some old but still presentable trousers out of her friends for a small boy so that he was not ashamed to go to school or to work, how to buy another boy some boots, or to get a third a job in a tele-graph office where there wasn't really a vacancy. She *paid poor boys' school fees . . .*

. . . which she was ashamed to confide in him and which (p. 160) worried her.

'I know you're kind,' she said after some thought. 'Well, if you're so keen then, lend me two hundred roubles.'

Laptev gestured impatiently.

'What's the use of talking to you?' He sighed. 'You remind me of the Ukrainian who said that if he'd been Tsar he'd have stolen a hundred roubles and run away.'

. . . sternly surveying her mother (p. 187). At that time we had a dog called Caro—a pointer or a setter—at our country cottage,' said Nina quietly, breath-ing heavily after each word. 'There was a walk we used to take—to the station, to see the trains arrive and leave. Well, we were walking along and laughing aloud as girls do, when some gentleman—tall, handsome, dignified—stroked Caro and said he was "a most expensive dog, madam". I was embarrassed. The gentleman lived with some relatives at Khimki, and he started taking me out.'

Panaurov took the candle . . .

(d) *Material on Panaurov*

He had started another family in town, which (p. 155) provoked much mur-muring in society since no secret was made of this illegitimate family. But he held local public opinion in utter scorn, saying that he would run ten families just to annoy these morons, imbeciles and dunderheads if he could afford it.

He suffered chronic shortage of cash. In recent years the Moscow office had, incidentally, been sending his legitimate family 250 roubles a month without the old man's knowledge, all the money being debited to the brothers—now to Theodore, now to Alexis.

... *as if begging a favour* (p. 157). He was forty-eight years old, but he still screwed up his eyes from old habit as he had fifteen or twenty years ago. He would sigh, languidly shake his head, smile benevolently and regally, all his movements and glances conveying patent self-satisfaction and the assumption that his presence and conversation were an enormous source of pleasure to others.

Laptev listened without interest, not trying to understand. 'What a popinjay!' was his only thought. In his ears echoed the words 'lymph', 'cells', 'bile'.

Bored in the end, he stood up.

'*I'm a bit peckish . . .*'

... *contrived to run through his own and his wife's property, and* (p. 157) was heavily in debt. He was said to have eaten himself out of house and home, to have squandered his substance on lemonade. He really did like *tasty food . . .*

... *the waiters to whom he nonchalantly tossed* (p. 157) five- or ten-rouble tips. A single rouble wasn't grand enough for him, it was an indecent scrap of paper and he was ashamed to give it. He liked to subscribe *to everything . . . canes, scents,* and only smoked because of his passion for cigarette holders, pipes and cigar cases. *His nightshirts . . .*

... *screwing up his dark eyes* (p. 158). 'If you fall in love, suffer, make mistakes, experience remorse, and if you fall out of love, then know that sooner or later a time will come when you'll have forgotten it all, or will look on it with the eye of a detached historian. Everything comes to an end. *You'll be deceived . . . you'll coolly reckon* that these infidelities are inevitable, that they don't mean a thing, actually, don't do anyone any harm.'

Tired, slightly drunk . . . clipped black beard and white waistcoat, and wished that he himself could cut such a figure, or have such manners. He could see his sister's point of view now *and felt he understood . . .*

... *wandering listlessly through the house* (p. 217). Panaurov arrived after dinner and talked to him about Mme Milan while he agreed without hearing.

'She's complained of my deserting her,' said Panaurov. 'But that's nonsense, my dear chap. I only want to make her see that my new job can't be squared with free love, and if I'm seen living with a common-law wife I may be asked to resign. It will be no worse for us and our children if we live in different towns.'

'Yes, yes, yes,' Laptev agreed.

'As for love, passion and all that—high time the old girl gave it all up. Why, it's all so silly. And the financial aspect, old son—that's been most splendidly settled by you. She tells me you've promised to send her 240 roubles a month. Jolly good of you, what? Er, I imagine you've given your office my new address?' he asked in honeyed tones.

'Yes, yes, yes.'

(e) *Material on Laptev's brother Theodore*

'*Local government people are all the rage there, old son, and* (p. 194) you'll run a department, believe you me—you might make junior minister. You'll be an under-secretary before you're fifty and wear a ribbon round your neck.' His eyes blazed, childlike joy was written on his face. *Realizing that . . . were Theodore's own ambitions*, he felt awkward, went away and sat by the fireplace.

'I'm sorry, but you've changed an awful lot lately,' he said after a short pause.

'Perhaps,' sighed Theodore.

(f) *Material on Dr. Belavin*

The doctor was relieved, but (p. 164) continued through inertia.

'I don't suppose it's all that amusing to share a house with a lunatic.' He threw up his arms in amazement.

'*. . . surely that's insanity in our age* (p. 164)! I've been fair and decent to people, but they've always thrown stones at me, walked all over me. Even from my nearest and dearest I've had no sympathy—none whatsoever.'

'Oh, this is too much!' Julia spoke with irritation. '*It's impossible to talk to you . . .*'

. . . how often her father was unfair to her (p. 164).

'I am a sick man,' went on the doctor. 'I haven't long to live. Soon, soon I'll make you all happy by freeing you from my presence.'

He was absolutely convinced that he had anaemia and a nervous indisposition because he ate and slept so little, whereas he was a hearty trencherman, drank his three glasses of vodka at lunch and dinner every day, and slept to his heart's content. This continual harping on ill health upset Julia because it was all so unfair.

She was irascible, often quarrelling with her father, often swearing to leave home once and for all. But she was easygoing by nature, she was always the first to go and make peace overtures. It was no different now. *But she soon . . .*

(g) Material on Polina Rassudin

. . . as if impelled from behind (p. 179). Her movements were angular, brusque. She was wholly womanly only when she sat at the piano or stood on one spot without moving. In the street, when she hurried to a lesson in her long overcoat and cap pulled down to her ears, you might have taken her for a young monk.

. . . but she ran into the hall (p. 183) and brought him back.
'But you've treated me cruelly, admit it.' She burst into tears and her head fell on his shoulder. 'I have lost you,' she said. 'And I feel as if I had died.'
She burst out sobbing and *frantically clutched his upper arm . . .*

(h) Material on Kostya Kochevoy

. . . large, reddish whiskers (p. 187). In his jersey tightly encircling his narrow chest, on his long legs, brandishing his long arms, he looked like a daddy-long-legs.
Panting, wiping the sweat off his face, he went to the telephone and ordered tea from the big house in a fruity bass. *Peter, a middle-aged odd-job man . . .*

. . . Julia had not liked Kostya at first (p. 189). She particularly disliked his deep voice and way of expressing himself when he was in a good mood—*all that* 'shove off' *. . . over his vodka.* As for his habit of clinking glasses and uttering lamentations over his drink, she found it trivial. Nor could she find any virtue in the poem about the senior porter which he often laughingly recited with malicious relish. But when she knew him better, finding him easy to get on with, not sly, fond of Laptev, of herself, of the little girls and even of Peter, she felt very much at ease with him and was even pleased when his deep voice resounded in the big house. *He was open with her . . .*

. . . a famous writer one day (p. 190). There were two especially notable features in his creative work. First, his *novels were all about the countryside . . . to Volokolamsk over a court case.* And, secondly, he only wrote on topical subjects. Thus, if some newly instituted official post was not to his liking, he would depict an unsympathetic hero as occupying that post.

. . . looking angrily at the jury (p. 203). After a long and totally superfluous exordium he drank some water, and weighed in about the atrociously hard life of the working class, ignorance, universal drunkenness, hunger, and how the poor had been left with nothing but their own integrity—how, even for an

insignificant little squirt like the accused, integrity was the most precious thing in the world.

He spoke circumstantially, convincingly (p. 203), gesticulating with both arms. As he listened, Laptev was surprised at the man's capacity for delivering—at length, in this earnest tone—nothing but platitudes and truisms which had long grated on people's nerves. Embarrassed, he simply could not fathom what Kostya was after. After all, from *his oration a juror* . . .

(*i*) *Material on Yartsev*

. . . *looked like a scientist* (p. 192). Familiarity with the natural sciences leaves a special mark on literary men—on their methods, on their way of defining things, even on their physiognomy.

Yartsev's main principle was to try to be loftier than his instincts and to live consciously. Believing, for instance, that Russia's hard climate disposes people to lying on the stove and dressing carelessly, he never permitted himself to lie down in daytime, rose early, never wore a dressing-gown or slippers, changed his shirt daily. All the same, his clothes always looked shabby, and his frock-coat had a clumsy hang.

Yartsev followed her (p. 204).

'I just can't see what you have against love, gentlemen. Argue as you will, but love's a great blessing in the last resort, isn't it? If it's cruel and destructive sometimes that's not love's fault but ours. So long as some people are well fed, intelligent and kind, while others are hungry, stupid and vicious, then every blessing leads only to dissension, increasing human inequality. *We keep talking* . . . *precious little loving*, and that I find an enormous gap in our lives.'

(*j*) *Material from conversations between Laptev and others*

. . . *with an angry look at Yartsev* (p. 192). 'In *A Sportsman's Sketches* [by Turgenev] we see a protest against serfdom, and in *Anna Karenin* the author [Tolstoy] takes up the cudgels against high society with its trivialities, and that's why these works are *significant and useful* . . . *and him falling out of love with her* and all the rest of the rigmarole—such works are insignificant, say I, and are only written to corrupt the imagination of schoolboys and priests' wives.'

'. . . *these acts of infidelity* (pp. 192–3), this stuff about how people can't love properly nowadays—and today I read that we're all dying of love, and that our only salvation lies in giving it up—*is there nothing else to say?*'

'*It must disgust them to read all this* (p. 193). Yesterday Alexis and I drove through the Khitrov Market, which was crowded with ragged, drunken, repulsive people with frozen cheeks. It would be better to write about them.'

Laptev knew what Kostya and Yartsev were going to say, having often taken part in such arguments before. The only novelty, an unpleasant one, was that his wife was *discussing love so earnestly . . .*

But he could guess why she did it (p. 193).

'One can't argue about matters of taste,' said Yartsev. 'And since that's just what we are arguing about we'll never be finished. If poetry doesn't solve the problems you think important, then leave it alone and refer to technical works, to criminal and financial law, read leading articles, read scientific articles. You want poetry to respond to current needs and to specialize, but what's the point when there are masses of specialist works at our disposal? For instance, why *should Romeo and Juliet . . .*'

'. . . *popularization of knowledge and humane ideals* (p. 193). Good God, if you don't like them leave them alone and read something that suits your needs and tastes. Myself, I'm bored by tales and stories with no love element. But when reading I always count on the author telling me something new and significant about love. Now, if he repeats something stale and delivers dull trivialities, then I yawn and put the book aside. But I don't have the least desire for this incompetent writer to take up science or homiletics.'

'. . . *culture is visibly striding ahead* (p. 194), and I'm absolutely certain that to have millions in the bank and make money by exploiting factory workers will be just as absurd, one day, for a civilized man as it now seems to swop serf girls for dogs. Education will gradually render capitalism absurd, and it will lose all importance.'

'That will be in five thousand years.' Kostya laughed. 'In five thousand years Rothschild will find *his gold vaults absurd . . .*'

'. . . we must fight (p. 194).'

'Struggle away if you want, but what will it lead to? If a civilized man, richer than yourself, isn't imbued with consciousness that money's an evil and an aberration, you can't do anything by force because force is on his side anyway.'

'Oh, really? Do you really think he'll make no concessions? *A cat eating from the same bowl . . .*'

'*It was forced to do it* (p. 194).'

'The things you hear all day—they're enough to make your head spin.' Laptev wiped his forehead with his palm. 'Now, see here, Ivan. I think most present-day capitalists have already learnt from experience that money doesn't buy happiness, that money is evil and so on. But they lack the confidence to

start a new life. None of them is a hundred per cent convinced that to renounce money is desirable. Not only am I not convinced of it myself, but I
even think sometimes that if my father gave me a million straight off I'd do a
lot of good with it.'

'Besides, you're used to luxury, my dear sir,' said Kochevoy.

'What luxury? What have I ever got out of my money, may I ask?' Laptev
looked sternly at Kostya. 'And in what way am I happier than you or Yartsev?
My childhood was . . .'

. . . *which had aroused her hatred* (p. 195).

'Life is forging ahead, according to you,' said Kostya to change the subject.
'But if you ask me it's constantly retreating.'

'Oh, chuck it,' said Yartsev angrily. 'A man with no ear for music thinks
musicians can't play properly, and that he's the only one to notice it. Life
follows its natural course, believe me, and it doesn't create discords—it's just
those without the ear for it who think everything's in an awful mess. Do
calm down, please!'

Going to his study after supper, Laptev tensely, *with pounding heart . . .*

(k) *Material on Dr. Belavin's and the Laptevs' employees*

. . . *began dressing* (p. 165). Owing to the doctor's ill nature the cooks and
maids were continually being changed in his house. Some were lazy, disobedient, impudent, utterly stupid, some could not tidy a room without
stealing a ring or a handkerchief. Three years ago one maid—red-haired,
freckled—had become abusive when given her notice, hinting that the doctor
had had an affair with her. And the female servants offended Julia's suscepti-
bilities. *When she had dressed . . .*

. . . *walk in front with the torch-bearers* (p. 192). At his recommendation a
governess—a Mary Vasilyevna—had been engaged by the Laptevs. She was a
skinny, dark-complexioned spinster represented by Kish as an intelligent,
intellectual, sensitive creature. It was agreed that she would help the girls with
their lessons, take them for walks, and—for a special honorarium—look after
Laptev's library. The sensitive creature began by writing on each book in an
atrocious hand: 'This book belongs to Alexis Laptev.' Then she turned out to
suffer from nerves. When she could not do one of Sasha's sums, or when
Kostya forgot to bow on his way upstairs through the room where she worked,
she would throw things, beat her breast with her fists, sob. The girls would
beg her to calm down, and then take her for a walk in Dmitrovka Street. And
now the Laptevs just couldn't think of a decent excuse to get rid of her.

NOTES

THE following notes, which have been kept as brief as possible, are designed to explain references in the text which might be obscure to English-speaking readers and to point out certain difficulties which have occurred in the translation.

Page

16 'like the old poet Derzhavin blessing the young Pushkin.' Reference is to the famous occasion of 8 January 1815 when the elderly poet Gabriel Derzhavin (1743–1816) heard the young poet Alexander Pushkin (1799–1837) recite his *Recollections of Tsarskoye Selo* at the Lyceum of Tsarskoye Selo near St. Petersburg.

23 'Schopenhauers.' Reference is to the well-known German philosopher Arthur Schopenhauer (1788–1860).

29 ' "Onegin, I cannot deny . . ." ' Aria from the opera *Eugene Onegin* (1877–8) by P. I. Tchaikovsky (1840–93), based on Pushkin's verse novel *Eugene Onegin* (1823–31); Chekhov's heroine Tanya (short for Tatyana) has the same name as Pushkin's.

31 'Braga's famous *Serenade*.' The vocal serenade by Gaetano Braga (1829–1907), Italian cellist and operatic composer.

34 'Gaucher.' N. Gaucher, a prominent French-born horticulturalist active in the 1880s.

34 'Pesotsky's king of his own little castle.' Literally, 'Rich and famous is Kochubey.' A line from Pushkin's narrative poem *Poltava* (1829).

39 ' "in my Father's house . . ." ' John, 14:2.

44 'The Assumption.' Assumption Day falls on 15 August.

45 'Polycrates.' Tyrant of Samos, crucified *c.* 522 B.C.

45 ' "Rejoice evermore." ' 1 Thess. 5:16.

46 'St. Elias' Eve.' On the eve of 20 July, which is St. Elias' (or Elijah's) Day.

49 'Sevastopol.' The Crimean port and naval base.

49 'Yalta.' The town and seaside resort on the Crimean coast.

61, 72 'the Old Religion . . . Reformed Orthodox rites . . . a Nonconformist.' Reference is to the schismatic branch of Russian Orthodoxy which adhered to the 'Old Belief'—the ritual of the Russian Church as practised before the reforms of the Patriarch Nikon in the mid-seventeenth century. Adherence to the Old Belief was extremely prevalent in the nineteenth-century Russian merchant class.

73 'over his uniform.' Uniforms were worn at this period by pupils and staff at state educational institutions; these included the universities and high schools (*gimnazii*).

Page

75 'a senior civil servant.' Literally, 'an Actual State Councillor'—the fourth class, in descending order of seniority, in the Table of Ranks instituted by Peter the Great in 1722.

75 'a St. Anne ribbon.' The orders (ордена), decorations for distinction in peace or war, had been instituted by Peter the Great in the early eighteenth century. The Order of St. Anne, second class, was worn on a ribbon round the neck.

76 'Leconte de Lisle.' The French poet Charles-Marie-René Leconte de Lisle (1818–94).

77 'Duse.' The Italian actress Eleonora Duse (1858–1924).

79 'her Nonconformist peasant instincts.' Those associated with the Old Belief—see note on pp. 61, 72, above.

79 'Jules Verne.' The French novelist (1828–1905).

80 'Maupassant.' The French novelist and short-story writer Guy de Maupassant (1850–93).

81 'Turgenev.' I. S. Turgenev, the novelist (1818–83).

85 'Kings.' Card game in which the player to win most tricks becomes 'King'.

96 'St. John's Day . . .' 8 May—the day of St. John the Evangelist.

96 'St. Nicholas's Day . . .' 9 May—the day of the Transference of the Remains of St. Nicholas the Miracle-Worker.

105 'Ryurik.' Rurik, or Ryurik, a late ninth-century Viking prince of Novgorod, was traditionally the founder of the Rurikid line—the Russian ruling house from 862 to 1598.

105 'Ivan the Terrible.' Ivan IV, Tsar of Muscovy; born 1530, acceded 1533, died 1584.

105 'Peter the Great.' Peter I, the first Russian emperor; born 1672, acceded 1682, died 1725.

106 ' "At the Last Supper . . ." ' In the account which follows Chekhov's student quotes or paraphrases material from the Gospels (Mark 14; Luke 22; John 18), and the translation draws on the Authorized Version at the appropriate points.

111 'Count Nulin.' The horse is named after the hero of Pushkin's comic poem *Count Nulin* (1825).

111 'Marie Godefroi.' A well-known equestrienne of the period, of whom A. A. Suvorin had written to Chekhov from Feodosiya in the Crimea, on 6 September 1888, as 'that *prima donna* of the ring, a rather handsome, well-built brunette—a truly fabulous horsewoman and a devastating trick rider' (*Works*, 1944–51, xiv, 512).

114 'Shchedrin.' M. Ye. Saltykov (1826–89), the well-known satirist who wrote under the pseudonym 'Shchedrin', and is often known as Saltykov-Shchedrin.

Page

114 'Dostoyevsky.' F. M. Dostoyevsky (1821–81), the novelist.

115 '*Eugene Onegin*.' Pushkin's verse novel.

115 '*Boris Godunov*.' Pushkin's historical play (1824–5).

115 'Lermontov.' The poet M. Yu. Lermontov (1814–41).

115 'Alexis Tolstoy's poem "*The Sinful Woman*".' This work by A. K. Tolstoy (1817–75) also figures in Act Three of Chekhov's *Cherry Orchard*—see *The Oxford Chekhov*, iii, 181.

116 'Lessing's *Hamburgische Dramaturgie*.' The treatise on drama (1769) by the German critic and dramatist G. E. Lessing (1729–81).

118 'Battle of Kalka.' At the battle by the River Kalka in south Russia, on 31 May 1223, the Russians were routed by a Mongol–Tatar army.

118 'Siberian capes.' Literally, 'Cape Chukotskys'—reference being to the Chukotsky Peninsula in the far north-east of Siberia, opposite the Bering Straits.

119 '*European Herald*.' *Vestnik Yevropy*, a historico-political and literary monthly of liberal complexion published in St. Petersburg/Petrograd, 1866–1918.

123 'Neglinny Drive.' Street leading north from the Maly Theatre in central Moscow.

124 'Gogol.' N. V. Gogol (1809–52), the novelist and short-story writer.

126 'the Consecration of the Waters.' Annual ceremony of the Orthodox Church held on 5 January, the Eve of Epiphany.

134 'your most churlish backwoods squire.' Literally, 'a bad Sobakevich', reference being to the notoriously curmudgeonly landowner of that name in Part One of Gogol's novel *Dead Souls* (1842).

135 'Goncharov.' I. A. Goncharov (1812–91), the novelist, author of *Oblomov*.

135 'Tolstoy.' L. N. Tolstoy (1828–1910), the novelist.

138 'Flammarion.' Camille Flammarion (1842–1925), French astronomer and popularizer of astronomy.

139 'Kharkov.' Large city in the Ukraine, frequently invoked in Chekhov's fiction as a dump for unwanted objects or persons.

143 'Ibsen.' The Norwegian playwright Henrik Ibsen (1828–1906).

143 ' "For in the fatness . . ." ' Shakespeare, *Hamlet*, Act III, Scene iv.

152 'Sokolniki.' District containing a large park, to the north-east of Moscow; a favourite place for out-of-town excursions.

154 'Pyatnitsky Road.' Long street in the merchant quarter south of the Moscow River, running north towards the river from Serpukhov Square.

154 'Khimki.' River port a few miles north-west of Moscow.

157 'picturesquely miserable bumpkins.' Literally, 'an Anton Goremyka'— reference being to the hero of the short story *Anton Goremyka* (1847) by D. V. Grigorovich (1822–99).

Page

159 ' "it will sort itself out." ' The phrase occurs in the novel *Anna Karenin* (1875–7) by L. N. Tolstoy.

168 'a comic figure from an operetta.' Literally, 'a Gaspard from *Les Cloches de Corneville*' (1877), the popular operetta by the French composer Robert Planquette (1848–1903).

173 'Tambov.' Town about 300 miles south-east of Moscow.

174 'Kashira.' Town about 70 miles south of Moscow.

174 'bold and proud is woman's heart.' Literally, 'for woman's heart is a Shamil.' The guerrilla leader Shamil (1797–1871) led the Caucasian tribesmen in their struggle against conquest by the Russians.

175 'Fley's.' A well-known *pâtisserie* on Neglinny Drive in the centre of Moscow.

176 'Vologda.' Town about 300 miles north of Moscow.

176 'Nikolsky Road.' In central Moscow, leading north-east from the Red Square.

176 'What sickening humbug!' Literally, 'how like Shchedrin's Iudushka'—the sanctimonious hero of the novel *The Golovlyov Family* (1876–80) by M. Ye. Saltykov-Shchedrin.

178 ' "The prophet Samuel . . ." ' The relevant passage occurs in 1 Sam. 17:4–5.

179 'Anton Rubinstein.' The composer (1829–94).

179 'the Conservatoire.' In Great Nikitsky Road in the west of central Moscow; founded by Nicholas Rubinstein (1835–81), brother of Anton.

180 'Guerrier's courses.' V. I. Guerrier (1837–1919), professor of history at Moscow University, 1868–1904.

181 'the Gentry Club.' On Great Dmitrovka Street, leading north-west from central Moscow.

181 'Ostozhenka.' Road running roughly south in south-west Moscow, beginning about half a mile from the Kremlin.

181 'Savelovsky Street.' A turning off Ostozhenka Road.

182 'Great Nikitsky Road.' West of the centre of Moscow.

182 '*Reinheit*.' German for 'purity'; often the subject of whimsical discussion in the unpublished letters between Chekhov and Lydia (Lika) Mizinov, this supposedly expressed one of the qualities which he required in his young female friends.

184 'Presnya.' District in the east of Moscow.

185 'the Second High School on Razgulyay Square.' An actual school in the north-west of central Moscow, a three- to four-mile walk from Pyatnitsky Road.

187 'Little Dmitrovka.' Street in the north-west of Moscow.

Page

187 'Old St. Pimen's Church.' A few hundred yards west of Little Dmitrovka Street.

189 'Strastnoy Boulevard.' In the north of central Moscow.

189 'Tver Road.' Running north-west from the Red Square in central Moscow.

189 'the Iverian Chapel.' Near the Red Square, site of the famous miracle-working Iverian Madonna.

189 'Filippov's Café.' On the corner of the Tver Road and Glinishchevsky Street.

190 'Volokolamsk.' Town about 60 miles north-west of Moscow.

190 'apply to be registered as gentlefolk.' More literally, 'to seek the status of *dvoryanin*' (gentleman), the most privileged of the various classes or estates to one or other of which all Russian citizens were assigned in law.

190 '*The Maid of Orleans*.' Opera (1881) by P. I. Tchaikovsky.

190 'Mariya Yermolov.' Noted Russian actress (1853–1928).

191 'the Maly Theatre.' In central Moscow, near the Bolshoy Theatre.

191 'Hotel Dresden.' On the Tver Road in central Moscow.

193 ' "In the sweat of thy face . . ." ' Gen. 3:19.

194 'an under-secretary.' Literally, 'a Privy Councillor'—Class Three in Peter the Great's Table of Ranks.

195 'Merchants' Club.' On Little Dmitrovka Street.

196 'The Yar Restaurant . . . the Strelna.' Both these establishments were located out of town in the Petrovsky Park to the north-west of Moscow. Both were, according to Baedeker, 'much frequented in the evening (not cheap)'.

201 'School of Art.' In north-west Moscow.

202 'Shishkin.' I. I. Shishkin (1832–98), Russian landscape painter.

203 'the Exaltation of the Cross.' Church festival, celebrated on 14 September.

203 'Yaroslavl.' Town about 200 miles north-east of Moscow.

206 'Muscovy.' Name commonly applied to the Moscow-ruled Russian state between the fourteenth and the early eighteenth century.

206 'Krasny Prud . . . at St. Alexis's Convent.' Reference is to the area of Krasny Prud ('Red Pond') in the north-west of Moscow, about 3 miles from the Red Square. The two friends were approaching the centre of the city, moving south-west past the convent and along Krasnoprudny (Red Pond) Road.

207 'Lyapunovs.' P. P. Lyapunov (d. 1611), hero of Russian national resistance against the Polish invader in the early seventeenth century; also his slightly less famous brother Z. P. Lyapunov.

207 'Godunovs.' Boris Godunov (1552–1605) was first Regent, and then—from 1598 until his death—Tsar of Muscovy.

207 'Yaroslav.' Yaroslav I, the Wise, prince of Kiev; ruled 1019–54.

207 'Monomakh.' Vladimir Monomakh, prince of Kiev; ruled 1113–25.

Page

207 'Pimen's soliloquy.' A famous speech from Pushkin's *Boris Godunov*.

207 'Dmitrovka Street.' Great Dmitrovka Street, leading north-west from Teatralny Square in central Moscow.

207 'Polovtsians.' Another name for the Cumans, a Turkic-speaking people engaged in sporadic struggle with Kievan Russia between 1054 and their defeat by the Mongol–Tatars in 1238.

208 'the St. Alexis Cemetery.' On the northern outskirts of Moscow.

209 ' "A person well may stupid be . . ." ' From Act Three of the celebrated play *Woe from Wit* (1822–4) by A. S. Griboyedov (1795–1829).

212 'valley in the Caucasus.' Literally, 'I feel as if I'm lying in a Daghestan valley.' Reference is to the first line of Lermontov's lyric *The Dream* (1841): 'In noontide's heat, in a valley of Daghestan, with a bullet in my breast, I lay motionless.' Daghestan is an area in the north-east Caucasus.

213 'a higher rank.' Literally, 'Actual State Councillor'—see note on p. 75, above.

215 'policemen of all kinds.' Literally, 'constables and gendarmes', the former representing the ordinary and the latter the political police.

221 'Bubnov's Inn.' Untraced.

221 ' "Old Nero." ' Literally, 'Malyuta Skuratov'. Reference is to Malyuta ('Babe') Skuratov, died 1573: the dreaded leader of the Oprichnina, Ivan the Terrible's private Mafia.

222 'south-bank Moscow.' In the original 'Zamoskvorechye'—literally 'the place beyond the River Moscow'. The merchant quarter south of the river.

223 'Butovo.' Village about twelve miles south of Moscow.

224 'the Exhibition.' Reference is to the World's Columbian Exposition at Chicago, Illinois (1893).

SELECT BIBLIOGRAPHY

I. BIBLIOGRAPHIES IN ENGLISH

Two useful, but now somewhat dated, bibliographies, published by the New York Public Library and containing in all nearly five hundred items, give a comprehensive picture of the literature relating to Chekhov published in English—translations of his writings, biographical and critical studies, memoirs, essays, articles etc. They are:

> *Chekhov in English: a List of Works by and about him.* Compiled by Anna Heifetz. Ed. and with a Foreword by Avrahm Yarmolinsky (New York, 1949) and
> *The Chekhov Centennial Chekhov in English: a Selective List of Works by and about him, 1949–60.* Compiled by Rissa Yachnin (New York, 1960).

Bibliographies in English will also be found in the books by David Magarshack (*Chekhov: a Life*), Ernest J. Simmons and Ronald Hingley mentioned in Section III, below. Magarshack provides a bibliographic index of Chekhov's writings in alphabetical order of their English titles, Simmons includes a list of bibliographies in Russian. Hingley (1950) gives a list of Chekhov's translated stories in chronological order, while Hingley (1976) has an appendix on 'Chekhov in English', and another which discusses the 'Shape of Chekhov's Work' as a whole.

II. TRANSLATIONS INTO ENGLISH OF THE STORIES IN THIS VOLUME

(Where the titles of translated stories differ from those in the present volume, the title adopted here is given in square brackets if the difference is so great as to make it difficult to identify the story.)

(a) TR. BY CONSTANCE GARNETT

The Darling, and Other Stories (London, 1916).
    Includes: *The Two Volodyas, Three Years.*

The Lady with the Dog, and Other Stories (London, 1917).
    Includes: *The Black Monk.*

The Party, and Other Stories (New York, 1917).
    Includes: *A Woman's Kingdom, The Teacher of Literature* [*The Russian Master*].

The Witch, and Other Stories (London, 1918).
Includes: *The Student.*

The Chorus Girl, and Other Stories (London, 1920).
Includes: *At a Country House, Rothschild's Fiddle.*

The Schoolmistress, and Other Stories (London, 1920).
Includes: *The Head Gardener's Story.*

(*b*) BY OTHER TRANSLATORS

The Black Monk, and Other Stories. Tr. R. E. C. Long (London, 1903).
Includes: *The Black Monk, Rothschild's Fiddle, At the Manor* [*At a Country House*].

The Kiss, and Other Stories. Tr. R. E. C. Long (London, 1908).
Includes: *The Head Gardener's Tale.*

Stories of Russian Life. Tr. Marian Fell (New York, 1915).
Includes: *The Head Gardener's Tale.*

Russian Silhouettes: More Stories of Russian Life. Tr. Marian Fell (London, 1915).
Includes: *Rothschild's Fiddle.*

The Grasshopper, and Other Stories. Tr. with Introduction by A. E. Chamot (London, 1926).
Includes: *The Black Monk.*

Three Years. Tr. Rose Prokofieva (Moscow, 1958?).

Anton Chekhov: Selected Stories. Tr. with Introduction by Jessie Coulson (London, 1963).
Includes: *The Black Monk, The Student.*

Seven Short Novels by Chekhov. Tr. Barbara Makanowitzky with Introduction and Prefaces by Gleb Struve (New York, 1968).
Includes: *A Woman's Kingdom, Three Years.*

The Image of Chekhov: Forty Stories by Anton Chekhov. Tr. with Introduction by Robert Payne (New York, 1963).
Includes: *Big Volodya and Little Volodya* [*The Two Volodyas*].

III. BIOGRAPHICAL AND CRITICAL STUDIES

Leon Shestov, *Anton Tchekhov and Other Essays* (Dublin and London, 1916).

William Gerhardi, *Anton Chekhov: a Critical Study* (London, 1923).

Oliver Elton, *Chekhov* (The Taylorian Lecture, 1929; Oxford, 1929).

Nina Andronikova Toumanova, *Anton Chekhov: the Voice of Twilight Russia* (London, 1937).

W. H. Bruford, *Chekhov and his Russia: a Sociological Study* (London, 1948).

Ronald Hingley, *Chekhov: a Biographical and Critical Study* (London, 1950).

Irene Nemirovsky, *A Life of Chekhov*. Tr. from the French by Erik de Mauny (London, 1950).

David Magarshack, *Chekhov: a Life* (London, 1952).

David Magarshack, *Chekhov the Dramatist* (London, 1952).

Vladimir Yermilov [Ermilov], *Anton Pavlovich Chekhov, 1860–1904*. Tr. Ivy Litvinov (Moscow, 1956; London, 1957).

W. H. Bruford, *Anton Chekhov* (London, 1957).

T. Eekman, ed., *Anton Chekhov, 1860–1960* (Leiden, 1960).

Beatrice Saunders, *Tchehov the Man* (London, 1960).

Ernest J. Simmons, *Chekhov: a Biography* (Boston, Toronto, 1962; London, 1963).

Maurice Valency, *The Breaking String: the Plays of Anton Chekhov* (New York, 1966).

Thomas Winner, *Chekhov and his Prose* (New York, 1966).

Robert Louis Jackson, ed., *Chekhov: a Collection of Critical Essays* (Englewood Cliffs, N.J., 1967).

Nils Åke Nilsson, *Studies in Čechov's Narrative Technique:* The Steppe *and* The Bishop (Stockholm, 1968).

Karl D. Kramer, *The Chameleon and the Dream: the Image of Reality in Čexov's Stories* (The Hague, 1970).

J. L. Styan, *Chekhov in Performance: a Commentary on the Major Plays* (Cambridge, 1971).

Siegfried Melchinger, *Anton Chekhov*. Tr. by Edith Tarcov (New York, 1972).

Virginia Llewellyn Smith, *Anton Chekhov and the Lady with the Dog*. Foreword by Ronald Hingley (London, 1973).

Harvey Pitcher, *The Chekhov Play: a New Interpretation* (London, 1973).

Sophie Laffitte, *Chekhov, 1860–1904*. Tr. from the French by Moura Budberg and Gordon Latta (London, 1974).

Donald Rayfield, *Chekhov: the Evolution of his Art* (London, 1975).

Caryl Brahms, *Reflections in a Lake: a Study of Chekhov's Four Greatest Plays* (London, 1976).

Ronald Hingley, *A New Life of Anton Chekhov* (London, 1976).

Beverly Hahn, *Chekhov: a Study of the Major Stories and Plays* (Cambridge, 1977).

Kornei Chukovsky, *Chekhov the Man*. Tr. Pauline Rose (London, n.d.).

IV. LETTERS AND MEMOIR MATERIAL, ETC.

Letters of Anton Tchehov to his Family and Friends. Tr. Constance Garnett (London, 1920).

The Note-books of Anton Tchekhov together with Reminiscences of Tchekhov by Maxim Gorky. Tr. S. S. Koteliansky and Leonard Woolf (Richmond, Surrey, 1921).

Letters on the Short Story, the Drama and other Literary Topics. By Anton Chekhov. Selected and ed. Louis S. Friedland (New York, 1924).

Konstantin Stanislavsky, *My Life in Art.* Tr. J. J. Robbins (London, 1924; New York, 1956).

The Life and Letters of Anton Tchekhov. Tr. and ed. S. S. Koteliansky and Philip Tomlinson (London, 1925).

The Letters of Anton Pavlovitch Tchehov to Olga Leonardovna Knipper. Tr. Constance Garnett (London, 1926).

Anton Tchekhov: Literary and Theatrical Reminiscences. Tr. and ed. S. S. Koteliansky (London, 1927).

Vladimir Nemirovitch-Dantchenko, *My Life in the Russian Theatre.* Tr. John Cournos (London, 1937).

The Personal Papers of Anton Chekhov. Introduction by Matthew Josephson (New York, 1948).

Lydia Avilov, *Chekhov in my Life: a Love Story.* Tr. with an Introduction by David Magarshack (London, 1950).

Konstantin Stanislavsky, *Stanislavsky on the Art of the Stage.* Tr. with an introductory essay on Stanislavsky's 'System' by David Magarshack (London, 1950).

The Selected Letters of Anton Chekhov. Ed. Lillian Hellman, tr. Sidonie Lederer (New York, 1955).

Letters of Anton Chekhov. Tr. Michael Henry Heim in collaboration with Simon Karlinsky. Selection, Commentary and Introduction by Simon Karlinsky (New York, 1973).

Letters of Anton Chekhov. Selected and edited by Avrahm Yarmolinsky (New York, 1973).

V. OTHER WORKS USED IN THE PREPARATION OF THIS VOLUME

P. Semyonov (compiler), *Geografichesko-istorichesky slovar Rossiskoy imperii* (St. Petersburg, 1862–85).

Vsya Moskva na 1911 god (Moscow, 1911) [gazetteer].

Karl Baedeker, *Russia with Teheran, Port Arthur and Peking: Handbook for Travellers* (Leipzig, 1914).

Polnoye sobraniye sochineny i pisem A. P. Chekhova, ed. S. D. Balukhaty, V. P. Potyomkin, N. S. Tikhonov, A. M. Yegolin, 20 vols. (Moscow, 1944–51).

Chekhov v vospominaniyakh sovremennikov: vtoroye, dopolnennoye izdaniye, ed. N. L. Brodsky and others (Moscow, 1954).

N. I. Gitovich, *Letopis zhizni i tvorchestva A. P. Chekhova* (Moscow, 1955).

Arthur Jacobs, *A New Dictionary of Music* (Harmondsworth, 1958).

Literaturnoye nasledstvo: Chekhov, ed. V. V. Vinogradov and others (Moscow, 1960).

Sovetskaya istoricheskaya entsiklopediya, ed. Ye. M. Zhukov and others (Moscow, 1961–76).